EGYPT Splendours of an Ancient Civilization

Thames & Hudson

Contents

Text
Alberto Siliotti

Editor
Valeria Manferto

Designer
Patrizia Balocco

Colour drawings
Luca Rossi

**Black-and-white
maps and drawings**
Monica Falcone
Cristina Franco

The publisher would
like to thank:
Yvonne Marzoni,
Fabio Bourbon,
Ahmed El Ebrashi
(Director of the
*General Cairo Press
Centre*), Ebtesam
Gamal El Den.

1 *Four stellar deities depicted on the ceiling of the tomb of Irinefer, 'the Servant in the Place of Truth'. (TT no. 290, Deir el-Medina, western Thebes)*

2–3 *Pale gold leaf plaque belonging to Queen Henut-tawy, the mother of Pharaoh Psusennes I (Twenty-First Dynasty, around 1000 BC). Plaques such as this, bearing the protective* udjat-*eye, were placed over the embalming incision made in the abdomen of the deceased to extract the viscera during mummification. (Cairo Museum)*

4–5 *Pectoral, of gold and blue faience, found in the tomb of Sheshonq II and formerly belonging to Sheshonq I (both Twenty-Second Dynasty). At the centre of the jewel is an image of the sun barque which sails across the primordial ocean, bearing the sun disk. (Cairo Museum)*

6–7 *Relief showing two guests at a banquet, in the tomb of Ramose, vizier during the reign of Amenophis IV (TT no. 55 at Sheikh Abd el-Qurna, western Thebes). These delightful portraits are among the finest examples of the art of the Eighteenth Dynasty.*

8 *A head of the hawk-god Horus. This masterpiece of the goldsmith's art of the Old Kingdom was found at the site of Hierakonpolis, the first capital of Upper Egypt during the Predynastic Period. (Cairo Museum)*

9 *The solid gold funerary mask of Psusennes I, found by Pierre Montet in 1939 at Tanis, is one of the greatest treasures of the Cairo Museum and is comparable to that of Tutankhamun.*

(Note: caption numbers refer to the pages where the illustrations appear.)

First published in the United Kingdom in 1994 by Thames & Hudson Ltd, 181A High Holborn, London WC1V 7QX

www.thamesandhudson.com

Paperback edition published in 2002

This new smaller format hardback edition first published 2005

© 1994, 2002, 2005 White Star S.p.a. Vercelli, Italy

British Library Cataloguing-in-Publication Data
A catalogue record for this book is available from the British Library

ISBN-13: 978-0-500-51264-7

ISBN-10: 0-500-51264-7

Printed and bound in Singapore

PREFACE

The civilization of ancient Egypt has for centuries captured the human imagination, and a vast array of studies has dealt with the subject in almost every conceivable way.

It might therefore seem at first glance unnecessary, or at least presumptuous, to offer another. Careful study of the remarkable number of books dealing with ancient Egypt, however, soon reveals that none of them uses its illustrations as true visual documentation – the ideal medium for presenting the treasures and monuments of Egypt, in all their richness, colour and overwhelming grandeur.

Here, a stunning collection of photographs recreates for the reader the excitement and wonder of a journey down the Nile and through the archaeology and geography of Egypt. The images are both evocative and intriguing, but also – and most importantly – informative. The accompanying text supplies a commentary, guiding the reader through the illustrations, filling in the necessary background, while a straightforward summary of the complex history of Egypt puts the buildings and artifacts in their context and explains their significance.

The major archaeological sites are revealed through photography and plans. Objects found at each site are also illustrated, so that works of art can be appreciated in their original setting, rather than simply as museum pieces.

An illustrated glossary explains the most important technical terms, and aspects of the mythology and religion of ancient Egypt. For to look at photographs of even the most beautiful monuments without an understanding of these details of ancient Egyptian life is to see only architectural structures, empty of meaning.

10 (above) The cartouche of Queen Nefertari Meri-en-Mut, whose name means 'the Lovely One, Beloved of Mut'.

11 (opposite) This beautiful portrait of Nefertari, wife of Ramesses II (Nineteenth Dynasty) was painted on one of the walls of her tomb in the Valley of the Queens. Technically and stylistically the paintings in the tomb of Nefertari are some of the finest in Egyptian art.

12–13 Two colossi of Ramesses II watch over the entrance to the temple of Luxor. The two obelisks which originally stood in front of these statues were given to France by Pasha Mohammad Ali in 1831. The French transported one of them to Paris and in 1836 it was erected in the Place de la Concorde, where it still stands today; the other remains in its original position.

14–15 The Nubian temple of Ramesses II at el-Sebua was threatened by the rising waters of the Nile following the construction of the High Dam at Aswan. The temple was saved – along with many others – by an international rescue campaign organized by UNESCO which dismantled the buildings and then reassembled them at higher sites a few miles away.

KEMET, THE BLACK LAND

The ancient Egyptians called their homeland *kemet*, or the 'black land', distinguishing it from the desert that surrounded it, which they called *deshret*, meaning the 'red land'. They referred to themselves as *remet-en-kemet*, the 'people of the black land'. The black land was arable earth, the fertile silt that the Nile deposited each year when it overflowed its banks, and that black land covered the same extent as the Nile's annual floods. During the Tertiary Period (around 45 million years ago) Egypt was entirely covered by the great ocean Tethys. When, towards the end of the Tertiary Period, the great mountain-building movements of the earth's continental plates led to the formation of the Himalayas and the Alps, the waters of the massive ancient sea dropped, the basin of the Mediterranean Sea was formed, and the territories now called Egypt and the Sahara emerged.

At the beginning of the Quaternary Period a huge system of equatorial lakes formed and changes in the climate led to the creation of what is now the Nile River. The Nile is in fact a product of the confluence of two great rivers, the White Nile and the Blue Nile, which merge in the Sudan, near the modern city of Khartoum.

The White Nile has its source in the great lakes – Lake Victoria, Lake Edward, Lake George – and its level and rate of flow vary only slightly through the year. The Blue Nile, with the Atbara River, gushes down from the mountains of Ethiopia, and its flow is swelled enormously by the monsoon rains, which cause it to run particularly high in late spring. This mechanism is the origin of the behaviour of the Nile and its floods, which had such an effect on the development of civilization. Along the Nile's course the river's waters sliced through soft limestone, once the bed of the ancient sea of Tethys, and thus carved out a broad valley. As the ancient river ran down to the sea, it encountered a number of outcrops of harder rock, made of the ancient granite of the continental plate. These granite obstacles formed the six cataracts (from a Greek word meaning waterfall) that mark the Nile's course. On approaching the Mediterranean, the Nile divides into a number of smaller streams, spreading out into a fan shape. The Greeks called this formation the Delta, because of its resemblance to the fourth letter of the Greek alphabet. To the east and west of the Nile stretch the Eastern or Arabian Desert (mountainous), sloping down towards the Red Sea, and the Western or Libyan Desert (sandy), forming the eastern edge of the Sahara. The Western Desert is broken, some 160 km (100 miles) from the Nile, by a series of shallow lens-shaped depressions, in a line roughly parallel to the river; these are the oases.

16 (below) The ritual of shai, *an Arabic word meaning tea, accompanied by the smoking of the* sisha, *the water pipe of Ottoman origin, is a popular custom among the people of Upper Egypt, and among those who live in the deserts to the east and west of the Nile.*

17 (opposite) A line of sand dunes extends in a lengthy cordon across the Western Desert, also known as the Libyan Desert; this is the tiny Egyptian fringe of the Sahara Desert.

18–19 A caravan of camels in the desert of Upper Egypt travelling in a stately fashion to market. The dromedary, usually simply referred to as a 'camel', was –

contrary to popular belief – completely unknown to the ancient Egyptians in the time of the pharaohs, and was probably introduced at a later period.

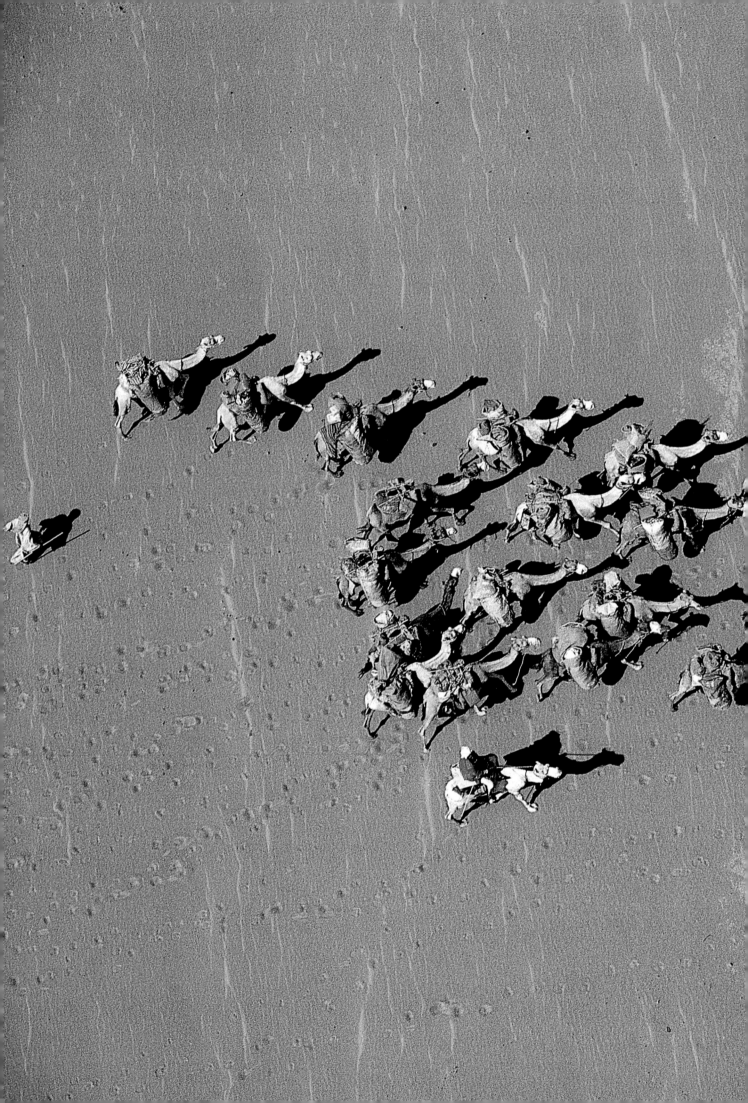

Were it not for the Nile, Egypt would simply be a desert, in which a number of nomadic communities might have developed and even prospered – as is the case in the Sahara – but where a lasting civilization could never have emerged. Some 10,000 years ago, the Nile flowed majestically along, its waters lapping at the edge of the so-called 'Green Sahara'. Land that is now desert sand was then, due to a far more humid climate (associated with the great glaciations of the Quaternary), a vast savannah teeming with water buffalo, gazelles, elephants and zebras. The river's yearly floods were disruptive events, but when the waters dropped, myriad lakes, ponds and marshes were scattered across the landscape, which re-emerged into the sunlight. In this watery terrain lived crocodiles and hippopotamuses, along with all sorts of fish and birds. It was an extremely hospitable environment, where bands of hunters and gatherers roamed, practising primitive forms of animal husbandry and agriculture,

hunting prey and collecting fruits and berries, and grazing animals and raising crops. Climate and nature favoured travel, both through what was later to become impassable desert, and along the river: raw materials and ideas were exchanged with equal frequency. Towards 5000 BC the climate began to grow more arid, gradually developing into that experienced today, and the native peoples, struggling for survival, sought refuge along the Nile Valley, where more favourable living conditions could be found. And so the first proto-urban settlements began to develop, gravitating towards two distinct areas – the north and the south.

In the south, the settlements tended to concentrate in an area just down-stream from what would become the city of Thebes, near Hierakonpolis, while to the north, they settled in the western area of the Nile Delta and the Faiyum, a lush region around Lake Qarun. The two groups developed differently and independently, each placing their own stamp on Egypt, which thus became known as 'the Double Land' or 'the Two Lands' – a dual nature reflected in the division into Upper and Lower Egypt.

These earliest communities soon required a more complex form of social organization, and the role of the chieftain emerged, who in time became the king – he who ensured the survival of his subjects, who organized his people's labour and who protected them from external enemies. The creation of a king and of a centralized power were the vital steps that allowed Egypt to develop into a dynastic state.

The Nile was the central feature upon which this state laid its foundations – it provided a constant supply of the life-giving water that no longer fell as rain from the sky, and the pattern of its floods provided the rhythm against

20 (left) The light of sunset highlights the delicate profiles of the feluccas *that ply the river waters near Aswan. The felucca is the typical boat of the Nile: equipped with an enormous sail, it can move on the lightest of breezes. River boats were the chief means of moving both people and goods in a country where, until the last century, transportation over land was virtually unknown.*

21 (right) The golden sands of the desert are bathed by the waters of the Nile at Aswan, known as Syene in ancient times. This city, an ancient trading centre through which the bounty of equatorial Africa flowed, marks the boundary of the region known as Nubia.

which the ancient Egyptians measured their seasons and determined the sequence of their labours. In the middle of July, when Sothis began to glitter once again in the morning sky, the ram-headed god Khnum opened the gates of his immense cave at the bottom of the First Cataract and allowed the waters to rush out. This marked the beginning of the season of *akhet* ('flooding') which lasted until the end of September. Then, when the waters began to drop and the river returned to its bed, the season of *peret*, that of planting and growth, began (November to March), followed by the ripening of the grains, and the harvest, which took place in the months of April, May and June, in the season of *shemu*.

The two grains most widely cultivated in Egypt, wheat and barley, were not enough to meet the nutritional needs of the community, but the cultivation of vegetables and legumes required the availability of a more dependable supply of water than the often irregular floods of the Nile. It therefore became necessary to tame the waters of the river. The Egyptians designed and built locks and canals possibly as early as the Predynastic Period, if the relief carved on the mace-head of King Scorpion is interpreted as a scene of a man intently excavating the bed of a canal. At the same time granaries and storehouses were built for the conservation of foodstuffs, a complex system that required a central authority – a king – and an efficient admin-istration in order to function properly.

Of course, the earlier economy, based on hunting, fishing and gathering, practised along the river, in the ponds and in the extensive marshes, was never entirely abandoned, and continued to be an important factor in the subsistence of the population living along the Nile Valley. The beneficent river, however, provided the Egyptians with more than just food. In a desert landscape where life was only possible in a narrow strip along the shores of the Nile, the river was also the only channel for communications.

Among the painted designs on ceramic vessels of the Predynastic Naqada II period (named after a site in the region of Abydos), are depictions of boats, some of them with oars and a kind of cabin. Travelling from one place to another automatically meant sailing – facilitated by the direction of the current when sailing downstream, that is northwards, and by the prevailing winds when sailing upstream, that is southwards. Interestingly, in hieroglyphs, travel was depicted in two different ways, according to the direction: the hieroglyph ⟨⟩, a sail, meant travel towards the south, while a boat with an oar ⟨⟩ indicated

travelling towards the north, with the assistance of the current. Relying both on the main body of the Nile and on the network of canals and secondary courses into which the Nile split, especially near the Delta, the Egyptians enjoyed enviable communications and transport facilities. These were so efficient and reliable that, in the entire history of ancient Egypt, the only roads built were within cities, not between them. This system of communications was undoubtedly a great unifying factor, promoting the formation of a consolidated state; at the same time, it was an obstacle to enemies attempting to penetrate a territory that had no means of communication east to west, from the desert, or northwards, from the marshes and wetlands of the Delta.

The Nile Valley, from the most distant prehistoric times, was like a broad corridor that connected remote peoples and cultures, a longitudinal highway linking Equatorial Africa with the Mediterranean. In philosophical and religious terms, the Egyptians conceived of the world as made in the image of their valley: a land with a vertical orientation, from south to north, and that drew its origin from the waters, just as the earth and heavens emerged from Nun, the Primordial Ocean.

The other essential element in this world was the sun – a sun whose power could dry the earth, shrivel the pastures and destroy the crops, and yet, at the same time, brought life, light and warmth. Unlike the waters of the Nile, which flowed from the south to the north, the inhabitants of Egypt observed that the fiery heavenly body followed a direction that intersected the direction of the river, from east to west, from Orient to Occident.

24 Raising water using a shadoof; *a scene in a painting from the tomb of Ipuy at Deir el-Medina, dating from the era of Ramesses II. This traditional method of irrigation has changed little over the centuries, as can be seen by comparing this painting with the modern version shown on the opposite page. (TT no. 217)*

24–25 (opposite) A farmer transporting sugar cane on a donkey. The donkey is even today one of the most common means of transport for short distances for the fellahs *(an Arabic word indicating peasants or farmers) of Egypt. Because of its remarkable endurance and its docility, this was the most widely used animal in the caravans that crossed the desert during the time of the pharaohs.*

25 (opposite, below) The saqya, *a form of water-wheel driven by an animal, and the* shadoof, *a system using human power, are the traditional methods for raising water from the Nile, or the numerous irrigation*

channels, to fields, orchards and small gardens. However, these old ways, which would probably be recognized by the ancient Egyptians, are rapidly being replaced by the increasing use of mechanical pumps.

26–27 The date harvest, in October, is an important event in the oases of the Libyan Desert and the palm groves of Upper Egypt. When the dates are spread out to ripen and dry in the sun, they form dazzling carpets of colour.

28–29 The Nile, the second longest river in the world at around 6500 km (4160 miles) long, has always been the principal channel of communications for the whole of Egypt. On its banks, the Egyptians built pyramids, temples, necropolises, cities and

villages. Herodotus, the Greek historian who visited Egypt around 450 BC, understood completely the vital importance of the river to the very existence of the land and the people, and wrote that Egypt was a gift of the Nile. The river has played a key

role in the largely agrarian economy of Egypt from the most remote antiquity until very recent times, fertilizing the country with its seasonal floods, which deposit a thick layer of humus on the farmland, thus making successful agriculture possible.

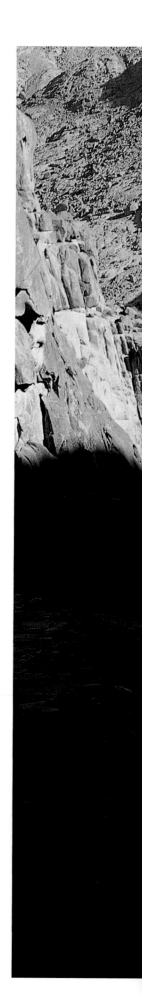

30 (above) The temple of Serabit el-Khadim, built on a rocky peak in the mountains that rise up in the centre of the Sinai Peninsula, was dedicated to the goddess Hathor, 'Mistress of Turquoise'. This semiprecious stone was quarried in this region in impressive quantities, along with copper, from the Old Kingdom period.

30 (below) On the peak of Gebel Mousa, or Mount Moses, identified as the Mount Sinai of the Bible, at 2132 m (7000 ft) above sea level, is a chapel built in 1934, reusing blocks of stone from the remains of a church dating from the reign of Justinian, around the middle of the sixth century AD.

Each evening the sun disappeared in the west, as if swallowed up by the heavens, but during the night it gathered its strength again, in a process of rebirth, reappearing the following day on the eastern horizon.

Based on these natural observations, the Egyptians conceived and developed a vision of the world that underlay their religious beliefs. This vision was closely connected with the axes of the universe, the terrestrial north–south axis and the celestial east–west axis. Fundamental though the Nile was to their existence, and vital though its role may have been in forming the Egyptian world-view, the Egyptians never gave the river a name. In fact, it is not known exactly how the name Nile – which comes from the word *Neilos*, by which the Greeks referred to the river – came to apply to it, though it is possible that the term derived from a corruption of the word *na-iteru*, meaning 'the rivers', a term that the Egyptians used to indicate the various branches of the Nile that divided in the Delta.

Likewise, the Egyptians never made the Nile a god, though they identified its various effects with different deities. In this way they attributed to the god Hapy, a divinity associated with the concept of abundance, the phenomenon of flooding. And the energy of the waters which rejuvenated and fertilized the earth was linked to the myth of the resurrection of Osiris.

This was the source of the connection between the cult of the dead, the concept of divine resurrection and the fertilization of the earth, a concept that had already evolved in the Predynastic Period.

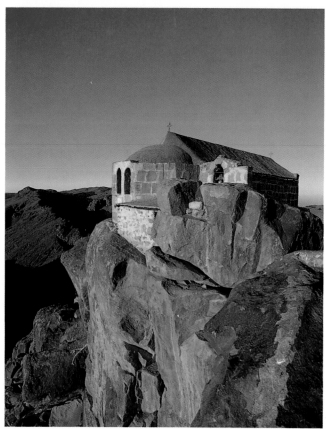

30–31 (right) The monastery of Saint Catherine, in a valley at the foot of Mount Moses at an altitude of 1660 m (5452 ft) above sea level, was first founded by Queen Helena in the fourth century AD. Enclosed within a strong enclosure wall, the monastery was enlarged and expanded several times during the succeeding years, and includes a large church, a mosque built during the tenth century, a celebrated library with over 3500 manuscripts and the Chapel of the Burning Bush, built on the site where, according to tradition, Moses saw the bush that burned brightly but was not consumed.

32–33 *The Bedouin
of the Sinai have
preserved many of
their ancient customs,
but the rapid growth
of tourism is a force
for change among the
inhabitants of the
peninsula.*

33 (above) The strange landscapes of the highlands of the Sinai Desert. These rocky formations, worn by the wind, create intriguing panoramas as the light changes.

33 (below) The camel is still the most common form of transportation for the Bedouin in the mountains of southern Sinai, even though cars and trucks are becoming more widely used.

34 (left) Ras Mohammad is the southernmost point of the Sinai Peninsula. The entire area was declared a National Park in 1983, and development has been strictly limited in order to preserve one of the most beautiful and untouched landscapes on the Red Sea. The coasts of Ras Mohammad are surrounded by coral formations that boast a rich aquatic life, where both reef and open-sea fish thrive.

34–35 *The Strait of Tiran, where the coasts of Sinai and of the Arabian Peninsula converge to within a mile of each other, marks the southern limit of the Gulf of Aqaba. Of great strategic importance are the two islands of Tiran (seen here) and Sanafir, under Saudi Arabian sovereignty, but for administrative purposes ceded to Egypt. The area is under the control of the multinational forces that patrol the Sinai. The seabeds off Tiran are one of the most popular destinations for scuba divers. Tiran and Sanafir are also stop-over areas in the migratory routes of many species of birds, and the beaches provide breeding grounds for sea turtles. In 1983 the two islands were declared Nature Reserves, incorporated into the National Park of Ras Mohammad.*

36–37 On one of the walls of the pronaos of the temple of Abu Simbel, Ramesses II is shown wearing the Khepresh, the blue ceremonial headdress, as he symbolically offers Ethiopian and Nubian prisoners to two of the deities of the Theban Triad: Amun-Re and his bride, Mut. Between the two deities is Ramesses II himself, deified and identified with the sun god. (Ippolito Rosellini, Monumenti Storici)

ABUSIR

ALEXANDRIA

EL-NIQRASH
Naukratis

SA EL-HAGAR
Sais

BEHBEIT EL-HAGAR
Hebyt

SAMANNUD
Sebennytos

MEDITERRANEAN SEA

N

RL94

46 On the eve of the battle of Qadesh, fought in the fifth year of his reign, Ramesses II is shown discussing with his officers the plan of attack against the Hittites. Below is a line of Egyptian soldiers (right) and foreign mercenaries (left) enlisted into the pharaoh's army – recognizable by their round shields and horned helmets. (Ippolito Rosellini, Monumenti Storici)

MEDINET MADI
Narmouthis

OASIS OF BAHARIYA

QASR QARUN
Dionysias

LAKE QARUN

MEDINET EL-FAIYUM
Arsinoe, Crocodilopolis

EL-FAIYUM

DIME
Soknopaiou Nesos

GIZA

HAWARA

KARANIS
Kom Aushim

EL-LAHUN

MEIDUM

SAQQARA

DAHSHUR

MEMPHIS

LIMESTONE QUARRIES AT TURA

HELIOPOLIS

RED SEA

SAN EL-HAGAR
Tanis

QANTIR
Pi-Ramesse

TURQUOISE AND COPPER
MINES

PELUSIUM

Second Intermediate Period
c. 1750–1550 BC

Royal power declined and Nubia became an independent state. A new dynasty (no longer tracing its descent from Theban kings) founded its capital in the western section of the Delta. The Hyksos gained control of the northern part of Egypt establishing their capital at Avaris in the Delta. In circa 1550 BC Amosis expelled the occupiers.

Thirteenth Dynasty
About 70 rulers

Fourteenth Dynasty
Groups of minor sovereigns, probably all contemporary with the Thirteenth or the Fifteenth Dynasty

Fifteenth Dynasty (Hyksos)

Sixteenth Dynasty

Seventeenth Dynasty
Numerous Theban kings

New Kingdom
c. 1550–1076 BC

Tuthmosis I conquered Upper Nubia. Hatshepsut built the great funerary temple of Deir el-Bahri. Tuthmosis III conquered Syria and extended his influence over the Near East. Tuthmosis IV freed the Sphinx of Giza from the sand that engulfed it. Amenophis III established diplomatic ties with the kings of Babylon, Syria and Mitanni. Amenophis IV replaced the old religion with the worship of a single god, the sun disk, and changed his name to Akhenaten. He moved his capital to Tell el-Amarna (Akhetaten). After his death, the new religion was abolished. Tutankhamun moved the capital back to Memphis. Ay replaced Tutankhamun. Sethos I fought against the Libyans, the Syrians and the Hittites; Ramesses II continued the war against the Hittites, and after the battle of Qadesh (1274 BC) he made a peace treaty with them.

Eighteenth Dynasty
(c. 1550–1295 BC)
Principal rulers
Amosis – Tuthmosis I
Tuthmosis III – Hatshepsut
Amenophis II – Amenophis III
Tuthmosis IV
Amenophis IV/Akhenaten
Tutankhamun – Ay – Horemheb

Nineteenth Dynasty
(c. 1295–1188 BC)
Principal rulers
Ramesses I – Sethos I
Ramesses II – Merneptah

Twentieth Dynasty
(c. 1188–1076 BC)
Principal rulers
Ramesses III – Ramesses IV
Ramesses IX – Ramesses X
Ramesses XI

Third Intermediate Period
c. 1076–712 B.C.

At Tanis, the royal residence in the Delta, a new dynasty was founded that shared power with the High Priests at Thebes. Nubia became independent and Egypt lost its control over Palestine. A number of kings of Libyan origin sprang up in the east of the Delta; their power grew strong and they carried out building works at Tanis and Bubastis. Thebes declined in importance. Egypt was split up into numerous small states. Nubian rulers of the kingdom of Kush took control over Upper Egypt, conquering Memphis as well.

Twenty-First Dynasty
(c. 1076–945 BC)
Principal rulers
Smendes – Psusennes I
Psusennes II

Twenty-Second Dynasty
(c. 945–712 BC)
Principal rulers
Sheshonq I – Osorkon I
Sheshonq II

Twenty-Third Dynasty
(c. 828–712 BC)
Various simultaneous dynasties of kings recognized at Thebes, Hermopolis, Heracleopolis, Leontopolis and Tanis; there is still disagreement among scholars as to their exact order and distribution

Twenty-Fourth Dynasty
(Saite)
(c. 724–712 BC)
Principal sovereigns
Tefnakhte – Bocchoris

Late Period
c. 712–332 BC

Despite continuous wars, this was a time of prosperity and cultural development. Following Nubian domination, Egypt fell briefly under Assyrian control. The Nubian kingdom of Kush was finally and definitively separated from Egypt. The Twenty-Sixth Dynasty saw a new period of prosperity; trade flourished, principally with the Greeks. Construction was begun on a canal from the Nile to the Red Sea, but the project was later abandoned. In 525 BC Psammetichus III was defeated by Cambyses, the king of Persia, and Egypt became a Persian province. The Thirtieth was the last native dynasty. Nectanebo I built temples at Philae and Medinet Habu, and a majestic pylon in front of the temple of Karnak.

Twenty-Fifth Dynasty
(c. 712–657 BC)
Principal rulers
NUBIA AND THEBES
Kashta – Piye
NUBIA AND EGYPT
Shabaka –Taharqa

Twenty-Sixth Dynasty
(c. 664–525 BC)
Principal rulers
Necho I – Psammetichus I
Necho II – Apries – Amasis
Psammetichus III

Twenty-Seventh Dynasty
(Persian)
(c. 525–405 BC)
Principal rulers
Cambyses – Darius I – Xerxes I
Artaxerxes I – Darius II

Twenty-Eighth Dynasty
(c. 405–399 BC)

Twenty-Ninth Dynasty
(c. 399–380 BC)

Thirtieth Dynasty
(c. 380–343 BC)
Principal rulers
Nectanebo I – Nectanebo II

Second Persian Period
(c. 343–332 BC)

Graeco-Roman Period
332 BC–AD 395

In 332 BC, Alexander the Great occupied all of Egypt. After the death of Alexander, the Macedonian general Ptolemy, satrap of Egypt, had himself proclaimed pharaoh under the name of Ptolemy I Soter I. In 163 BC, Roman influence began to extend to Egypt. In 48 BC, Julius Caesar landed in Egypt to defend Cleopatra VII, who had been deposed by her brother Ptolemy XIII Philopator. In 31 BC, Octavian (Augustus) arrived in Egypt to fight Mark Antony, who had been declared an enemy of the Roman people by the Roman Senate. Octavian defeated Mark Antony in the battle of Actium, and conquered Alexandria. Egypt became a Roman province, and in AD 395 it became part of the Eastern Roman Empire.

Macedonian Dynasty
(c. 332–304 BC)
Principal rulers
Alexander the Great
Philip Arrhidaeus
Alexander IV

Ptolemaic Dynasty
(c. 304–30 BC)

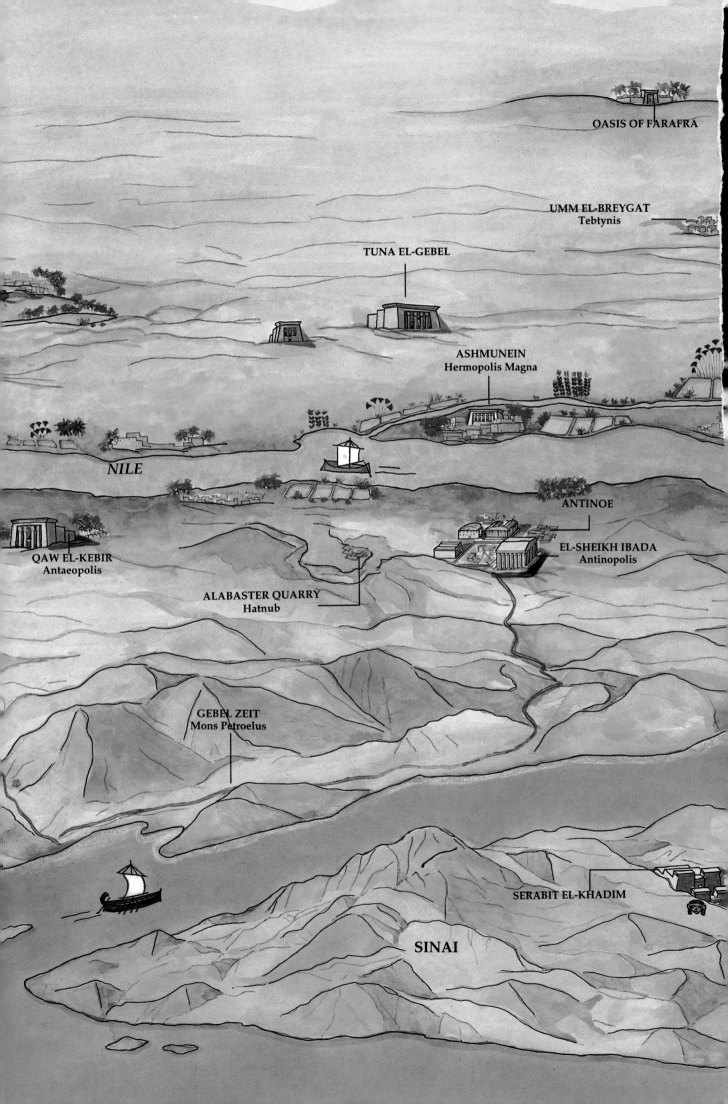

OASIS OF FARAFRA

UMM EL-BREYGAT
Tebtynis

TUNA EL-GEBEL

ASHMUNEIN
Hermopolis Magna

NILE

ANTINOE

QAW EL-KEBIR
Antaeopolis

EL-SHEIKH IBADA
Antinopolis

ALABASTER QUARRY
Hatnub

GEBEL ZEIT
Mons Petroelus

SERABIT EL-KHADIM

SINAI

EGYPT BEFORE THE PHARAOHS

It is difficult to say when humans first appeared in the Nile Valley, but the earliest stone tools found there date from the Palaeolithic, about 200,000 years ago. Much later, in the Neolithic, groups living in the Libyan Desert, the Delta, the Faiyum and Upper Egypt, practised an economy based on herding and other early agricultural activities.

The change to a more arid climate forced these people to seek refuge along the banks of the Nile, where the earliest proto-urban settlements were established. This is the phase of Egyptian history known as the Predynastic Period. The population began to concentrate around two main centres – one to the north, in the Delta region, and the other to the south, at Hierakonpolis. Documentation, in the form of reliefs on palettes and mace-heads, exists for a number of kings in the south, such as Scorpion and Narmer. It was Narmer, the last king of the Predynastic Period, who conquered Lower Egypt and first united the country. His successor, Horus Aha – who is probably the same as King Menes – founded the First Dynasty.

The first two dynasties were also called 'Thinite', because, according to Manetho, a Greek historian responsible for the division of the rulers of Egypt into 30 dynasties, their kings were all natives of the city of This, a site that has never been identified, but which must have been in the region of Abydos. The accession of Menes marked the beginning of the Early Dynastic Period, which was to last for around three centuries, from the beginning of the third millennium BC until 2658 BC.

During the reign of Menes, a second capital was founded in the north, to ensure control over the enlarged territory that could not have been effectively governed from the southern

city of Hierakonpolis. And so the city of White Walls was founded (the name probably referring to a dam built to keep out the Nile's floods), later to become Memphis, the Old Kingdom capital. The rituals of coronation were celebrated in Memphis, rituals which soon became quite complex, focusing on the power that unified Upper and Lower Egypt, embodied in the person of the king. From the little information available concerning the reign of Menes, it seems that he waged wars against the peoples of the neighbouring territories – Nubians and Libyans – and that trade was well established with the nearer regions of the Middle East. Menes was buried in Abydos, where all the kings of the First Dynasty and two kings of the Second Dynasty were buried, and was succeeded by Djer, who was in turn succeeded by Djet – known also as the Serpent King because of the pictogram that represented his name.

Qaa was the last king of the First Dynasty. A period of confusion ensued, with serious internal disorder, until Hetepsekhemwy succeeded to the throne. He was the founder of the Second Dynasty, whose kings were probably natives of the Delta. Unlike the kings of the First Dynasty, those of the Second were unable to preserve the unity of the Two Lands, and Egypt returned to being a divided monarchy with two kings, until a certain Khasekhem took the throne of Hierakonpolis, reuniting the country and taking the name of Khasekhemwy. He was the last king of the Second Dynasty; his wife is thought to have been the mother of Djoser, the second ruler of the Third Dynasty. With Djoser, who re-established Memphis as the capital, Egypt emerged from the Early Dynastic Period, and entered the period known as the Old Kingdom: the age of the pyramids.

48 (above) Flint tool, dating to the Upper Palaeolithic, found in the Theban region. The earliest stone artifacts discovered in Egypt date from over 200,000 years ago, that is in the Lower Palaeolithic, but it was not until the Upper Palaeolithic (about 30,000 years ago) that the first blade tools manu-factured using a fairly sophisticated technology appeared.

48 (below) Human head, modelled in terracotta then painted. Possibly religious in function, it is one of the earliest sculptures produced in Egypt, probably dating to the end of the fifth millennium BC. It was found at the Neolithic site of Merimda Beni Salama, on the edge of the Delta, where a community of hunters and gatherers lived. (Cairo Museum)

49 *The famous palette of Narmer, found at Hierakonpolis at the end of the nineteenth century. This remarkable artifact, dating from around 3000 BC, depicts the deeds of King Narmer, who probably unified the kingdoms of Upper and Lower Egypt. The pharaoh is shown on this side of the palette wearing the white crown of Upper Egypt, as he subjugates an enemy from Lower Egypt.*
(Cairo Museum)

THE OLD KINGDOM AND THE AGE OF THE PYRAMIDS
(2658–2150 BC)
FIRST INTERMEDIATE PERIOD
(2150–2100 BC)

50 (left) This imposing diorite statue of Chephren was discovered by the French archaeologist Auguste Mariette in 1860, in the Valley Temple of the pyramid of Chephren, at Giza. The pharaoh, who was the son and successor of Cheops, is depicted sitting on his throne dressed in the characteristic pleated skirt, known as the scendyt, *and wearing the* nemes, *a headcloth that drapes over the chest. A hawk with spread wings enfolds the head of Chephren in a protective embrace. The bird is a symbol of Horus, the hawk-god who protected the pharaoh, his earthly representative. (Cairo Museum)*

51 (right) A small ivory statuette, found at Abydos, is the only known representation of the pharaoh who ordered the building of the largest of all the pyramids of Egypt. Khufu, better known as Cheops, the name handed down by tradition and by Herodotus, reigned between 2560 and 2537 BC. (Cairo Museum)

Djoser moved the capital to Memphis and built the first pyramid in Egypt, at Saqqara. Formed of a series of superimposed *mastabas* (Arabic for 'bench') in a stepped arrangement, the pyramid seemed like a stairway leading up to the sky, by which the pharaoh could ascend to the heavens.

At the beginning of the Fourth Dynasty, the pharaoh Snefru built the first geometrically true pyramids, initially adding a smooth outer casing over the steps of the pyramid built by his predecessor Huni at Meidum, and then building two true pyramids at Dahshur, just to the south of Saqqara.

In the second half of the third millennium BC, the pharaohs Cheops (or Khufu), Chephren (Khafre) and Mycerinus (Menkaure) built the three great pyramids at Giza. In 2465 BC, Userkaf founded the Fifth Dynasty, during which the worship of the sun god Re grew increasingly important, with the pharaoh gaining the status of earthly son of the solar god. The pharaohs Sahure, Neferirkare and Nyuserre built their pyramids at Abusir, midway between Giza and Saqqara.

Unas, the last pharaoh of the Fifth Dynasty, built his pyramid at Saqqara, and for the first time texts were carved on the interior, in the burial chamber. These were the Pyramid Texts, which were later to develop into the Coffin Texts, and then, in the New Kingdom, into the Book of the Dead.

During the Sixth Dynasty (circa 2311–2150 BC) the power of the pharaohs declined while that of provincial officials strengthened. The rulers of this period (Teti, Pepy I, Merenre and Pepy II) built their pyramids at Saqqara. The reign of Pepy II was followed by the First Intermediate Period (circa 2150–2100 BC; Seventh to Tenth Dynasties) during which there was a clear weakening of centralized power.

The sovereigns of the Ninth and Tenth Dynasties took up residence at Heracleopolis, while in Thebes the local dynasty of the Intefs (I, II and III) held power.

THE MIDDLE KINGDOM
(2100–1750 BC)
AND SECOND INTERMEDIATE
PERIOD
(1750–1550 BC)

The princes of Thebes re-established central power and reunified the country. With the Middle Kingdom, founded by Nebhepetre Mentuhotep, a period of great prosperity began. The pharaohs of the Twelfth Dynasty (including Amenemhat I, Sesostris I, Amenemhat II, Sesostris II, Sesostris III, Amenemhat III) continued the task of subjugating Nubia started by Mentuhotep and built the southern pyramid of el-Lisht, two pyramids at Dahshur and the pyramids at the southern end of the Faiyum (el-Lahun and Hawara). Land reclamation work was undertaken in the Faiyum and a new royal residence established at el-Lisht.

Around 1750 BC, at the end of the Twelfth Dynasty, domestic rebellions brought about a decline of royal power. Nubia became an independent state while a rival dynasty (no longer descended from the Theban kings) established its capital in the western section of the Delta. Thus Egypt entered the Second Intermediate Period, which lasted until 1550 BC; a

troubled time when the country was taken over by foreign rulers, the Hyksos (a Greek name derived from the Egyptian, *heqau-khasut*, meaning 'Rulers of Foreign Lands'). The Hyksos assimilated Egyptian culture to some extent, but they also introduced major technological developments, including the use of the horse-drawn chariot for warfare. The new rulers established their capital in the Delta, where they founded the city of Avaris (Tell el-Daba). In about 1550 BC, the pharaoh Amosis, a prince of Thebes, succeeded in expelling the invaders and reconquered the Nubian territories, reorganizing the country; he was the founder of the Eighteenth Dynasty, which marks the beginning of the New Kingdom.

52 *A company of 40 painted wooden Nubian archers, from the tomb of Mesehti, a prince from the region of Assiut (Middle Kingdom, Eleventh Dynasty, about 2000 BC); their dark skin is a clear indication of their Nubian origin. Foreign troops such as these were no doubt recruited to reinforce the local troops. The army was particularly crucial at this period of political instability, when the lack of a strong central power was accompanied by the development of numerous autonomous local potentates. (Cairo Museum)*

53 *The spearmen of Assiut advance menacingly, carrying leather shields and spears; their light complexion shows that these are local troops. Found in the same tomb as the Nubian archers (opposite), both objects are evidence that the practice of placing miniature painted models in tombs was already known in the early Middle Kingdom period. Such models depicted themes or particular moments from the everyday life of the deceased. (Cairo Museum)*

THE NEW KINGDOM AND THE AGE OF THEBES
(1550-1076 BC)

With the Eighteenth Dynasty (circa 1550–1295 BC), founded by Amosis, the city of Waset, better known by its Greek name of Thebes, became the capital of Egypt. It was in this period that the temples of Luxor and Karnak were built, along with the royal necropolises of the Valley of the Kings and the Valley of the Queens. During the reign of Tuthmosis I, Egypt reached its greatest territorial extent: in the north all the way to the Euphrates, and to the south as far as the Fourth Cataract. Tuthmosis III, one of the greatest Egyptian rulers, campaigned in Syria, where the kingdom of Mitanni had grown powerful, but was forced to cede part of the territories on the Euphrates.

Tuthmosis also led expeditions to Nubia, where he established a provincial capital at Napata. Amenophis II continued the war against Mitanni, a war which was not to end until the reign of Tuthmosis IV, the pharaoh who freed the Sphinx of Giza from the sands that were engulfing it. Amenophis III succeeded in establishing diplomatic relations with the kings of Babylonia, Syria and Mitanni. Under his rule, there was a remarkable flourishing of the arts and architecture. Nothing remains now of his great funerary temple on the west bank at Thebes but two great statues, known as the Colossi of Memnon. Amenophis IV, who changed his name to Akhenaten, replaced the traditional religion with the sole worship of a single god, Aten, 'the Sun Disk'; he moved the capital from Thebes to Tell el-Amarna (Akhetaten), a new city that he founded in Middle Egypt, and married Nefertiti, making her his queen.

54 Amenophis III, the 'Sun Pharaoh', reigned from 1391 to 1353 BC, at the peak of the splendour of the Eighteenth Dynasty. This was a time distinguished by remarkable developments in architecture and an innovative style in statuary, the result of influence from the east, which is discernible in the increased flexibility and freedom in form.

55 Considered to be one of the masterpieces of New Kingdom sculpture, this splendid statue depicts pharaoh Tuthmosis III (Eighteenth Dynasty, 1479–1425 BC). It was uncovered in 1904 in the cache found in the courtyard in front of the seventh pylon of the temple of Karnak. Tuthmosis III was a great general who led a series of victorious military campaigns in Syria and also expanded Egyptian power in the south, where he established a second capital at Napata, not far from the Fourth Cataract. (Museum of Luxor)

During the reign of Tutankhamun, the young pharaoh, son of Akhenaten, who came to the throne aged about seven, and who died ten years later, the old religion was re-established, and the capital was moved to the north, to Memphis, by now the most important city in Egypt. During this period, the real reins of power were held by the priest Ay, who took the throne on Tutankhamun's death and ruled for four years, and by the general Horemheb, who succeeded Ay.

Horemheb was the last ruler of the Eighteenth Dynasty; Ramesses I was the first pharaoh of the Nineteenth, which lasted for about a century, from 1295 to 1188 BC. Sethos I, Ramesses' son, waged war against the Libyans, Syrians and Hittites, and at the end of his reign, he governed jointly with his son, Ramesses, who became pharaoh Ramesses II. After his accession he continued the war against the Hittites, and, following the battle of Qadesh (1274 BC), fought in Syria on the banks of the Orontes, he signed a peace treaty with them. In his incredible 67-year rule, Ramesses was a prolific builder. Aside from the hundreds of statues erected, many temples were built (Abu Simbel, Memphis, Bubastis, Abydos), while others were enlarged and embellished (Abydos, Karnak, Luxor). Moreover, Ramesses founded a new capital in the Delta, on the former capital of the Hyksos, Avaris; he named it Pi-Ramesses. Among his numerous consorts, two stood out above all the rest: Nefertari, well known for her tomb in the Valley of the Queens and for the temple dedicated to her at Abu Simbel; and Isis-Nofret. It was Isis-Nofret, the location of whose tomb is unknown, who bore Ramesses' successor: Merneptah. Merneptah was succeeded by Sethos II, and then for two years a woman reigned: Tawosre, the widow of Sethos II. With the brief reign of the pharaoh Setenakhte, the Twentieth Dynasty began (circa 1188 to 1076 BC), dominated by the figure of Ramesses III, who was succeeded by a long line of Ramessids, ending with Ramesses XI. Ramesses III built important temples, including that of Medinet

56 Sethos I, the father of Ramesses II, continued the task of restoring the cult of Amun, begun by Horemheb after the brief interruption of the Amarna period. He also waged a series of campaigns against the Hittites in Syria and was responsible for the construction of a number of religious buildings, including part of the great hypostyle hall at the temple of Karnak. (Cairo Museum)

Habu, and he successfully waged war against the Libyans and the 'Sea Peoples'.

Towards the end of the dynasty, central power weakened, and the High Priest of the god Amun at Karnak became one of the most powerful figures in the land. The High Priest Herihor even claimed royal powers for a brief period.

57 A close-up view of
one of the four colossi
of Ramesses II on the
façade of the great
temple of Abu Simbel.
The pharaoh is shown
with a ceremonial
beard and wearing the
classic headcloth, the
nemes. On the
pharaoh's forehead
sits the uraeus, the
sacred serpent, a
protective symbol and
one which indicates
royal rank.

THE THIRD INTERMEDIATE PERIOD
(1076 – 712 BC)

The end of the Twentieth Dynasty was followed by the Third Intermediate Period: a lengthy and extremely complex period, during which, at certain times, several different dynasties governed the country simultaneously. In the city of Tanis in the Delta, not far from the capital of the Ramessids, a new Tanite dynasty emerged, the Twenty-First, which shared power with the High Priests of Thebes. Egypt was in effect divided again into two kingdoms and lost its hold over Palestine, while Nubia gained its independence.

Subsequently, a number of kings of Libyan descent established themselves to the east of the Delta (the Twenty-Second Dynasty) and grew very powerful. The importance of Thebes declined; Egypt was split up into tiny states, and any local warlord could have himself proclaimed king and receive the acclamation of the people.

The various dynasties, up to the Twenty-Fifth, governed at the same time in different parts of Egypt. Between 724 and 712 BC, in Sais (modern-day Sa el-Hagar), in the western Delta, the local princes Tefnakhte and Bocchoris reigned (the Twenty-Fourth or Saite Dynasty).

Previously, around 770 BC, the king Kashta, of the Kushite Dynasty, had been acknowledged as ruler at least as far north as Aswan. His successor Piye, who founded the Twenty-Fifth (Nubian) Dynasty, received the submission of the sovereigns of Sais.

THE TWILIGHT OF THE PHARAOHS: THE LATE PERIOD
(712 – 332 BC)

Despite incessant wars, this was a time of prosperity and cultural development. The new kings considered themselves the legitimate successors of the first pharaohs, and they worked to preserve and enhance their cultural legacy. Egypt, however, was to lose its independence for several centuries. Under Nubian rule, Egypt enjoyed a period of great affluence and became once again a major power, whose only rival was Assyria. Assyrian kings, helped by the rulers of Sais, occupied the country briefly. Psammetichus I (Twenty-Sixth Dynasty) defeated the Assyrians towards 653 BC, and forced the smaller independent states into submission, establishing Egyptian unity once again. The Twenty-Sixth Dynasty (664–525 BC) was a period of renewed prosperity when trade flourished, especially with the Greeks.

The pharaoh Necho began the construction of a canal from the Nile to the Red Sea, but the project was finally abandoned. In 525 BC, Psammetichus III was defeated by Cambyses, king of Persia, and Egypt became a Persian province dominated by Persian rulers: Cambyses, Darius I, Xerxes I, Artaxerxes and Darius II. It was not until around 380 BC with the Thirtieth Dynasty (circa 380–343 BC), founded by Nectanebo I, that Egypt regained its independence. This was the last native Egyptian dynasty. In 343 BC, under Artaxerxes III, the Persians reconquered Egypt but maintained control over the country for only ten years, until 332 BC (the Second Persian Period).

58 A splendid uraeus, made of solid gold inlaid with cornelian and glass paste, has pride of place on the forehead of the coffin of Pharaoh Amenemope, who succeeded Psusennes I. The coffin was discovered by Pierre Montet at Tanis in 1940.

THE WEST AND EGYPT: THE GRAECO-ROMAN PERIOD
(332 BC–AD 395)

In 332 BC, Alexander the Great triumphantly entered Egypt, where he was acknowledged as divine. His Macedonian Dynasty, however, lasted only until 304 BC, when the general Ptolemy had himself proclaimed pharaoh under the name of Ptolemy I Soter I. He founded the Ptolemaic dynasty, which, with alternating successes and failures, was to last until 30 BC, when Egypt fell under the sway of the Roman Empire. During the reign of Ptolemy XII Neos Dionysos, also known as Ptolemy Auletes, the construction of the temple of Edfu was completed, and work began on the temple of Dendera. In 48 BC, Julius Caesar landed in Egypt to defend the queen, Cleopatra VII, who had been deposed by her brother Ptolemy XIII Philopator.

Later, in 31 BC, Octavian, the future emperor Augustus, arrived in Egypt in pursuit of Mark Antony, now Cleopatra's lover, who had been declared an enemy of the Roman people by the Senate. Octavian defeated Mark Antony at the battle of Actium and Egypt became a Roman province.

Roman emperors presented themselves to the Egyptian people as successors to the pharaohs. Egyptian religion continued to survive, spreading to other parts of the Mediterranean region – even to Rome itself. Around AD 200, Christianity began to grow in popularity, and in AD 379 it was made the official religion of the Empire. The end of the ancient period is conventionally dated as AD 395, when Egypt became part of the Eastern Roman Empire.

60 *In the innermost recess of the temple of Horus, at Edfu, there is chapel of granite – a naos – that once contained the cult statue of the falcon-god in his terrestrial form.*

THE BYZANTINE PERIOD
(AD 395–640)

The Eastern Roman Empire was too weak to exert effective control over all its subject states, and Egypt was left to its own devices, being afforded no protection against invaders: Nubians from the south and North Africans from the west, until the arrival, in AD 640, of the Arabs, led by Amr Ibn al-As, the lieutenant of Caliph Omar.

THE ISLAMIC PERIOD
(AD 640–1517)

The Arabs brought their religion to Egypt, though they also allowed some freedom of worship. A succession of different caliphates (Umayyads 658–750, Abbasids 750–868, Tulunids 868–905, Ikhitids 905–969, Fatimids 969–1171) ended in 1171, when the warlord of Kurdish descent, Salah-ed-Din (the notorious Saladin), deposed the last Fatimid caliph and took the title of sultan, founding the Ayyubid dynasty (1171–1250). This was the most glorious period of Egyptian history during the Middle Ages.
In 1176, after the destruction of much of Cairo by Crusaders, Saladin began the fortification of the city, building the Citadel and the city walls. To defend the city, he hired an army of Turkish mercenaries, the Mamelukes, who seized power in 1250, and held sway for over two centuries.

THE OTTOMAN PERIOD
(AD 1517–1798)

In 1517, when the power of the Mamelukes was weak, Egypt was absorbed into the Turkish Ottoman Empire, and the government of the country was entrusted to a pasha, appointed by the sultan. The authority of the Ottoman Empire (the 'Sublime Porte') declined rapidly, however, while the political power of the Mamelukes increased once again. The pashas were forced to ask the Mamelukes for their support in order to be able to rule effectively; the absence of a central power affected the country seriously, in both political and economic terms.

61 The celebrated zodiac of the temple of Dendera, as illustrated in 1837 in the Atlante Monumentale del Basso e dell'Alto Egitto, by the Italian traveller Girolamo Segato. The zodiac, which was painted on the ceiling of one of the eastern chapels located on the roof of the temple, was removed during Napoleon's Egyptian expedition and was shipped to the Louvre, where it is now on display.

THE BIRTH OF MODERN EGYPT

In 1798, Napoleon Bonaparte landed in Egypt, a move in his campaign against British power in the Mediterranean. He defeated the Mameluke army in the celebrated Battle of the Pyramids, near Aboukir Bay, but the French fleet was then destroyed by that of the British, commanded by Admiral Nelson. The French found themselves virtual prisoners in the land they had just conquered. In 1801 they left Egypt.

At this time of war and confusion, an officer in charge of the Albanian regiment, Mohammad Ali, seized power and had himself named Pasha by the Ottoman sultan (1805). He eradicated all Mameluke influence within the country, conquered the Sudan, Palestine and Syria, and began a vast project of modernizing Egypt. He was succeeded by his nephew Abbas in 1848, who was in turn succeeded by his two sons: Said (1854–1863) and Ismail (1863–1879). In 1867 Ismail was named viceroy. It was during his reign that the Suez Canal was inaugurated, in 1869.

The modernization begun by Mohammad Ali, however, led to massive foreign debt, and the country slipped into economic difficulties. Egypt was forced to submit to the interference of the great European powers – especially the British.

62–63 The Battle of Aboukir, painted by Louis François Lejeune, and now in the collection of the National Museum of France at Versailles. On 25 July 1799, near the fort of Aboukir, Napoleon's troops routed the Turkish soldiers commanded by Mustapha Pasha, who were supported by the English. Despite victory on land in the famous Battle of the Pyramids on 21 July 1798, Napoleon's fleet had already been destroyed by the English, under the command of Admiral Horatio Nelson on 1 August, in a great naval battle just off Aboukir. Victory in the land battle of Aboukir was therefore insignificant in strategic terms. The French army was held virtual prisoner in the territory that it had conquered, and on 2 September 1801, General Menou was obliged to surrender.

THE BRITISH PROTECTORATE
(AD 1882–1922)

The English re-established domestic order through a military occupation of Egypt, but the country's development was subordinated to British economic interests. In 1918, the Wafd, the first popular Egyptian nationalist party, founded and led by Saad Zaghlul, demanded independence. British rejection of the demand led to revolt and, in 1922, Britain was forced to accede.

THE KINGDOM OF EGYPT
(AD 1922–1952)

Ahmed Fuad Pasha, or King Fuad I, was responsible for Egypt's first constitution, establishing the country as a parliamentary monarchy. During the reign of his son, Farouk, Egypt became a member of the League of Nations, in 1937. After the Second World War, in a nation impoverished by inflation and unemployment, and plagued by serious problems of civil disorder, the power of an Egyptian officer named Gamel Abdel Nasser grew, and in 1952 Nasser forced Farouk to abdicate.

64 (above, left) The minarets of the mosque of Mohammad Ali in Cairo rise above the Citadel, the imposing fortress that dominates the entire city. The mosque, begun in 1824, was completed in 1857, during the rule of Said. It was built in an Ottoman style reminiscent of the great mosques of Istanbul.

64 (left) Mohammad Ali is considered the founder of modern Egypt. An officer of Albanian birth sent to Egypt by the sultan of Constantinople during Napoleon's Egyptian expedition, he succeeded in having himself made Pasha. After doing away with the last Mameluke chiefs – he had them slaughtered wholesale after

inviting them to the Citadel under pretext of a dinner of reconciliation – Mohammad Ali became the unrivalled ruler of Egypt. During his reign the country prospered thanks to his policy of developing cotton plantations; the country's military might and international influence also grew.

THE ARAB REPUBLIC OF EGYPT

On 18 June 1953, Egypt was declared a republic. Nasser was named Prime Minister, and, later, President. In terms of foreign policy, Nasser moved away from the Western powers and looked instead towards the then Soviet Union and the People's Republic of China. In 1956, he nationalized the Suez Canal, and used the revenue thus obtained to build the Aswan High Dam. Nasser

65 This view of modern Cairo shows one of the many bridges that connect the two sides of the city – the western side, built at the foot of the Citadel and Mt Mokkatam, and the eastern quarters – and the two large islands, Gezira to the north and Roda to the south. With its 14 million inhabitants, Cairo is one of the largest cities in the world, and its population is growing rapidly.

followed a Pan-Arabic philosophy, and in 1958 he founded the United Arab Republic (UAR), with Yemen and Syria, which lasted until 1961. After the war against Israel in 1967, Egypt lost Sinai, and, at the same time, the revenue from ships passing through the Suez Canal, which had been made impassable. Nasser agreed to recognize the state of Israel in exchange for the restitution of the occupied regions.

Nasser died in 1970 and was

succeeded by his vice-president Anwar al-Sadat. After a lightning attack against the Israelis in 1973, Sadat implemented a liberal domestic policy and sought closer ties with the West. During his presidency, in March 1979, the Camp David Agreement was signed, establishing Egyptian links with Israel; one effect of this was a deterioration of Egypt's relations with other Arab nations. Sadat was assassinated on 6 October 1981 and was succeeded by Hosni Mubarak.

Voyages and Voyagers
The rediscovery of Egypt

Around 450 BC, the Greek historian Herodotus visited Egypt and wrote an historical account of the country, describing with great precision its traditions, customs and religious beliefs. A few centuries later, in 57 BC, the historian Diodorus Siculus also visited Egypt, and wrote a survey of the country's history. The Roman geographer Strabo sailed up the Nile as far as the First Cataract in 30 BC, and devoted an entire book of his *Geographica* to a description of the land. In the first century AD Plutarch travelled to Egypt, enquiring into its religious beliefs, which he described in his book, *De Iside et Osiride*. Egypt and its extraordinary monuments then plunged into obscurity in the West.

The travellers and merchants – often Venetians – who visited the country in their dealings with the Middle East never ventured further south than Cairo. It was not until 1589 that an unknown merchant, referred to as the Anonymous Venetian (Anonimo Veneziano), sailed up the Nile as far as Thebes and wrote the earliest surviving European account of a journey to Upper Egypt. In 1638, John Greaves, an English astronomer, visited the pyramids at Giza and performed the first accurate measurements of the monuments, later published in his book, *Pyramidographia*. A few years later, in 1672, the Dominican friar J.B. Vansleb described the ruins of Antinoë, the city built by the Roman emperor Hadrian in memory of his young favourite, Antinous, who drowned in the Nile. Between 1708 and 1726, the French Jesuit Claude Sicard made five trips to Upper Egypt, and drew the first scholarly map of Egypt, indicating the principal monuments and the locations, real or supposed, of the ancient cities.

Another Frenchman, Benoît de Maillet, published a thorough description of Egypt in 1735, including a fairly accurate cross-section of the pyramid of Cheops. Three years later, in 1738, a Danish sea captain, Frederik Ludwig Norden, was sent to Egypt by King Christian VI, to write a complete report on the country, and in 1760, the Paduan botanist Vitaliano Donati ventured beyond Aswan and the First Cataract. Around the same time, in 1766, Jean Baptiste Bourguignon

66 (left) In the Mappamondo of Fra Mauro Camaldolese of 1459, because of the particular orientation the cartographer monk gave to his map, north, and hence the Mediterranean Sea, appears at the bottom of the image, while the course of the river, drawn with a surfeit of fancy, winds its way through the country. (Venice, Marciana Library)

67 (right) The Nautical Atlas by Battista Agnese, dating from 1554, maps the course of the Nile and the Red Sea. The Nile is shown following the classical course suggested by the Alexandrian geographer Claudius Ptolomaeus, better known as Ptolemy; two spring-fed basins serving as southern sources are indicated. Along the river's course, the cities of Meroë, Napata and Syene are illustrated; to the north Cairo and Alexandria can be seen. (Venice, Marciana Library)

demascus
hierusalem

babilon nüc
cairo

aleyandria

AEGYP
IVS.

altos porto dlfoldan
ARA
mecha

siene

zidan

napata
regia

lmyona

REGI N A CAD
ACES
AETHYOPIA
SVB AEGYPTO
meroe
regia

REGINA
AVSTRIA.
meroe regio elfaba hodie
dicitur in qua diuum mat heu
euangeliu predicaffe ferut
hacc iofepho tefte eft illa
faba inde ad falamone
profecta eft regina

amamtrea ualif filua

PRETE IAN

coloa ciuitas

d'Anville published a map of Egypt that was used by most later explorers. In 1768, the English traveller James Bruce visited Luxor and Karnak, finding, in the Valley of the Kings, the tomb of Ramesses III (also known as 'Bruce's Tomb' or the 'Harper's Tomb'). The most exhaustive study of Egypt's monuments came as a result of the great expedition of Napoleon Bonaparte. In 1798, Dominique Vivant Denon and the teams of scholars accompanying Napoleon and his army to Egypt roamed the entire country, cataloguing and drawing everything they came across. Their work was published in 1809 as the *Description de l'Égypte*, a monumental work, with nine volumes of text and eleven of plates, with more than 3000 drawings by some 200 artists.

The monuments of ancient Egypt, although covered with writing, remained silent to Europeans. Despite

numerous attempts, the task of deciphering the writing of the pharaohs seemed impossible. In 1799, as Napoleon's Egyptian expedition was coming to an end, a Lieutenant Bouchard came across, by chance, at Rosetta in the Delta, a stela, which, a few years later, proved fundamental in solving the problem. Other major discoveries were also being made: in

1813 the Swiss orientalist Johann Ludwig Burckhardt came upon the temple of Abu Simbel, and in 1815 the Paduan explorer Giovanni Battista Belzoni landed in Egypt where, between 1816 and 1818, he achieved a series of remarkable successes, among which were the opening of the temple of Abu Simbel and the finding of Sethos I's tomb and of the entrance to the pyramid of Chephren. Also in 1818, another Italian – Girolamo Segato – came to Egypt. He located the entrance to the step pyramid of Djoser at Saqqara and charted vast territories in Upper Egypt and Nubia, reaching as far as the oasis of Siwa. Meanwhile, a then-unknown French scholar had devoted himself to the study of the stela with a triple inscription found by Bouchard at Rosetta.

This young scholar was named Jean François Champollion, and in 1822 he announced to an astonished world that he had deciphered hieroglyphs. In 1828 he organized the Franco-Tuscan Expedition, with the assistance of his prize pupil, Ippolito Rosellini. The purpose of the expedition was to test the validity of his deductions by deciphering new epigraphic texts on the spot. This was the birth of modern Egyptology.

In 1838, the Scottish painter David Roberts sailed up the Nile and systematically sketched the sites of ancient Egypt. It was through his paintings that most Europeans became acquainted with the ancient Egyptian monuments. The Prussian Richard Lepsius carried on Champollion's scientific work; in 1842, he organized an expedition that sailed up the Nile as far as Meroë and later published his fundamental work, *Denkmäler aus Ägypten und Äthiopien*. In 1858, the French archaeologist Auguste Mariette set up the Egyptian Antiquities Service and the Egyptian Museum of Cairo. His greatest work was at Saqqara, where he uncovered the catacomb of the sacred Apis bulls, known as the Serapeum. At Giza, Mariette found the magnificent Valley Temple of the pyramid of Chephren, which yielded numerous statues, the best known of which is the life-sized

diorite portrait of the pharaoh seated on his throne. Gaston Maspero, Mariette's successor, carried on his work and, in 1881, made suspicious by a sudden abundance on the market of objects of very high quality, which certainly came from a royal tomb, he managed to track down a band of tomb-robbers in the Luxor region. His detective work brought to light the celebrated cache of Deir el-Bahri, hidden in a tomb in a narrow fissure in a cliff-side, not far from the temple of the same name. Here, priests of the Twenty-First Dynasty, alarmed at the repeated looting of royal tombs by robbers, had placed the mummies of the most important pharaohs of Egypt, including Amenophis I, Tuthmosis III, Ramesses II and Sethos I.

In 1880, the British Egyptologist Sir William Matthew Flinders Petrie came to Egypt. Over many years he carried out important excavations, mostly in Upper Egypt, where he discovered the great Predynastic necropolis of Naqada and the royal tombs of Abydos, containing the burials of the kings of the First Dynasty.

At the beginning of the twentieth century, in 1904, a disciple of Maspero, the Italian Ernesto Schiaparelli, established the Missione Archeologica Italiana, and in two decades of excavation he uncovered numerous tombs, the best known of which was that of Nefertari.

Perhaps the greatest archaeological discovery of all took place in 1922, when the English archaeologist Howard Carter discovered the almost intact tomb of a little-known pharaoh: Tutankhamun. Surprises did not end there, however, and, less than 20 years later a French archaeologist made the only discovery that can claim to rival that of Tutankhamun's tomb.

68 (left) It was thanks to Napoleon's Egyptian expedition (here at the head of his troops just before landing in Egypt) that Europe rediscovered the civilization of the pharaohs at the dawn of the nineteenth century.

69 (right) Scientists of Napoleon's expedition, shown here as they measure the Great Sphinx of Giza, systematically studied, documented, described and analysed all the major monuments of Egypt for the first time.

In 1939, the Egyptologist Pierre Montet was working in the eastern Delta, at San el-Hagar, the site of the ancient city of Tanis. Here he discovered the almost untouched tombs of pharaohs of the Twenty-First and Twenty-Second dynasties, during which time the city was the Egyptian capital, sometimes referred to as 'Thebes of the North'. The extremely lavish array of funerary articles from the tomb of Pharaoh Psusennes I, including spectacular jewels, gold and silver vases, a gold mask and a rare silver coffin, displays an extremely high level of artistry and craftsmanship.

Alongside the pharaoh's tomb, Montet discovered four other tombs, which had belonged to Osorkon II, Amenemope – son and successor of Psusennes – General Undebaunded, and King Heka-kheper-re Sheshonq, known as Sheshonq II.

The discovery of the royal necropolis of Tanis, and its abundant treasures, marked the end of an era in the history of Egyptology in the first half of the twentieth century, an era that had begun with the discoveries of Schiaparelli and Carter. But Egypt held yet more secrets and discoveries are still being made today.

GIOVANNI BATTISTA BELZONI, THE TITAN OF PADUA

Born on 5 November 1778 in Padua (Italy), in 1803 Giovanni Battista Belzoni arrived in England, a country where he lived for seven years, finally taking British citizenship. To make a living, Belzoni took to the stage as the 'Patagonian Samson', utilizing his gigantic stature and Herculean strength to lift ten or more people at once in an iron frame.

In 1815, Belzoni, returning from a theatrical tour that had taken him to Spain, Portugal and Sicily, reached Malta, where he met with Ishmael Gibraltar, the emissary of the Pasha of Egypt, who was carrying out a number of land-reclamation schemes and irrigation projects. Belzoni, who had trained as a hydraulic engineer, offered his assistance. And so the

70 (left, above) Although the Greek historian Herodotus clearly stated that the second pyramid of Giza, that belonging to Chephren, had no interior chambers, the Paduan-born traveller Giovanni Battista Belzoni would not admit defeat and, on 2 March 1818, after extensive and painstaking research, he succeeded in finding an entrance to the corridor that led to the burial chamber. Belzoni met with bitter disappointment when he realized that the pyramid had already been despoiled. The only object he found inside the pyramid was a plain stone sarcophagus, without decoration or inscription.

70 (left) The removal and transport of one of the colossal heads of Ramesses II, which once stood in the pharaoh's memorial temple in western Thebes, the Ramesseum. This was Belzoni's first great undertaking in Egypt, completed in 1816. Previously, even Napoleon's troops, who had attempted to remove the head, had been unable to achieve this remarkable feat. In a few days of hard labour, Belzoni managed to move the statue as far as the Nile, where it was loaded on board a ship and transported to the British Museum in London, where it still remains today.

MODE IN WHICH THE YOUNG MEMNONS HEAD (NOW IN THE BRITISH MUSEUM.) WAS REMOVED.

Paduan sideshow performer and inventor set off for Egypt. Once he had arrived there, after a number of adventures, he presented the Pasha with a hydraulic machine of his own invention, a type of water wheel for irrigating cultivated fields.

Unfortunately, a mishap occurred during his demonstration of the device, and this, together with opposition at court, meant that Mohammad Ali, the Pasha, was persuaded to decline the offer of the new machine, and Belzoni found himself out of a job. At this point he made the acquaintance of Henry Salt, the new consul general of England, who, like other diplomats of the period, was occupied in assembling collections of antiquities for his national museum. Belzoni offered his services to transport a colossal granite bust of Ramesses II, weighing more than 7 tons, from the funerary temple of Ramesses II in Thebes, the Ramesseum (then called the Memnonium), an undertaking which had been beyond the ability of the troops of Napoleon's expedition. His offer accepted, on 30 June 1816 Belzoni took ship from Bulaq, the river port of Cairo, and headed for Thebes, thus setting out on his first amazing adventure in Egypt.

When he arrived in Thebes he eventually succeeded in enlisting the help of some 80 locals, and, on 27 July, he began the daunting operation with the sole assistance of levers, pulleys and ropes made of palm leaves. On 12 August 1816, the 'Younger Memnon', as the bust had come to be called, stood on the banks of the Nile. Hoisted on to a boat heading for Cairo, and then on to

Alexandria, the bust was finally sent off to London, and placed in the Egyptian Gallery of the British Museum, where it remains today.

After returning to Cairo the following year, Belzoni undertook a second journey to Upper Egypt, with the intention of freeing the temple of Abu Simbel of the sands that almost enveloped it. Abu Simbel had been

discovered four years earlier by the Swiss orientalist and traveller Johann Ludwig Burckhardt, but Belzoni wished to be the first to penetrate the interior. Once again Belzoni's efforts were crowned with success, and on, 1 August 1817, he made his way into the interior of the monument. After returning to Thebes, Belzoni decided that he next wanted to begin research

71 Giovanni Battista Belzoni, born in Padua, Italy, in 1778, worked in Egypt from 1815 to 1819. During these few years, he associated his name with the most important monuments in Egypt, succeeding in making his way into the great temple of Abu Simbel and into the pyramid of Chephren, and discovering the tomb of Pharaoh Sethos I in the Valley of the Kings. The finds that he brought to light on behalf of the English consul Henry Salt constitute an important part of the collection of Egyptian antiquities of the British Museum in London.

in the Valley of the Kings, and, on 18 October 1817, he stumbled upon a tomb that was to prove to be one of the finest and largest tombs ever found in Egypt: that of Sethos I, still known as the 'Belzoni Tomb'. The tomb, which Belzoni – who of course could not read hieroglyphs – attributed to a pharaoh named Samathis, was decorated with very fine paintings and remarkable reliefs. In the burial chamber stood a splendid alabaster sarcophagus, which was removed and transported to England. Returning again to Cairo, Belzoni next became interested in the great pyramids of Giza, in particular

the pyramid of Chephren, which, according to Herodotus, had no internal chambers. After making a number of comparative observations with the pyramid of Cheops, on 2 March 1818 Belzoni found the entrance corridor leading into the monument – thus one of the wonders of the ancient world finally disclosed its mystery. After completing, in the same year, a journey through the Arabian Desert and along the coasts of the Red Sea, he discovered the ruins of the ancient city of Berenice, the port built by Ptolemy II Philadelphus, and in the following year, during an expedition into the Libyan Desert he

72 (left) Sethos I in the presence of the goddess Hathor, in a copy of a painted relief from the pharaoh's tomb by Alessandro Ricci, an excellent draughtsman and fellow adventurer of Belzoni's. The drawing was made immediately after the discovery of the tomb by Belzoni, who himself executed plaster casts and life-size drawings of almost the entire tomb of Sethos I; he later exhibited these to the public in a hugely popular exhibition in London. Belzoni never attempted to remove any of the murals, and the most he did was to take away the alabaster sarcophagus of the king. The bas-relief shown here, along with another similar one, was in fact removed later by Jean François Champollion and Ippolito Rosellini during the Franco-Tuscan Expedition of 1828.

reached the ancient oasis of Jupiter
Ammon, whose oracle had been
consulted by Alexander the Great.
During this voyage Belzoni became
the first European to visit the oasis of
Bahariya. The great adventurer then
took ship to return to Europe, bidding
what proved to be a final farewell to
Egypt. Belzoni had many opponents
during his life and after his death.
Many criticized his rough and ready
methods, forgetting that at that time
Egypt was full, not of archaeologists,
but of collectors of antiquities, whose
only interest was not the study of
Egyptian civilization, but rather the

gathering of artifacts.

The most balanced and impartial
judgment, however, is that offered by
Who Was Who in Egyptology, published
by the Egypt Exploration Society of
London: 'He cannot be judged by the
standards of later excavators, such as
Petrie or even Mariette, but must be
seen in the context of the period before
decipherment [of hieroglyphs]; at the
start of his career he was neither better
nor worse than other contemporary
figures, but he later evolved
techniques and acquired knowledge
that raised him above the general
level.'

*73 Belzoni was
responsible for
discovering the largest
and most beautiful
tomb in the Valley of
the Kings, that
belonging to Pharaoh
Sethos I, father of
Ramesses II. The
Paduan traveller, after
locating the entrance*
*of the tomb, succeeded
in entering it in
October 1817. Over
120 m (393 ft) in
length, the tomb was
entirely decorated
with very fine
polychrome paintings
and bas-reliefs of
great interest and
refinement.*

GIROLAMO SEGATO, DRAUGHTSMAN AND GEOGRAPHER

Girolamo Segato, born at Vedana, near Belluno (Italy), in 1792, came to Egypt almost by chance, as did so many travellers of his time. Segato, like Belzoni, immediately fell prey to the allure of the ancient and unexplored world of the pharaohs.

At first, however, he did not devote himself to the search for antiquities, but rather to employment of a topographical nature, drawing – on behalf of the son of Mohammad Ali, Khedive Ismail – maps and topographical charts of Cairo. Now and then he extended his interests to the great monuments built by the pharaohs not far from the city, especially those in the area of Saqqara and Abusir. Then, in 1820, Segato took part in the great military expedition led by another son of Mohammad Ali, Ibrahim Pasha, around Sennar, in the eastern Sudan. Segato, going ahead of the expedition, left Cairo on 6 May and reached Aswan on 17 May. A month later the Italian traveller was at the Second Cataract of Wadi Halfa, and from here he set out for the Arabian Desert, having been excluded from the expedition to Sennar, probably as a result of intrigues that never fully came to light.

After travelling south for a while, passing the Fifth Cataract and reaching Suakin, Segato returned to Cairo on 29 November, and sailed back down the Nile, stopping at the most important archaeological sites. When Segato, by now completely exhausted, returned to Cairo, he had accumulated an enormous number of charts and drawings. In the following year, Segato undertook another major journey, accompanying the expedition of the Prussian Baron von Minutoli into the Libyan Desert west of the Nile, and making his way as far as the remote oasis of Siwa, the oasis of

Jupiter Ammon, where the famous 'Fountain of the Sun' was located, mentioned by classical authors for its remarkable property of flowing cold by day and warm by night.

Segato returned once again to Cairo and devoted himself to exploring the archaeological zone of Saqqara, and in particular the step pyramid. The step pyramid at Saqqara was the first funerary structure of this type built in Egypt and dates from the reign of Pharaoh Djoser. Much like Belzoni with the pyramid of Chephren, Segato wished to find the entrance to Djoser's pyramid and unveil its long-held secrets. The discovery of a shaft led Segato to the main entrance of the pyramid, buried beneath some 15 m (50 ft) of sand. After freeing the entrance, Segato entered the pyramid, the first to do so in modern times. Unfortunately, he found that tomb-robbers had preceded him thousands of years before, as was the case in all the great pyramids.

After the successful exploration of this monument, he returned to his calling as a draughtsman, and in April 1822 he accurately sketched two cubit measures (the basic unit of measurement of the ancient Egyptians), one found by Nizzoli and the other by the French consul Drovetti. Segato's last archaeological work is recorded at this time, and it seems he spent the final part of his stay in Egypt in other fields of study, perhaps connected with botany, chemistry and the processes of mummification and petrification, which all played an important role in the second half of his life, after his return to Italy in April 1823. Embittered by the loss of his collection of antiquities, which had been packed in 90 cases

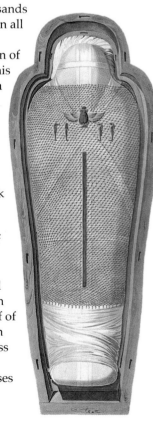

74–75 (right) The Italian traveller and cartographer Girolamo Segato, worked in Egypt from 1818 until 1823, completing a vast number of sketches and drawings all over the country and taking part in adventurous travels to Sennar (Sudan), in the entourage of Ibrahim Pasha, and to the oasis of Siwa in the Libyan Desert. He was responsible for the discovery of the entrance to the step pyramid of Saqqara, and the first scientific documentation of this monument. (Civic Museum of Belluno, Italy)

74 (left) A mummy and its protective amulets – a drawing by Girolamo Segato. The winged scarab is a symbol of the sun god, and the four sons of Horus guard the viscera of the mummy. (From the Atlante Monumentale dell'Alto e del Basso Egitto)

and loaded on a ship for Berlin that was lost at sea, Segato moved to Florence. In 1827 he published a work, or at least the first volume, called *Saggi pittorici, geografici, statistici e catastali dell'Egitto*, or *Pictorial, Geographic, Statistical and Demographic Essays on Egypt*. In 1833 he began preparing a second, the *Atlante Monumentale dell'Alto e del Basso Egitto*, or *Atlas of the Monuments of Upper and Lower Egypt*, published in 1837, a year after he died.

75 (left) View of el-Mansura in Lower Egypt. Original drawing by Girolamo Segato in Saggi pittorici, geografici, statistici e catastali dell'Egitto. (Civic Museum of Belluno, Italy)

JEAN FRANÇOIS CHAMPOLLION, THE VOICE OF ANCIENT EGYPT

76 Jean François Champollion le Jeune, painted by the artist Léon Cogniet in 1831. Champollion began to work on the trilingual texts of the Rosetta Stone at the age of 18, in 1808, and he succeeded in unlocking the mystery of hieroglyphs after 14 years of study, in 1822.

In 1808 the French scholar Jean François Champollion began to work on what was already known as the Rosetta Stone, the stela inscribed with three different versions of the same text: two versions in Egyptian – one in hieroglyphs and one in demotic Egyptian – the third in ancient Greek, found in 1799 near the small town of Rosetta, in the Nile Delta. Born at Figeac (France) in 1790, Jean François Champollion soon concentrated his studies on languages and the East in general, at the *lycée* of Grenoble and, later, in Paris, at the Collège de France and at the École Practique des Langues Orientales. His thorough knowledge of numerous different languages (he spoke about ten) and especially Coptic was of great use to him in his studies.

At the precocious age of 18, Champollion was made a professor at the University of Grenoble, and he then spent the next 14 years studying the writing system of the ancient Egyptians: hieroglyphs. He based his approach to the decipherment of this obstinate code, which had been taxing scholars for over a century, on three fundamental and brilliant intuitions: first of all, that Coptic, a language which was well known, represented the final stage of the Egyptian language; second, that hieroglyphs had a two-fold value, both as ideograms and as phonetic building-blocks; and third, that the hieroglyphs enclosed in cartouches were phonetic transcriptions of the names of pharaohs.

Therefore, postulating that every hieroglyphic sign might correspond to a letter of the alphabet, and knowing from the Greek text of the Rosetta Stone that the pharaoh in question was a Ptolemy, he succeeded in reading the symbols that could be transcribed as the name

Ptolmys. Later, in 1821, while analysing the bilingual text (hieroglyphs and Greek) on an obelisk found on the island of Philae by Belzoni and transported to England, he succeeded in reading the name Cleopatra, thus obtaining the alphabetic value of 12 hieroglyphs. Extending this method to other cartouches, Champollion succeeded in establishing the values of other signs, and in 1822, he presented his discovery to the world

by writing the famous work, *Lettre à M. Dacier*; Dacier was the secretary of the Académie des Inscriptions et Belles Lettres in Paris. Champollion followed this, in 1824, with a book called *Précis du système hiéroglyphique*, in which he set out the fundamental concepts of hieroglyphic writing. After studying inscriptions on numerous objects in collections and museums all over Europe, Champollion – with support from King Charles X of France and the

Archduke Leopold II of Tuscany, and assisted by his best pupil Ippolito Rosellini – organized the Franco-Tuscan Expedition, which set out for Egypt from Toulon in July 1828.

When Champollion arrived in the land of the pharaohs, he received confirmation of his discovery, which restored language to the silent monuments of ancient Egypt. This was the true birth of a new discipline: Egyptology.

77 Members of the Franco-Tuscan Expedition, led by Champollion, are portrayed here by the painter Giuseppe Angelelli, standing among the ruins of the temple of Karnak. In the centre, the 'Great Decipherer'

of hieroglyphs, Champollion, is shown seated, with a beard and wearing oriental-style dress. Standing alongside him is the Pisan scholar, Ippolito Rosellini, his disciple and collaborator. (Archaeological Museum, Florence)

78 (below) Painting of a relief made by the painter Bertin in the tomb of Ramesses III (Valley of the Kings) during Champollion's expedition. The reliefs and drawings executed during

Champollion's only trip to Egypt were published under the title Monuments de l'Égypte et de la Nubie, *from 1835 to 1845. (Paris, Bibliothèque Nationale)*

78 Champollion's notes of his study of the cartouche of Cleopatra, inscribed on an obelisk found at Philae by Belzoni. The names of Cleopatra and Ptolemy were the first words deciphered by Champollion. By analysing the texts of the Rosetta Stone and comparing them with

those on the obelisk of Philae, Champollion had the brilliant intuition that the names of the pharaohs in cartouches were in hieroglyphs with a phonetic value, and that it was therefore possible to establish an equivalence between hieroglyphic and alphabetic signs.

78 (left) The celebrated Rosetta Stone, which has an inscription in three different forms of writing (hieroglyphic, demotic and Greek), was discovered in 1799 by an officer of Napoleon's Egyptian expedition near Rosetta, now called Rashid, a place not far from Alexandria. The precious find fell into the hands of the

English in the wake of the defeat of Napoleon's army in Egypt in 1801, and was taken to the British Museum. It was his study of this artifact – or rather a copy of it – that led Jean François Champollion to the discovery of the key to deciphering hieroglyphs. (London, British Museum)

79 (right) A page from Champollion's notes for his work Grammaire égyptienne, *published between 1836 and 1841. (Paris, National Library)*

Dans le premier Système applicable *seulement* aux Caractères Sculptés en Grand, on cherchait, par des teintes plattes, à rappeler à peuprès, la couleur naturelle des objets représentés : Ainsi les Caractères figurants le Ciel. (1) étaient peints en bleu, la terre (2) en Rouge ; la Lune(3) en Jaune, le Soleil(4) en Rouge, l'Eau(5) en bleu ou en Verd (6.)

Les Figures d'Hommes en pied, sont peintes, sur les grands monuments d'après des règles assez constantes : Les chairs sont en Rouge plus ou moins foncé, les coëffures *généralement* en bleu et la tunique blanche, les plis des draperies étant indiqués par des traits rouges

On donnait ordinairement des chairs jaunes aux figures de Femmes et leurs Vêtements Variaient en blanc, en Verd ou en Rouge.

Les mêmes règles sont suivis dans le coloriage des hieroglyphes dessinés en petit sur les Stèles et les Sarcophages : mais les Vêtements sont tous de couleur verte.

IPPOLITO ROSELLINI, THE FIRST ITALIAN EGYPTOLOGIST

The Italian Ippolito Rosellini, born in Pisa, Italy, in 1800, was Champollion's prize student. The two met when the 'Great Decipherer' travelled to Italy in 1825. Rosellini shared with his mentor the effort and difficulties of the Franco-Tuscan Expedition, which set out for Egypt on 21 July 1828. During his Egyptian travels, which lasted until October of the following year, Rosellini oversaw the copying of numerous epigraphic reliefs and the sketching of the most important monuments of ancient Egypt – amounting to 14 manuscript volumes. He also collected interesting archaeological artifacts, which now form the core of the Egyptological collection of the modern-day Archaeological Museum of Florence. On his return to Italy Rosellini published the material he had assembled in his great work, *I Monumenti dell'Egitto e della Nubia*, between 1832 and 1844.

In 1834, the University of Pisa asked him to teach a course in the Coptic and Egyptian languages, the first in Europe. This picture, taken from *I Monumenti dell'Egitto*, shows Ramesses II, in his battle chariot drawn by galloping horses, richly adorned with multicoloured caparisons and plumed crests, as he prepares to fire an arrow at the Hittite positions at the battle of Qadesh. (Ippolito Rosellini, *I Monumenti dell'Egitto e della Nubia*, I, *Monumenti Storici*)

81

DAVID ROBERTS, A PAINTER ON THE NILE

Among the Europeans who travelled in Egypt, exploring and documenting the monuments of the land of the pharaohs in the early nineteenth century, a particularly important role belongs to the Scottish painter David Roberts. Roberts was born in Stockbridge, not far from Edinburgh (Scotland), in 1796. He was a stage designer of some talent, establishing a great reputation, and became the friend of personalities of the period, including the novelist Charles Dickens and the artist J.M.W. Turner. It was a friend, John Wilkie, who persuaded Roberts to give up scenic painting and work as an artist, taking trips abroad to expand his artistic experience.

It was on a trip to Spain and the north of Morocco that he first came into direct contact with the world of the East, and with the world seen in the illustrations of travellers such as Vivant Denon and, above all, Belzoni, which had greatly fascinated him. Roberts then set out for Egypt, landing in Alexandria in September 1838. Losing no time, Roberts rented a river vessel in Cairo for a period of three months.

The boat became many things to the artist over the coming months – a home, a workshop, as well as a means of transport. He sailed up the Nile to Abu Simbel, a structure that he described as a temple that by itself was well worth the journey to Nubia. On his journey, Roberts halted to study, analyse and sketch the most important archaeological sites and monuments of Egypt. He was intrigued by the architecture of the pharaohs and enchanted by the subtle magic exuded by the great river and the lands it flows through.

The Nile – with its continual changes of light and colour – particularly charmed the Scottish painter, who wrote : '[The Nile] dons in turn all of the colours of the rainbow, of the stars in the firmament, and it wends its way like a long winding sheet spangled with silver tears'. When on land Roberts spent long hours sketching and painting under the shade of a large umbrella.

Precise in every detail, Roberts' watercolours of Egyptian temples are excellent documents of the state of conservation of the monuments in the last century; moreover, they provide crucial information about the colours of many reliefs which have since almost entirely disappeared. Roberts returned to Cairo with hundreds of sketches and stirring memories, where he remained over a month, painting streets and alleyways, and scenes of the everyday life of the inhabitants. The intrepid Scotsman even obtained special permission to paint the interior of a mosque, where he worked disguised as an Arab.

In February 1839, Roberts took a long journey by camel, riding through the Sinai, where he also spent time at

82 (below) The great orientalist painter David Roberts was born near Edinburgh in 1796. After working as a decorator, he left London in 1838 and sailed for Alexandria, and from there proceeded to Cairo. He hired a boat and sailed up the Nile, visiting all the most important monuments in Egypt and sketching them in his travel journals. After taking a lengthy trip through the Holy Land, during which he gazed upon the Sinai, Petra and the ruins of Baalbek, he returned to London and set about transforming his drawings, made on the spot, into 247 spectacular water-colours, which were then published in six large volumes entitled Views in the Holy Land, Syria, Idumea, Arabia, Egypt and Nubia.

82 (above) The kiosk of Trajan on the island of Philae. It was called by David Roberts an 'hypaethral temple', since it had no roof, and was described by the natives of the area as the 'bed of the pharaoh'. In reality, the building, with perfect architectural proportions, was originally covered by a wooden roof, and was a wayside chapel for the sacred barque of Isis carried in procession during the great ceremonies held in honour of the goddess.

83 (right) A water-colour by Roberts of the decorations of the hypostyle hall of the temple of Isis at Philae, which he described as 'the great portico'. During the rule of Emperor Justinian (sixth century AD) this part of the hall was transformed into a church, as is evident from the crosses cut into the columns.

the Monastery of Saint Catherine, visited the ruins of Petra, toured Jerusalem and saw the majestic temples of Baalbek, in Lebanon.

From Beirut, Roberts took ship to Alexandria, and, after this last journey, left Egypt and the Middle East for good. On his return to London, the artist devoted himself to finishing his watercolours, which he showed to the public in a major exhibition, receiving great critical acclaim and was made a member of the Royal Academy. At the same time, Roberts entrusted to one of the finest lithographers in London, a certain Louis Haghe, the task of preparing lithographic reproductions of his watercolours. The publication of the precious visual material, gathered into a series of volumes entitled *Views in the Holy Land, Syria, Idumea, Arabia, Egypt and Nubia*, was issued between 1842 and 1849. The three-volume set, with a total of 272 lithographs, won him a lasting, world-wide fame that endures today.

David Roberts went on travelling extensively, in Italy, France, Belgium and Holland, but he never again set foot in those lands that he had so wonderfully portrayed. He died in London in 1864, and many of his paintings and sketches were sold at an auction at Christie's the following year.

His precious travel journal, in two volumes, written in Egypt and in the Holy Land, was entrusted to the National Library of Scotland, but was never published. *The Times* of London, in a lengthy obituary, wrote of him: '...he was certainly the finest architectural painter that our nation ever knew, and in the artistic specialty he was practically unrivalled...'

84–85 A painting by David Roberts of the Great Sphinx of Giza and the pyramid of Chephren entitled, Approach of the Simoon. *The simoon is a powerful wind that raises dense clouds of sand, cutting visibility drastically. In order to highlight the dramatic effect of this scene, Roberts placed the setting sun to the south, instead of the west where it should be, behind the hindquarters of the Sphinx.*

86 The obelisk and first pylon of the temple of Luxor, with the two colossi, partially buried by sand, depicting Ramesses II, painted by David Roberts. A second obelisk, which once stood in line with the western tower of the pylon, had already been donated to France by Pasha Mohammad Ali. It was erected in 1836 in the Place de la Concorde in Paris.

86–87 (opposite) Nothing remains of the temple of Esna, built during the Ptolemaic Period (second century BC), but this hypostyle hall, dating to the rules of Tiberius and Vespasian (first century AD). It was used as late as the end of the nineteenth century as a cotton warehouse and later still as an arsenal.

87 (below, left) When Roberts painted the portico of the temple of Horus at Edfu it was still partly buried in sand. This Ptolemaic temple was not uncovered until 1860, when it was excavated by the Egyptologist Auguste Mariette.

87 (below, right) The second courtyard of the Ramesseum, the memorial temple of Ramesses II in western Thebes, which Roberts called the Memnonium. The giant colossus of Ramesses II, the 'Sun of the rulers', lies toppled in the sand.

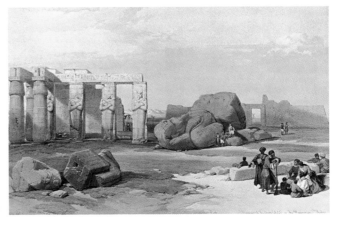

The Great Temple of Aboo-simble, Nubia
David Roberts, R.A.

88 The four colossi depicting Ramesses II, carved into the rock and almost covered by sand, adorned the façade of the great temple of Abu Simbel built by Ramesses II. It was rediscovered by the Swiss orientalist and traveller Johann Ludwig Burckhardt in 1813. Four years later, in 1817, the first Europeans penetrated the interior of the temple. One of Belzoni's feats was to free the façade of the monument from the enormous mass of sand engulfing it.

89 The interior of the impressive temple of Abu Simbel has a pronaos with eight giant Osiride pillars, each standing about 10 m (33 ft) tall, depicting the pharaoh as Osiris, Lord of the Under-world. Although it had been discovered only 25 years prior to the visit by David Roberts, the temple was a popular destination for many visitors, and the Scottish painter was shocked at the amount of graffiti left by tourists on the walls of the monument, which, according to Roberts, was alone worth the difficult trip to Nubia.

THE GREAT DISCOVERIES OF MARIETTE, MASPERO AND SCHIAPARELLI

In 1858, the French archaeologist Auguste Mariette founded the Egyptian Antiquities Service. Previously, in 1851, he had made the exciting discovery at Saqqara of the underground burial chambers of the bulls sacred to Apis, the famous Serapeum. Another of Mariette's discoveries was the magnificent Valley Temple of the pyramid of

Chephren at Giza. This temple yielded numerous statues, chief among them the celebrated life-sized diorite statue of the pharaoh seated on his throne, certainly one of the masterpieces of Old Kingdom statuary.

Gaston Maspero, successor to Mariette, continued his work with energy and tenacity. In 1881, suspicious over the appearance on the antiquities market of objects of extremely high quality, certainly funerary furnishings belonging to a royal tomb, Maspero set out on the track of a gang of tomb-robbers working in the region around Luxor. His enquiries finally led him to the renowned cache of Deir el-Bahri, from which a local family had already begun stealthily to pilfer priceless artifacts. The spectacular cache of royal mummies was hidden in a narrow fissure in the side of the Theban mountains, not far from the temple of Deir el-Bahri. The High Priests of the Twenty-First Dynasty, worried at the continual looting of royal tombs had concealed here the mummies of the most important pharaohs of Egypt, including those of Amenophis I, Tuthmosis III , Sethos I, and his son, Ramesses II.

90 Auguste Mariette began his activities in Egypt in 1850, making a number of discoveries, including the famous Serapeum at Saqqara (above, right) and the Valley Temple of the pyramid of Chephren. He was also behind the setting up of the Egyptian Antiquities Service and the first Egyptian Museum of Cairo, and was named an honorary pasha. When Mariette died in 1881 he was buried in the courtyard of the modern-day Cairo Museum.

91 (right) Ernesto Schiaparelli, the director of the Egyptian Museum of Turin, was also the founder of the Missione Archeologica Italiana. Between 1903 and 1920, Schiaparelli carried out countless digs and surveys throughout Egypt on behalf of the Missione. It was he who discovered the tomb of Nefertari and the tombs of the sons and daughters of Ramesses III in the Valley of the Queens; he also discovered the tombs of Kha and Maya at Deir el-Medina, as well as the tomb of Iti at Gebelein. The numerous artifacts found or acquired by Schiaparelli greatly expanded the collection of the Egyptian Museum in Turin, which ever since has been considered one of the best Egyptological museums in the world.

At the turn of the twentieth century, the Italian archaeologist Ernesto Schiaparelli, born in Biella (Italy), was made director of the Egyptian Museum of Turin. In order to enrich the collection of the museum he directed he undertook a long series of digs in Egypt, between 1903 and 1920. His earliest excavations were in the Valley of the Queens and at Deir el-Medina, which he followed by work at Heliopolis (the city sacred to the sun god), Giza, Qaw el-Kebir, Ashmunein and in the necropolis of Asyut, in central Egypt. Schiaparelli's most notable achievements were his discoveries of the tombs of Nefertari and of the princes Khaemwaset and Amun-(her-) khepshef, children of Ramesses III; the tomb of Maya; the intact tomb of the architect Kha at Deir el-Medina; and the tomb of Iti, a Twelfth-Dynasty official, at Gebelein. The priceless funerary furnishings of the tomb of Kha, the paintings from that of Maya, and those from the tomb of Iti, removed in order to save them from certain destruction, are among the most significant treasures now in the Egyptian Museum of Turin.

91 (below, right) The interior of the intact tomb of the architect Kha and his bride Merit, who lived during the Eighteenth Dynasty, during the reign of Amenophis III. This is how the tomb, in the necropolis of Deir el-Medina, appeared to the members of the Missione Archeologica Italiana on its discovery in 1906.

91 (above, right) A colleague of Schiaparelli's at work in the tomb of Nefertari, the bride of Ramesses II. The tomb, located in the Valley of the Queens, was discovered by the Missione Archeologica Italiana in 1904. Although it had *already been violated in antiquity and was practically empty, the decorations and the wall paintings were the most beautiful works that had ever been found in a royal tomb, despite having suffered somewhat through the passage of time.*

92 (above) The tomb of Tutankhamun, located just a few yards from the great tomb of Ramesses VI, is visible at the centre of this photograph, as it appeared following the initial work done by Howard Carter and his team. The discovery of the stairway leading down to the royal tomb took place on 4 November 1922, but Carter waited for Lord Carnarvon, the sponsor of the dig, to arrive from England before opening the tomb on 26 November. Howard Carter, Lord Carnarvon, his daughter Lady Evelyn and the engineer Arthur Callender were the first people to pass through the door that led to the Antechamber.

92 (below) On the seal of a small shrine-shaped box was a depiction of the god Anubis, in the shape of a jackal, with eight prisoners.

About 40 years after the finding of the Deir-el Bahri cache, another discovery shook not only the world of Egyptology, but caught the imagination of a much wider public. In November 1922, the English archaeologist Howard Carter opened the virtually intact tomb of a largely unknown pharaoh: Tutankhamun. Carter was born in Kensington, England, in 1874, and was on his way to joining his father's profession, commercial artist, when he was hired in 1891 by the Egyptologist Percy Newberry to finish a series of drawings of reliefs that Newberry had made in Egypt. Carter then travelled to Egypt, where he worked for the Egyptian Exploration Fund, a society founded in London to promote archaeology in Egypt, and as an assistant to the celebrated archaeologist William Flinders Petrie, making facsimiles at the temple of Hatshepsut at Deir el-Bahri, copying reliefs and executing a number of watercolour drawings. Although Carter had never taken a degree, he was highly thought of by Gaston Maspero, the successor to Auguste Mariette as the head of the Egyptian Antiquities Service, and in 1899 Carter was offered the job of Inspector-General of Monuments in Upper Egypt, with headquarters at Luxor.

93 (right) Carter and Callender opening the doors of the four shrines made of gilded wood containing the quartzite sarcophagus of Tutankhamun, located on the eastern side of the burial chamber. The doors of the first shrine had no seals; they may have been broken by the tomb robbers who had partially stripped the tomb, not once, but twice, during Pharaonic times. The door of the second shrine had its seals still intact – for the first time after 3245 years, a human gaze would penetrate that barrier.

He continued as an inspector until 1905, when he resigned following a dispute with a party of French tourists visiting the Serapeum at Saqqara.

In 1907, Carter met Lord Carnarvon, a wealthy English aristocrat with a passion for archaeology, who hired Carter to work for him. Carter and Carnarvon carried out a number of excavations, making interesting though not spectacular discoveries, when, in 1914, they received from the Egyptian Antiquities Service a licence to dig in the Valley of the Kings. Until the previous year, the American enthusiast Theodore Davis had been working there. Davis had declared the site to be exhausted from an archaeological point of view; Carter, on the other hand, piecing together the evidence, felt certain that the valley still held the tomb of a pharaoh called Tutankhamun, whose name had been found on a stela uncovered at the temple of Karnak, and on a number of artifacts found in the Valley itself by Davis. The outbreak of the First World War prevented Carter from proceeding, and he was only able to begin work in 1917, in the area between the tomb of Ramesses II and that of Ramesses VI. Not far from the latter tomb, he discovered the remains of huts used by the workers who had built this tomb. Carter soon stopped excavating these structures, and decided to investigate instead the immediately surrounding areas. This work, which went on in campaign after annual campaign, lasted until 1921, when still nothing had been discovered. In that year, Lord Carnarvon, who had already spent a huge amount of money, was about to give up the search and withdraw

94 (left) On the eastern wall of the chamber containing the sarcophagus was the entrance to a small annex. This room was called 'the Treasury' by Carter. It was mostly occupied by a statue of Anubis mounted on top of a carrying shrine. The room also contained numerous small chests and a magnificent gilded wooden shrine containing viscera of the pharaoh.

95 (top) On the northern side of the Antechamber, in front of the sealed door, stood two life-sized wooden statues intended to protect the eternal rest of the pharaoh. In the centre, a wicker basket and some rushes cover the small hole made by Carter in order to determine the contents of the burial chamber, situated beyond the wall, prior to the official opening of the chamber itself.

95 (centre) An alabaster vase with a particularly elaborate shape, containing aromatic ointments, found behind the door of the first of the gilt wooden shrines that enclosed the pharaoh's sarcophagus.

95 (bottom) One of the ritual beds found in the Antechamber, with sides in the form of a cow. Underneath it was a large number of wooden containers painted white, which held foodstuffs (for the most part various joints of meat), placed there for the nourishment of the pharaoh in the Afterworld.

96–97 After using an
elaborate system of
pulleys to hoist the
second gilded wooden
coffin off the ground,
Carter had it lowered
on to a platform and
proceeded to open it.
At that point, before
the astonished eyes of
the gathering of
archaeologists, his
assistants and
colleagues, there
appeared, hidden only
by an extremely thin
linen veil, the cover of
the third and final
coffin, made entirely
of solid gold, and
containing the royal
mummy of
Tutankhamun, which
was protected by the
gold mask that has
become so emblematic.
Howard Carter is seen
here cleaning, with
extreme care, the third
coffin, with the
assistance of a small
scalpel, removing the
incrustations of resin,
unguents and
bitumen. This
spectacular coffin
weighed 110.4 kg
(243 lbs) and was
118cm (74 in) in
length. In his account,
Carter mentioned the
great difficulty
involved in opening
the cover of the third
coffin, saying: 'This
pitch like material
hardened by age had to
be removed by means
of hammering,
solvents and heat'.

financing. Carnarvon told Carter that he could carry out one final year's digging, beginning in autumn 1922.

This campaign was intended to cover the area around the workmen's huts found previously. On 4 November, one of Carter's labourers stumbled upon a stone step, the first step in a stairway that ran down into the rock. Carter, sensing that this might be the long-awaited discovery, covered up the hole, and sent a telegram to Carnarvon in England, informing his sponsor of what had been found, and summoning him to the site with the utmost urgency. On 24 November, work resumed, in Carnarvon's presence. The stairway was cleared of rubble, and Carter and Carnarvon found themselves before a walled-up door, followed by a second inner door, which bore both the seals of the necropolis and the long dreamed-of name: Tutankhamun.

On 26 November, Carter, Carnarvon, and his daughter Evelyn, with the engineer Callender, who had just joined the dig, were finally able to pierce a hole through the second door and observe the interior of the tomb and the treasures it contained. This was the first, and to date the finest royal tomb found virtually intact in the history of Egyptology, even though careful study showed that there had been no fewer than two attempts in ancient times to rob the tomb, the consequences of which had fortunately been minor.

It took almost a decade of meticulous and painstaking work to empty the tomb of Tutankhamun. Around 3500 individual items were recovered. Clearly, this was the most exceptional archaeological discovery ever made in Egypt.

97 (right, top and bottom) The artifacts found in the tomb were carefully packed for shipment by Carter and his team. They could then be moved to the workshop that had been set up in the nearby tomb of Sethos II, where the objects were photographed and subjected to preliminary cleaning and consolidation, before being taken to Cairo. The enormous quantity of objects in the funerary equipment of the pharaoh forced work to proceed at a relatively slow pace, and the emptying of the Antechamber alone, begun on 27 December 1922, required about 50 days. The four large gilt shrines which contained the sarcophagus were the last finds to leave the tomb, and were not removed until November 1930.

98/103 A view of the western and southern sides of the Antechamber, immediately following the opening of the tomb. On one side are the four disassembled chariots belonging to the pharaoh and two of the three large ritual couches in the shape of animals (a lioness, a cow and a composite creature with the head of a hippopotamus), linked to three deities. They must have had a religious significance; perhaps the soul of the pharaoh could rest and regenerate on them.

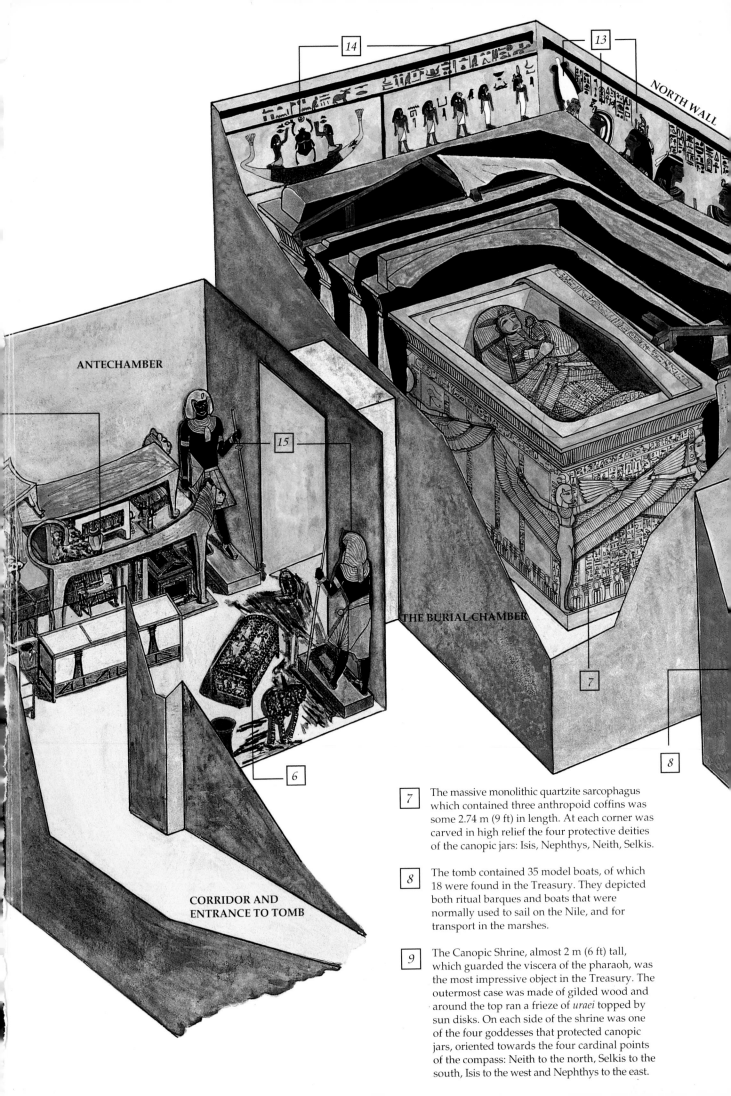

14

13

NORTH WALL

ANTECHAMBER

15

THE BURIAL CHAMBER

7

6

8

CORRIDOR AND
ENTRANCE TO TOMB

7   The massive monolithic quartzite sarcophagus which contained three anthropoid coffins was some 2.74 m (9 ft) in length. At each corner was carved in high relief the four protective deities of the canopic jars: Isis, Nephthys, Neith, Selkis.

8   The tomb contained 35 model boats, of which 18 were found in the Treasury. They depicted both ritual barques and boats that were normally used to sail on the Nile, and for transport in the marshes.

9   The Canopic Shrine, almost 2 m (6 ft) tall, which guarded the viscera of the pharaoh, was the most impressive object in the Treasury. The outermost case was made of gilded wood and around the top ran a frieze of *uraei* topped by sun disks. On each side of the shrine was one of the four goddesses that protected canopic jars, oriented towards the four cardinal points of the compass: Neith to the north, Selkis to the south, Isis to the west and Nephthys to the east.

THE TREASURE
OF THE UNKNOWN PHARAOH

It had been decided: the campaign of autumn 1922 was to be the last Howard Carter would lead in search of the fabled tomb of a pharaoh, about whom all that was known was his name and a few elusive hints. Lord Carnarvon, the sponsor of the digs, after eight years of work that was as expensive as it was fruitless, had come to the reluctant conclusion that the unhappy project should be brought to an end. However, on 4 November 1922 Carter's labourers uncovered the first step in a staircase that led down into the rock. Nobody could have dreamed that this was the beginning of what was destined to be the most important and – for want of a more accurate term – fabulous discovery ever made in Egypt. Although tomb-robbers had entered the tomb twice in antiquity, the remarkable funerary furnishings had been left virtually intact. On 26 November, Carter pierced a small hole in the wall, through which he could see into the chamber. He was the first to look inside, and, asked if he could see anything, he replied: 'Yes, wonderful things'.

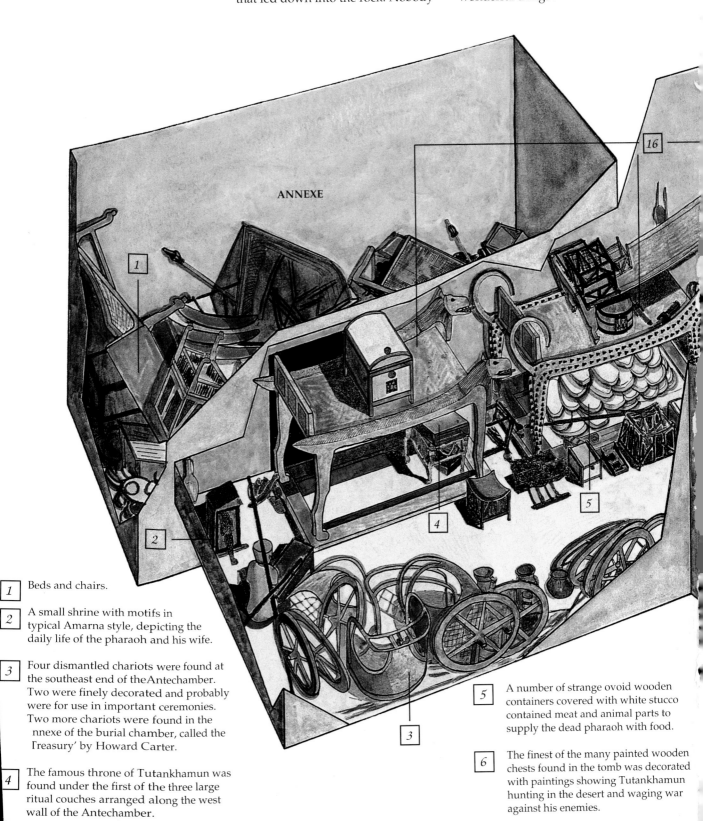

ANNEXE

1. Beds and chairs.

2. A small shrine with motifs in typical Amarna style, depicting the daily life of the pharaoh and his wife.

3. Four dismantled chariots were found at the southeast end of theAntechamber. Two were finely decorated and probably were for use in important ceremonies. Two more chariots were found in the nnexe of the burial chamber, called the Treasury' by Howard Carter.

4. The famous throne of Tutankhamun was found under the first of the three large ritual couches arranged along the west wall of the Antechamber.

5. A number of strange ovoid wooden containers covered with white stucco contained meat and animal parts to supply the dead pharaoh with food.

6. The finest of the many painted wooden chests found in the tomb was decorated with paintings showing Tutankhamun hunting in the desert and waging war against his enemies.

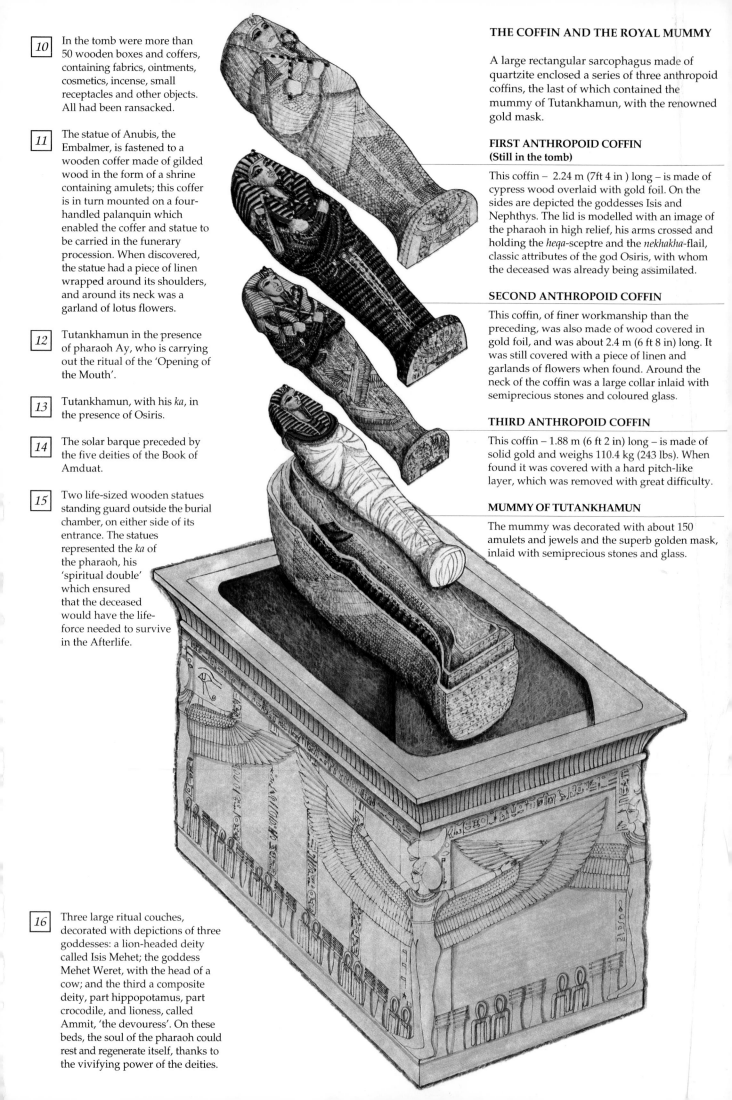

10 In the tomb were more than 50 wooden boxes and coffers, containing fabrics, ointments, cosmetics, incense, small receptacles and other objects. All had been ransacked.

11 The statue of Anubis, the Embalmer, is fastened to a wooden coffer made of gilded wood in the form of a shrine containing amulets; this coffer is in turn mounted on a four-handled palanquin which enabled the coffer and statue to be carried in the funerary procession. When discovered, the statue had a piece of linen wrapped around its shoulders, and around its neck was a garland of lotus flowers.

12 Tutankhamun in the presence of pharaoh Ay, who is carrying out the ritual of the 'Opening of the Mouth'.

13 Tutankhamun, with his *ka*, in the presence of Osiris.

14 The solar barque preceded by the five deities of the Book of Amduat.

15 Two life-sized wooden statues standing guard outside the burial chamber, on either side of its entrance. The statues represented the *ka* of the pharaoh, his 'spiritual double' which ensured that the deceased would have the life-force needed to survive in the Afterlife.

16 Three large ritual couches, decorated with depictions of three goddesses: a lion-headed deity called Isis Mehet; the goddess Mehet Weret, with the head of a cow; and the third a composite deity, part hippopotamus, part crocodile, and lioness, called Ammit, 'the devourers'. On these beds, the soul of the pharaoh could rest and regenerate itself, thanks to the vivifying power of the deities.

THE COFFIN AND THE ROYAL MUMMY

A large rectangular sarcophagus made of quartzite enclosed a series of three anthropoid coffins, the last of which contained the mummy of Tutankhamun, with the renowned gold mask.

FIRST ANTHROPOID COFFIN
(Still in the tomb)

This coffin – 2.24 m (7ft 4 in) long – is made of cypress wood overlaid with gold foil. On the sides are depicted the goddesses Isis and Nephthys. The lid is modelled with an image of the pharaoh in high relief, his arms crossed and holding the *heqa*-sceptre and the *nekhakha*-flail, classic attributes of the god Osiris, with whom the deceased was already being assimilated.

SECOND ANTHROPOID COFFIN

This coffin, of finer workmanship than the preceding, was also made of wood covered in gold foil, and was about 2.4 m (6 ft 8 in) long. It was still covered with a piece of linen and garlands of flowers when found. Around the neck of the coffin was a large collar inlaid with semiprecious stones and coloured glass.

THIRD ANTHROPOID COFFIN

This coffin – 1.88 m (6 ft 2 in) long – is made of solid gold and weighs 110.4 kg (243 lbs). When found it was covered with a hard pitch-like layer, which was removed with great difficulty.

MUMMY OF TUTANKHAMUN

The mummy was decorated with about 150 amulets and jewels and the superb golden mask, inlaid with semiprecious stones and glass.

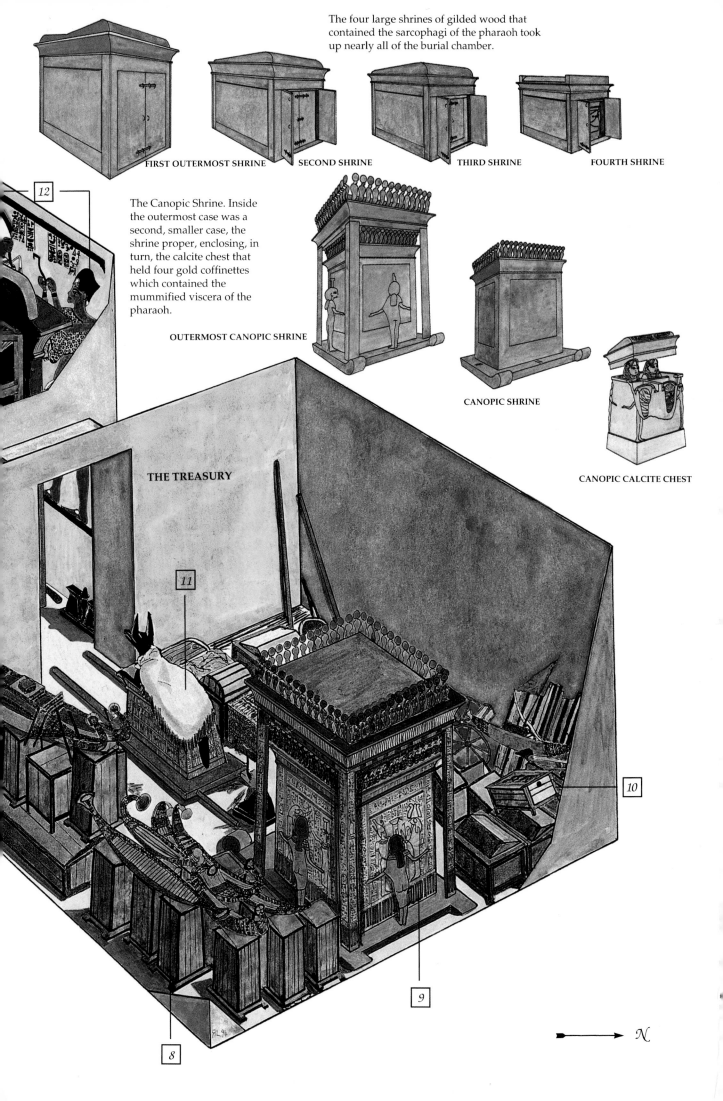

The four large shrines of gilded wood that contained the sarcophagi of the pharaoh took up nearly all of the burial chamber.

FIRST OUTERMOST SHRINE

SECOND SHRINE

THIRD SHRINE

FOURTH SHRINE

The Canopic Shrine. Inside the outermost case was a second, smaller case, the shrine proper, enclosing, in turn, the calcite chest that held four gold coffinettes which contained the mummified viscera of the pharaoh.

OUTERMOST CANOPIC SHRINE

CANOPIC SHRINE

CANOPIC CALCITE CHEST

12

THE TREASURY

11

10

9

8

N

RECENT DISCOVERIES

THE BARQUES OF RE

104 (below) A new royal barque revealed. A tiny probe fitted with a video camera was inserted into the suspected boat pit and an extremely clear image appeared on the screen the researchers were anxiously watching. The trench contained a second ship, similar to the previously known one, in an excellent state of preservation.

104–105 (opposite) In 1985 a team of American and Egyptian scientists and technicians begin operations to bore a microscopic hole through the limestone blocks covering the mysterious trench found in front of the pyramid of Cheops. Using extremely sophisticated technology, it was possible to drill a hole without allowing air from outside to penetrate the trench, thus avoiding any contamination.

After the disruption caused by the Second World War, research and excavations were resumed in Egypt at the beginning of the 1950s; the first discovery was so spectacular and sensational that it shook the world of Egyptology and attracted the attention of the world's press. In May 1954 labourers of the Egyptian Antiquities Organization, under the direction of a young architect named Kamal el-Mallakh, were cleaning an area of the south face of the pyramid of Cheops when they found two rectangular surfaces covered with a hardened plaster crust. Kamal el-Mallakh investigated the layer of chalky material to determine its consistency, and rapidly found that it covered two rows of immense limestone blocks. Since on the east side of the pyramid there were no fewer than six large boat-shaped pits, which originally must have contained boats either used during the funerary rituals or connected with them, Kamal el-Mallakh guessed that these blocks might cover more trenches containing royal barques, in which case, these vessels might well be intact.

When, at the end of January 1955, one of the huge limestone blocks covering the trench

was finally lifted, this hypothesis proved to be correct: before the amazed eyes of those present, and just as it had been placed there more than four thousand years before, the planking of a great ship appeared, carefully dismantled and arranged in thirteen layers stacked one on top of the other. A programme of investigation – the first to be run entirely by Egyptians without the direction or participation of non-Egyptian archaeologists – was immediately set in hand. Once all the components of the vessel had been removed from their tomb and arranged in a huge warehouse-laboratory not far away, the archaeologists realized the full extent of the task before them. There were 1224 pieces and no one had the slightest idea of how the elements of this gigantic puzzle could be fitted together, since next to nothing was known at that time about the construction of ships in ancient Egypt.

The job of rebuilding the ship of Cheops was given to the senior restoration expert at the Egyptian Antiquities Organization, Ahmed Yussuf, with the assistance of a conservator named Zaki Iskander.

It was not until 16 years later, years fraught with many disappointments and dashed hopes, that, in June 1970 the vessel was finally completely reassembled, and put on display in a museum built specifically to house it, next to the pit in which it had been found. Built mostly of cedars of Lebanon, the royal barque of Cheops was a full 43 m (142 ft) long, close to 6 m (20 ft) in width, with a draught of just over 1.5 m (5 ft) and a displacement of around 50 tons. The planks

had been fastened together using only vegetable fibres: a true masterpiece of naval architecture of the third millennium BC. It seemed a reasonable assumption that the second pit also contained a similar vessel. But its precise contents remained a mystery until 1985, when, through an agreement between the Egyptian Antiquities Organization and the *National Geographic Magazine*, it became possible to gain some idea about what lay in the closed pit.

With the assistance of the most advanced technology, in the form of a tiny probe equipped with a micro-camera, it was possible for a human eye – albeit through the assistance of an optical instrument – to examine the interior of the pit for the first time since it had been sealed. The images that appeared on the monitors of the researchers confirmed, at last, their hopes: there is another ship, also perfectly intact, lying buried beneath the desert sands.

THE HIDDEN STATUES OF LUXOR, THE PRINCESS MERITAMUN AND THE TREASURE OF DUSH

In 1989, the columns lining the great courtyard of Amenophis III in the temple of Luxor were found to be unstable and the Egyptian Antiquities Organization decided to undertake a survey to investigate the solidity of the surrounding ground. The workers began to dig down on the western side of the courtyard, but when they reached a depth of almost 3 m (10 ft), their shovels struck something smooth and hard. The object was quickly freed from the crumbling dirt: the features of a face, belonging to a statue, appeared in the bright sunlight, after their long dark sleep. The director of antiquities in Upper Egypt, Mohammed el-Saghir, was informed

immediately, and he ordered the statues to be covered with earth again, shortly afterwards sending a telegram to the headquarters in Cairo of the Egyptian Antiquities Organization. At that point, an excavation was begun, and to everyone's amazement, more than 20 statues emerged, most of them dating from the reign of Amenophis III, the Sun Pharaoh and great builder. The goddess Hathor, the god Atum, a great *uraeus*, the sacred cobra that protected royalty, came to light.

One statue in particular aroused the excitement of the archaeologists. Standing about 2 m (6 ft) feet tall, and cut from a block of red quartzite, it depicted the striding pharaoh. The face of the figure is particularly handsome, with the eyes and other features slightly orientalized, in accordance with the tastes of the period. The expression of the king gazes far off into the distance, and seems to bridge the yawning gulf of time. This statue is probably one the greatest masterpieces of New Kingdom sculpture. To display these new 'statues of Luxor', the Museum of Luxor was enlarged, with a new hall added in 1992. In the same fortunate year, another impressive discovery was made, on the boundary between Upper and Middle Egypt, in the city of Akhmim, once sacred to the god Min, identified by the ancient Greeks with Pan – in fact the Greeks called the city Panopolis. Here, in the sacred precinct of the temple in the ancient city, during an excavation carried out by the Egyptian Antiquities Organization, an immense statue – it stood about 8 m (26 ft) tall – came to light. This statue depicted a princess, but since the enormous block of stone lay face-down on the ground, it was impossible to see her features. Once the archaeologists had dug sufficiently around the face to be able to slide a mirror underneath it, they were astonished to see an exquisite face with delicate features, a woman whose lips were still painted red. This was Princess Meritamun, daughter of Ramesses II and Nefertari.

An enormous scaffolding was then built in order to raise the statue, which was temporarily enclosed in a wooden structure, and a base was constructed on which the lower section of the statue could be fastened to ensure its stability. The operation

was completed between 1992 and 1993, and the statue of Princess Meritamun is now on display and can be admired, not just by the few tourists who travel as far as Akhmim, a city that is not exactly on the main routes, but by Egyptians also, who are increasingly interested in the ancient history of their ancestors.

Discoveries are not limited to the banks of the Nile, however. In the oasis of Dush, at the southern extremity of the great oasis of Kharga,

surrounded by the sands of the Western Desert, Michel Reddé, of the Institut Français d'Archéologie Orientale of Cairo, created during Napoleonic times to oversee French research in Egypt, was excavating a Roman military camp, built here to protect the *limes* (frontiers) of the Empire. In March 1989 he uncovered a veritable treasure: a trove consisting of jewels and a solid gold crown that had belonged to a high priest of the god Serapis.

THE LATEST DISCOVERIES AT SAQQARA, THE FAIYUM AND IN THE DELTA

One thing is certain, the discoveries are not over. Throughout Egypt, excavation and research are being undertaken, by both Egyptian archaeologists and the numerous foreign missions that work there. France, Germany, Great Britain, Italy and the United States of America, among others, are currently involved in research and restoration – a central issue in the preservation of this huge cultural heritage, which belongs to the nation of Egypt but which also forms part of the cultural inheritance of everyone. UNESCO emphasized this by including a large number of the archaeological monuments of Egypt in its list of World Heritage Sites.

Among the archaeological work now under way in the region between the Faiyum and the Delta, particular mention should be made of the dig being conducted by the University of Pisa, directed by Edda Bresciani. This focuses on the southern Faiyum at Khelua, where an important tomb of the Middle Kingdom has been uncovered. The tomb belonged to a high official named Wage, and is now undergoing preliminary study with a view to possible restoration.

At Saqqara, Jean Leclant, Secretary of the Académie des Inscriptions et Belles Lettres, was working on the interesting hieroglyphic texts found inside the pyramid of Pepy I, when his team discovered a new pyramid to the south. This belonged to a queen, and the French team is now involved in the restoration of the burial chamber. Another Frenchman, Alain Zivie of the Centre National de la Recherche Scientifique, is excavating, again at Saqqara, the mysterious tomb of a vizier, Aper-el, which casts new light on certain aspects of Egyptian history. Also at Saqqara, an English team from the Egypt Exploration Society, led by Geoffrey Martin, discovered the important tombs of Horemheb, a powerful general who later became pharaoh, and of the treasurer of Tutankhamun, Maya. Just north of Saqqara, the Egyptians, under the direction of Ali Hassan, general director for Pharaonic Antiquities of Egypt, have found the first tomb of a hitherto unknown necropolis of the Nineteenth Dynasty.

At Giza Egyptian archaeologists discovered, in 1991 and 1992, the village where the labourers who worked on the Great Pyramid lived, and also new tombs from the Old Kingdom, one of which contained painted statues.

Lastly, the Austrian archaeologist Manfred Bietak is working in the eastern Delta at Tell el-Daba, where he has found the remains of a palace decorated with Minoan frescoes, unique in Egypt. Its study is casting new light on relations between Minoans and Egyptians in the second millennium BC.

108 (above) Alain Zivie, of the Centre National de la Recherche Scientifique, has been working at Saqqara for many years, studying the tomb of the Vizier Aper-el, who lived during the reigns of Amenophis III and Amenophis IV. In the course of his exploration Zivie found hundreds of cat mummies in the tomb, placed there in in the third century BC by the priests of the goddess Bastet, a guardian deity of the hearth.

108 (below) A relief in the tomb of Horemheb, a general under Tutankhamun, at Saqqara. The tomb was studied and restored by Geoffrey Martin, of the Egypt Exploration Society, who is now at work on the tomb of Tutankhamun's treasurer Maya.

109 (opposite) Archaeologists of a French archaeological mission, led by Jean Leclant, are here working on hieroglyphic texts on the interior of the pyramid of Pepy I at Saqqara.

TEMPLES AND TOMBS IN THE LAND OF THE PHARAOHS

A VOYAGE OF DISCOVERY ALONG THE NILE, FROM THE DELTA TO ABU SIMBEL

110–111 The goddesses Wadjet and Nekhbet placing the double crown of Upper and Lower Egypt on the pharaoh's head in a relief from the temple of Edfu.

TANIS,
THE ANCIENT CAPITAL
IN THE DELTA

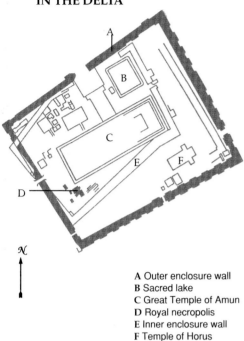

N

A Outer enclosure wall
B Sacred lake
C Great Temple of Amun
D Royal necropolis
E Inner enclosure wall
F Temple of Horus

Tanis, the Greek name for the city the ancient Egyptians called *Dja'ni*, is today referred to as San el-Hagar (el-Hagar meaning 'the stones'), a reference to the quarry where building stone was extracted for many centuries. Located in the Delta, about 160 km (100 miles) to the northeast of Cairo and about 65 km (40 miles) from the Mediterranean, the town's ruins now form an immense *tell* (or 'mound'), with a surface area of 177 ha (440 acres), and rising to a height of 32 m (105 ft). It was to this site that the pharaohs of the Twenty-First Dynasty moved the religious and political capital of Egypt.

Thus Tanis displaced Pi-Ramesses, the capital established by Ramesses II near modern-day Qantir – 24 km (15 miles) from San el-Hagar. The long reign of Ramesses II (1279–1212 BC) saw the power of the pharaohs at its peak, and Egypt extend its borders to Asia, but by the Twentieth Dynasty (1188–1076 BC) Egypt was losing its Asiatic empire and

112 (below, left) Excavations at the city of Tanis, at the site currently called San el-Hagar. The history of this site is a long and complex one, but it reached its greatest prominence during the Third Intermediate Period, at the time of the Twenty-First Dynasty, when it became the capital of Egypt. In the foreground the royal necropolis is visible, discovered by Pierre Montet between 1939 and 1940.

112–113 (right) A vast number of blocks of granite, fragments of obelisks and other architectural elements that bear the name of Ramesses II are scattered around the site. These come from the buildings of Pi-Ramesses, the former capital, and were reused at Tanis.

was troubled by internal conflict. Rival power centres were supplanting the pharaohs: the Libyan warriors who moved into the Nile Valley; and priests of Amun-Re, the god of Thebes, worshipped in the immense temple of Karnak. This god was believed to govern, through his oracle, all earthly matters and Amun-Re's possessions were more important than the State's.

THE SECRET NECROPOLIS OF TANIS

When the young French archaeologist Pierre Montet began in 1929 to dig at San el-Hagar, the site of ancient Tanis, the Delta capital during the Twenty-First Dynasty, he did not hope for major discoveries. Montet, however, had the great luck to stumble upon the royal necropolis, part of which had been left intact, and to find a treasure that could be compared only with that of Tutankhamun.

This cross-section reveals the layout of the royal tombs at Tanis. More than a necropolis, this is a funerary complex which included seven sepulchres, including those of pharaohs Psusennes I, Osorkon II and that of General Undebaunded. The body of Psusennes was protected by three coffins, the innermost of which was made of silver, the second of black granite and the third of pink granite.

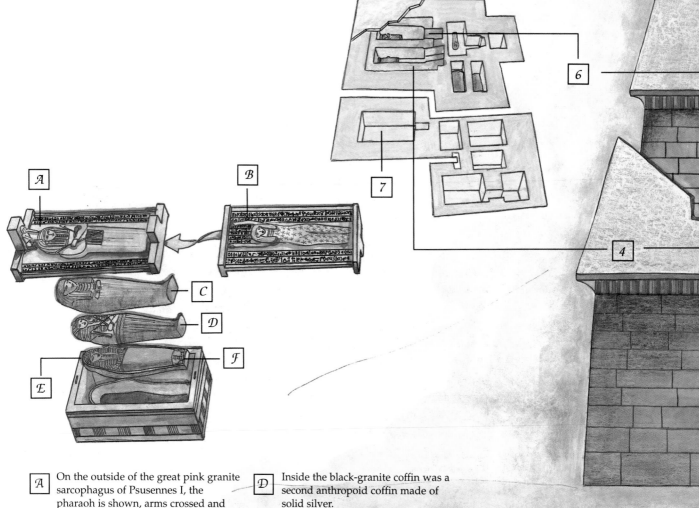

A On the outside of the great pink granite sarcophagus of Psusennes I, the pharaoh is shown, arms crossed and holding the royal and divine attributes.

B The features of the goddess Nut, 'Lady of the Heavens', were carved on the inner side of the sarcophagus of Psusennes. In the funerary cult, she has a protective role over the deceased and is a also a source of regenerative energies.

C When the outer sarcophagus was opened, the team saw an anthropoid coffin made of black granite; this had been usurped, but the archaeologists were unable to establish just who had been the previous proprietor. Between the two coffins were weapons and a sceptre.

D Inside the black-granite coffin was a second anthropoid coffin made of solid silver.

E The golden funerary mask rivalled that of Tutankhamun in beauty.

F When the archaeologists opened the silver coffin, after great effort, they found the mummy of Psusennes I.

1 The burial chamber with the sarcophagus of the general Undebaunded, commander of the archers of Psusennes I, was opened on 13 February 1946.

2 In the tomb of Psusennes I, the plundered sarcophagus of the general Ankhefenmut, the son of the pharaoh, was also found.

3 In the vestibule of the tomb of Psusennes, the archaeologists also found a silver coffin adorned with a hawk-head. The coffin had belonged to a ruler of the Twenty-Second Dynasty, hitherto unknown. This ruler's name was Heka-kheper-re Sheshonq (Sheshonq II), who ruled around 890 BC. The sarcophagus was opened a few days after its discovery – on 21 March 1939 – in the presence of Egypt's King Farouk.

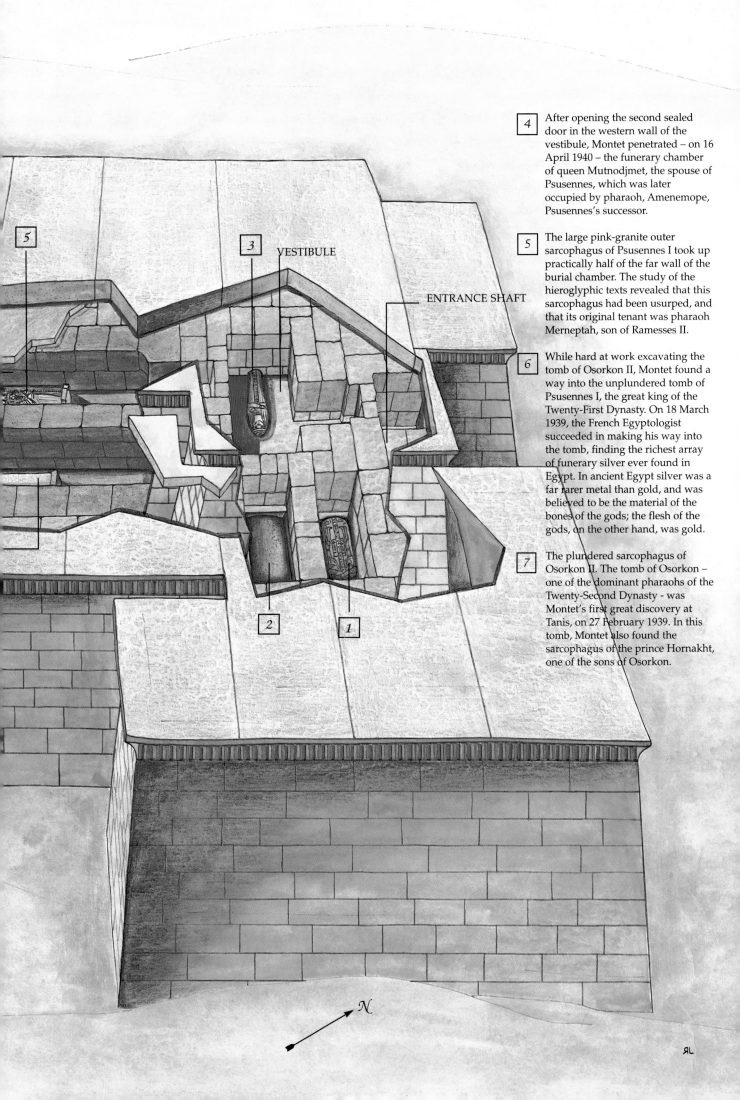

4 After opening the second sealed door in the western wall of the vestibule, Montet penetrated – on 16 April 1940 – the funerary chamber of queen Mutnodjmet, the spouse of Psusennes, which was later occupied by pharaoh, Amenemope, Psusennes's successor.

5 The large pink-granite outer sarcophagus of Psusennes I took up practically half of the far wall of the burial chamber. The study of the hieroglyphic texts revealed that this sarcophagus had been usurped, and that its original tenant was pharaoh Merneptah, son of Ramesses II.

6 While hard at work excavating the tomb of Osorkon II, Montet found a way into the unplundered tomb of Psusennes I, the great king of the Twenty-First Dynasty. On 18 March 1939, the French Egyptologist succeeded in making his way into the tomb, finding the richest array of funerary silver ever found in Egypt. In ancient Egypt silver was a far rarer metal than gold, and was believed to be the material of the bones of the gods; the flesh of the gods, on the other hand, was gold.

7 The plundered sarcophagus of Osorkon II. The tomb of Osorkon – one of the dominant pharaohs of the Twenty-Second Dynasty - was Montet's first great discovery at Tanis, on 27 February 1939. In this tomb, Montet also found the sarcophagus of the prince Hornakht, one of the sons of Osorkon.

VESTIBULE

ENTRANCE SHAFT

𝒩

116 (below) A gold pendant in the form of the goddess Bastet, found in the tomb of General Undebaunded (Twenty-First Dynasty, circa 1000 BC), at Tanis. The pendant, which formed part of a group of six deities arranged in a necklace upon the chest of the deceased, shows the goddess Bastet with the head of a lion, surmounted by a sun-disk and the uraeus, the sacred serpent, the symbol of royal power and of the power of the sun. Bastet, 'mistress of the heavens and eye of Re', is a deity with a dual aspect: she can have a protective function while at the same time representing a danger for enemies. (Cairo Museum)

117 (opposite) The gold funerary mask of Psusennes I, with lapis lazuli and glass inlays, is a marvellous example of ancient Egyptian art. Its beauty rivals that of Tutankhamun's mask, although its style is more sober and austere. Gold was considered the flesh of the gods, and its use in funerary rituals was linked to the process of conferring immortality upon the deceased. This priceless artifact was found by Pierre Montet in the tomb of Psusennes at Tanis (Tomb 3) and was placed directly upon the king's mummy. Many other funerary items of the finest workmanship were also found in Psusennes' tomb. (Cairo Museum)

Thus the New Kingdom came to an end and the Third Intermediate Period (circa 1076–712 BC) began: a turbulent time, during which Egyptian culture survived but was radically changed. At the beginning of the eleventh century BC, Upper Egypt became a theocratic and almost independent state, ruled by the 'first prophet of Amun', a civil and military leader as well as a religious authority. Smendes, the delegate of Amun in Lower Egypt, took up residence in Tanis and founded the Twenty-First Dynasty (circa 1076–945 BC). Under the pharaoh Psusennes I (possibly of Theban origin) Tanis became a second Thebes. Pharaohs were now buried here, in the temple of Amun. The Tanite kings dismantled the monuments of Pi-Ramesses, using the material to build temples to Amun, Mut and Khonsu, and removing obelisks, columns and statues to embellish the new capital. Hebrew tradition, anachronistically, identifies Tanis as the location of the deeds of Moses and the suffering of his people.

Towards 945 BC, kings of Libyan descent of the Twenty-Second Dynasty (circa 945–712 BC) took power. Besides Tanis, Bubastis, also in Lower Egypt, rose to prominence. Pharaohs Sheshonq I and Osorkon I succeeded in restoring some military lustre to Egypt with an expedition to Palestine, but a few generations later the country had broken down into several warring states, governed by parallel royal dynasties. In the seventh century BC, the Kushite kings of Ethiopian descent came from Sudan and annexed Upper Egypt, but were unable to end the turmoil, which was exacerbated by the various Assyrian attempts to invade Egypt. Unity was re-established only from the year 664 on, by a pharaoh from Sais, Psammetichus I.

Once the princes of Sais succeeded in establishing control, the dominant role of Tanis came to an end and it was reduced to the status of a prefecture, remaining occupied until Roman times. The last major monuments in the city date from the period of the last Ptolemies.

Although the site was abandoned, it was easily identified by the scholars accompanying Napoleon's Egyptian expedition. In 1825, the Marseilles sculptor Jean-Jacques Rifaud came to the site and enriched the Louvre with two large sphinxes in pink granite; other digs were ordered by Henry Salt, the British consul general in Egypt. Auguste Mariette undertook new expeditions between 1860 and 1864, which yielded still more splendid items, including the head from the statue of General Panemerit (a contemporary of Ptolemy Auletes, the father of Cleopatra), whose torso is in the Louvre. Flinders Petrie also worked there, on behalf of the Egypt Exploration Fund in 1884, but thereafter the attention of archaeologists was attracted by the great classical sites of Upper Egypt, and Tanis remained in obscurity until the arrival of Pierre Montet.

At Tanis today there are three groups of ruins: a) the great temple of Amun, with the temple of Khonsu and the Sacred Lake; b) the eastern temple, adorned with monolithic columns with palm-shaped capitals, and the nearby temple of Horus dating from the time of the Thirtieth Dynasty; c) the royal necropolis containing the tombs of Osorkon II (no. 1); the tomb of Psusennes I (no. 3) which also contained the sepulchres of his successor, Amenemope, and of General Undebaunded and King Heka-kheper-re Sheshonq, more commonly referred to as Sheshonq II; the incomplete tomb of Amenemope (no. 4); and the tomb of Sheshonq III (no. 5).

118–119 Psusennes' silver coffin is a unique object, given the rarity of the metal of which it is made. Silver was far less common in ancient Egypt than gold, and was considered to be the bones of gods. The cover of the coffin reproduces the form of the pharaoh, arms crossed and hands holding the attributes of royalty and divinity: the heqa-sceptre and the nekhakha-flail. The gold band around the forehead of the pharaoh supports a solid-gold uraeus. (Cairo Museum)

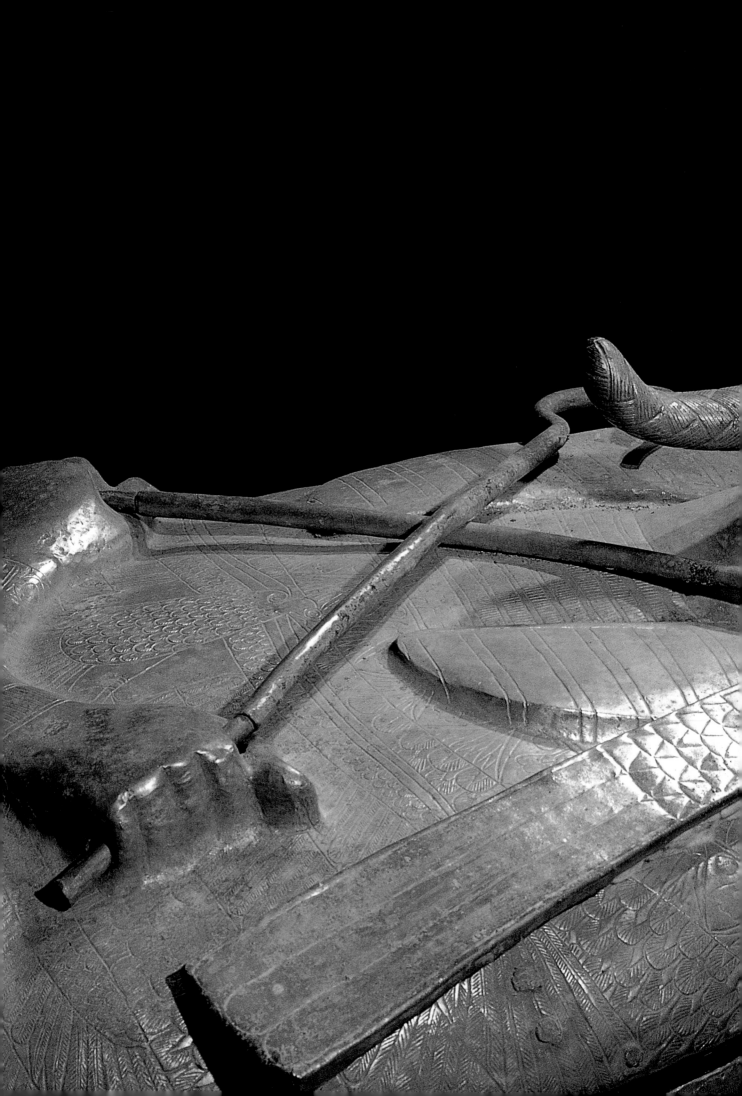

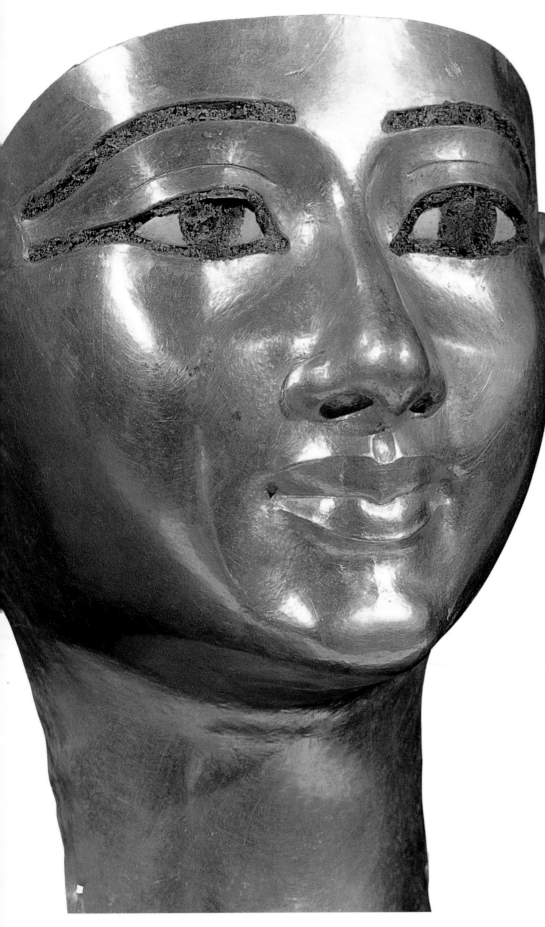

120 The golden mask of General Undebaunded displays a certain realism in the depiction of the face, contrasting with the tendency towards idealization. A slight, almost imperceptible smile seems to enliven the features of this general, who served under Psusennes I. The gold foil of which it is made was chased with remarkable craftsmanship by the artist, who shaped it with a hammer – the marks can still be seen.
(Cairo Museum)

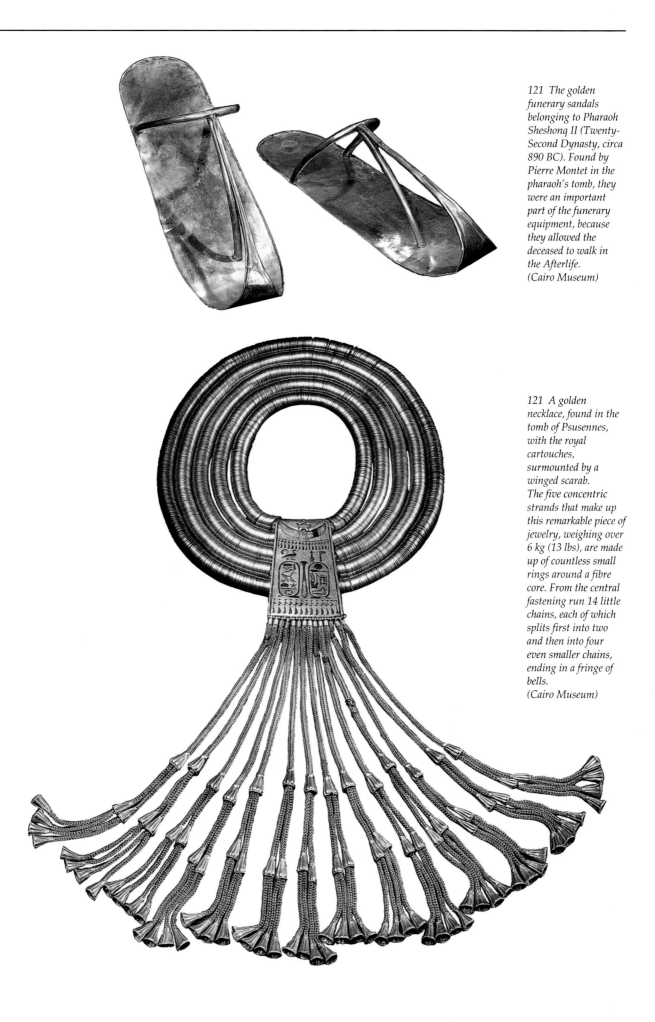

121 The golden funerary sandals belonging to Pharaoh Sheshonq II (Twenty-Second Dynasty, circa 890 BC). Found by Pierre Montet in the pharaoh's tomb, they were an important part of the funerary equipment, because they allowed the deceased to walk in the Afterlife. (Cairo Museum)

121 A golden necklace, found in the tomb of Psusennes, with the royal cartouches, surmounted by a winged scarab. The five concentric strands that make up this remarkable piece of jewelry, weighing over 6 kg (13 lbs), are made up of countless small rings around a fibre core. From the central fastening run 14 little chains, each of which splits first into two and then into four even smaller chains, ending in a fringe of bells. (Cairo Museum)

122 (below) Pectoral of gold, lapis lazuli and turquoise, found at Tanis and belonging to General Undebaunded. Set within a depiction of a pylon, the monumental gate that leads into a temple, the winged scarab lifts the name of the deceased towards the sun-disk and the heavens. The image is a reference both to the sun god at the exact moment of his morning rebirth and also to the theme of the resurrection of the deceased. The goddesses Isis and Nephthys, who stand on either side of the scarab, assist in this heavenly ascent. (Cairo Museum)

123 (right) A detail of one of the two exquisite pectorals, made of gold with polychrome inlays, found on the mummy of Psusennes. The goddess Isis spreads her winged arms both to protect and to give the breath of life to the cartouche that bears the name of the pharaoh. At the centre of the pectoral (only partly visible here) is the scarab, the image of Khepri, the form of the sun deity that is reborn and regenerated each morning. On the head of the goddess is the set-throne that transcribes her name. (Cairo Museum)

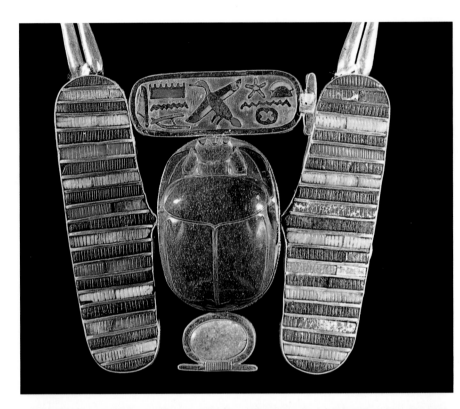

124 (above) One of the four pendants with a winged scarab found on the mummy of Psusennes. The winged scarab is a symbol of the eternal rebirth of the sun and of the pharaoh himself. The pharaoh's name is engraved in the cartouche that surmounts the green jasper scarab, itself flanked by two large geometric wings inlaid with semi-precious stones (cornelian and turquoise) and glass paste. The scarab stands in turn on a shenu-seal, a powerful protective amulet. On the reverse of the seal are inscribed passages of Chapter 30 of the Book of the Dead, calling on the heart of the deceased to refrain from testifying against its owner during the final judgment in the presence of Osiris. (Cairo Museum)

124 (below) One of the numerous rings discovered on the mummy of Psusennes. The cartouche of the pharaoh is engraved on lapis lazuli, and is framed by two rows of semiprecious stones (cornelian and lapis lazuli). The whole ring is decorated with a geometric motif in lapis lazuli and glass paste. (Cairo Museum)

125 This exquisite decorative motif – of an udjat-eye above a neb sign – adorns a bracelet made of gold, faience, cornelian and lapis lazuli, found on the mummy of Pharaoh Sheshonq II (Twenty-Second Dynasty). The bracelet, which is remarkably modern in style, was found with six others on the arms of the pharaoh. It served a protective function and was meant to ensure the immortality of the deceased. The udjat-eye was a powerful amulet. (Cairo Museum)

GIZA, THE LAST WONDER OF THE ANCIENT WORLD

Located some 16 km (10 miles) southwest of the centre of Cairo, on the edge of a desert plateau, the three great pyramids of Giza rise up majestically. They were built by pharaohs of the Fourth Dynasty (Cheops, Chephren and Mycerinus) and are the only one of the Seven Wonders of the Ancient World to have survived to the present day. As so often happens with the great monuments of humankind's distant

This is the core of the tale as told by Herodotus, who entertains us with other fanciful details about the perversity of the pharaohs of the Fourth Dynasty, and in particular the famed Cheops, who went so far as to prostitute his daughter in order to finance the building of his pyramid, according to the Greek historian.

The reality is somewhat different: the pyramids were not built by masses of toiling slaves, as Herodotus tells it, but rather by free citizens, craftsmen or peasants, who, during the period of the Nile's floods (from June to September), when the river's waters covered the country's arable land, performed a sort of obligatory 'community service', that was paid for by the pharaoh. The precise construction techniques used by the ancient builders of the pyramids are still much debated, and there are no documents to shed any light. One current theory is that they were built with overlapping ramps, that were extended and raised as the pyramid rose higher. Recent research suggests that the enormous limestone blocks of the body of the pyramid were quarried locally on the Giza plateau itself and then dragged to the construction site by teams of labourers using huge wooden sledges. The blocks were subsequently covered with a casing (long since lost) of harder limestone slabs, mostly taken from the quarry at Tura, on the opposite, east bank, of the Nile.

past, the pyramids are shrouded in an aura dense with mystery and have attracted innumerable myths, which are now deeply rooted in the popular imagination. The pyramids are often linked with a picture of thousands of slaves who, goaded and whipped by pitiless overseers, toiled endlessly to satisfy the vast ambitions and dreams of eternal greatness of a cruel pharaoh.

126 (left) The Grand Gallery in the pyramid of Cheops leading to the King's Chamber. A narrow north–south corridor opens out into this spacious rising passage, about 45 m (150 ft) long and 8 m (26 ft) high, a genuine *architectural wonder and contrasting sharply with all the other, much smaller, corridors in the pyramid. The blocks of limestone, arranged in seven vertical courses, are fitted together with remarkable accuracy.*

126–127 The pyramid of Cheops, the most imposing monument ever built in Egypt. It is 140 m (460 ft) tall and made from over 7.7 million tons of rock – more than 2.5 million *blocks cut with such precision that the joints between them are no wider than half a millimetre. Each face is 230 m (755 ft) long, and the base covers an area of around 5 ha (12 acres).*

127 (right) The sun barque of Cheops, over 42 m (138 ft) long and more than 5 m (16 ft) wide, was discovered in 1954, near the south face of the pyramid in a boat pit. The boat had been assembled without the use of a single nail, and was held together entirely by fibre ropes.

It is not known whether this boat ever sailed, nor what its real function may have been, though it is reasonable to suppose that it was intended to enable the soul of the pharaoh to sail eternally through the afterlife. The boat was not alone: there are three other large pits which must originally have contained three further barques, on the eastern side of the pyramid. Recently, a new pit was found unopened, and in it was a boat similar to the first, shown here, now conserved in a museum specially built near its original resting place.

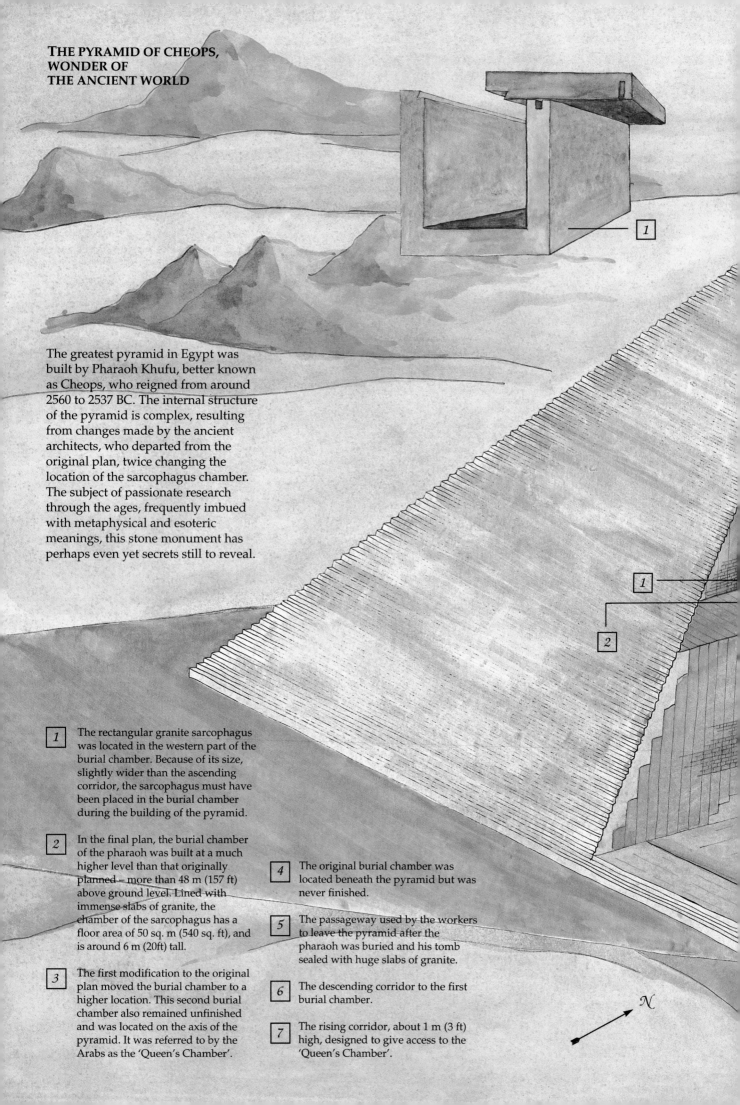

THE PYRAMID OF CHEOPS, WONDER OF THE ANCIENT WORLD

The greatest pyramid in Egypt was built by Pharaoh Khufu, better known as Cheops, who reigned from around 2560 to 2537 BC. The internal structure of the pyramid is complex, resulting from changes made by the ancient architects, who departed from the original plan, twice changing the location of the sarcophagus chamber. The subject of passionate research through the ages, frequently imbued with metaphysical and esoteric meanings, this stone monument has perhaps even yet secrets still to reveal.

1 The rectangular granite sarcophagus was located in the western part of the burial chamber. Because of its size, slightly wider than the ascending corridor, the sarcophagus must have been placed in the burial chamber during the building of the pyramid.

2 In the final plan, the burial chamber of the pharaoh was built at a much higher level than that originally planned – more than 48 m (157 ft) above ground level. Lined with immense slabs of granite, the chamber of the sarcophagus has a floor area of 50 sq. m (540 sq. ft), and is around 6 m (20ft) tall.

3 The first modification to the original plan moved the burial chamber to a higher location. This second burial chamber also remained unfinished and was located on the axis of the pyramid. It was referred to by the Arabs as the 'Queen's Chamber'.

4 The original burial chamber was located beneath the pyramid but was never finished.

5 The passageway used by the workers to leave the pyramid after the pharaoh was buried and his tomb sealed with huge slabs of granite.

6 The descending corridor to the first burial chamber.

7 The rising corridor, about 1 m (3 ft) high, designed to give access to the 'Queen's Chamber'.

N

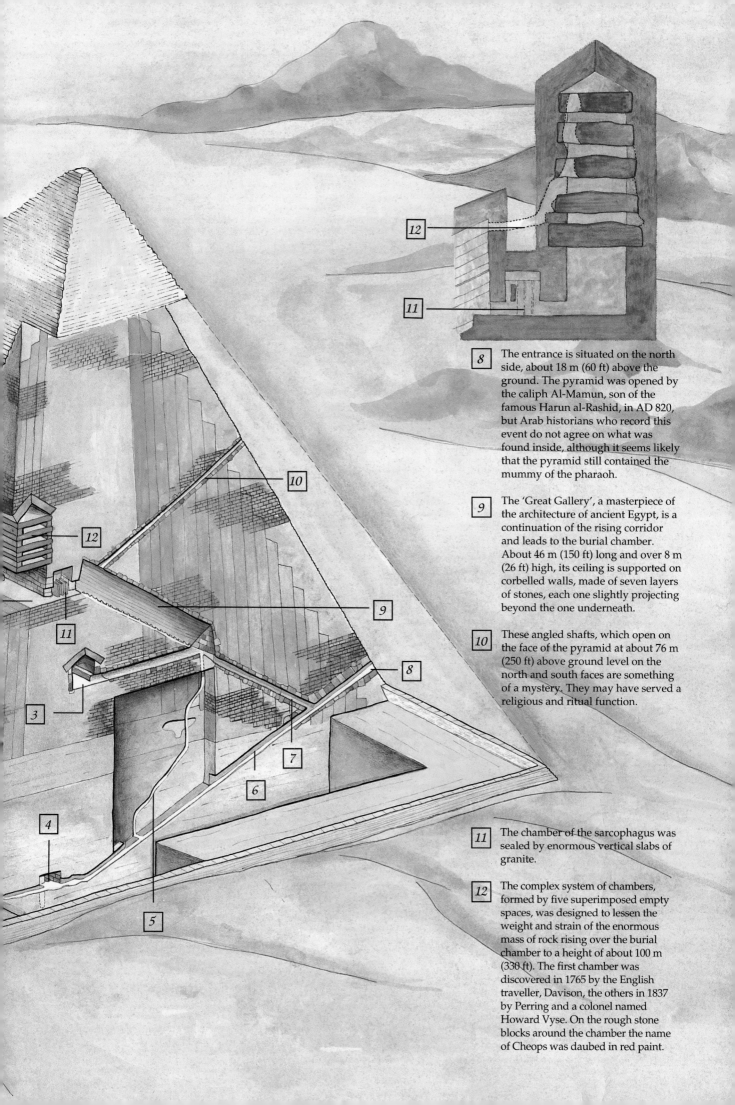

8 The entrance is situated on the north side, about 18 m (60 ft) above the ground. The pyramid was opened by the caliph Al-Mamun, son of the famous Harun al-Rashid, in AD 820, but Arab historians who record this event do not agree on what was found inside, although it seems likely that the pyramid still contained the mummy of the pharaoh.

9 The 'Great Gallery', a masterpiece of the architecture of ancient Egypt, is a continuation of the rising corridor and leads to the burial chamber. About 46 m (150 ft) long and over 8 m (26 ft) high, its ceiling is supported on corbelled walls, made of seven layers of stones, each one slightly projecting beyond the one underneath.

10 These angled shafts, which open on the face of the pyramid at about 76 m (250 ft) above ground level on the north and south faces are something of a mystery. They may have served a religious and ritual function.

11 The chamber of the sarcophagus was sealed by enormous vertical slabs of granite.

12 The complex system of chambers, formed by five superimposed empty spaces, was designed to lessen the weight and strain of the enormous mass of rock rising over the burial chamber to a height of about 100 m (330 ft). The first chamber was discovered in 1765 by the English traveller, Davison, the others in 1837 by Perring and a colonel named Howard Vyse. On the rough stone blocks around the chamber the name of Cheops was daubed in red paint.

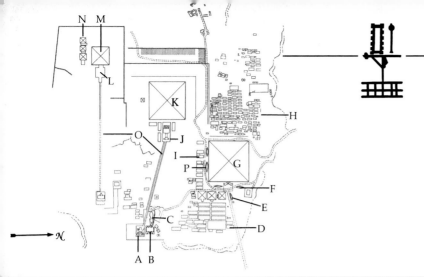

A Valley Temple
B Temple of
 the Sphinx
C Great Sphinx
D Eastern cemetery
E Satellite pyramids
F Boat-pits of the
 solar barques
G Pyramid of Cheops
H Western cemetery
I Solar barque
 (as yet unexcavated)

J Mortuary temple
K Pyramid
 of Chephren
L Mortuary temple
M Pyramid
 of Mycerinus
 (Menkaure)
N Satellite pyramids
O Pyramid ramp
P Museum of
 the Solar Barque

130 (above) Of the renowned Seven Wonders of the Ancient World, the only one that has survived to modern times is the complex of the great pyramids of Giza. Their majestic splendour has excited universal amazement and admiration ever since ancient times; the Greek historian Diodorus Siculus wrote that the pyramids astounded all those who saw them, by their massive size and their beauty. The scholars who accompanied Napoleon's Egyptian expedition calculated that with the material used in the construction of the three pyramids of Cheops, Chephren and Mycerinus, it would have been possible to build a wall about 3 m (10 ft) high and 30 cm (1 ft) thick around the whole of France.

131 (opposite) The great pyramids, supreme examples of the monumental architecture of the Fourth Dynasty, were expressions of a philosophical and religious culture that associated the worship of the sun with the pharaoh cult, and viewed the pyramid, a materialization in stone of the sun's rays, as a means by which the soul of the pharaoh could rise to heaven and rejoin the sun god Re. The pyramid of Chephren, in the centre, is slightly smaller than that of Cheops, though its sides are steeper and it was built on higher ground, giving it the impression of being slightly the largest of the three pyramids. The Greek historian Herodotus, who discussed the pyramids in his Histories, stated, wrongly, that the pyramid of Chephren, unlike that of Cheops, had no interior chambers.

132 (below) This so-called 'reserve head', found in a mastaba of the western cemetery of Giza, belonged to a member of the family of Pharaoh Chephren. It is not known exactly what significance was attached to these life-size heads with extremely realistic features, found in the burial chamber or nearby, but they may either have served as substitutes in case the body of the deceased was damaged, or they were used as models for the funerary mask of the dead person. (Cairo Museum)

132 (above) The dignified figure of Chephren (2529–2504 BC), found in the Valley Temple of the pyramid of Chephren by Auguste Mariette in 1860. This diorite statue is one of the finest achievements of Old Kingdom sculpture. The stiff pose and idealized perfection of the pharaoh successfully convey the concept of royal divinity. The king is depicted sitting upon a throne supported by two lions; his head is adorned with the nemes, a ceremonial headcloth, on the back of which the artist has carved an image of the god Horus in the shape of a hawk, identifying the king as the earthly representative of the god: the Living Horus. (Cairo Museum)

133 *The famous triad of Mycerinus, which formed one of a set of five group statues discovered in the Valley Temple of the pyramid of Mycerinus. Here, the pharaoh is shown wearing the white crown of Upper Egypt and is dressed in the* scendyt, *a distinctive pleated loincloth. He is flanked by two deities: the goddess Hathor, 'Lady of the Castle of the Sycamore', who was associated with concepts of fertility and abundance, on the left, and on the right the tutelary deity of the seventeenth nome (a word used to indicate the different administrative districts) of Upper Egypt, identifiable by the attribute above her head.*
(Cairo Museum)

THE SPHINX, GUARDIAN OF THE NECROPOLIS OF GIZA

134 (left) The face of the Great Sphinx, with the characteristic royal and divine headdress, known as the nemes, *is 4 m (13 ft) wide, and its eyes are 2m (over 6 ft) high. Part of the nose, the* uraeus *(the sacred cobra) which adorned its forehead, and the ritual beard – a fragment of which is in the British Museum – are now missing. The Sphinx, like the gods and the pharaoh, fulfilled a protective function.*

The sphinx – a Greek word taken from the Egyptian expression, *shesep ankh*, meaning 'living image' – is a figure with a lion's body and a human head or the head of an animal, itself representing a deity. One of the most typical forms of statuary under the pharaohs, the sphinx was a depiction of royal power – and hence only the pharaoh could be shown in this way – or of a protective deity. With its ancient, enigmatic gaze, seemingly contemplating the rising sun on the eastern horizon, the Great Sphinx of Giza has always intrigued visitors to Egypt from the earliest times. The strange figure has exercised particular allure for those attracted by esoteric and pseudo-scientific archaeology.

The Sphinx was carved during the reign of Chephren (2529-2504 BC), from a limestone spur that may already have been roughly shaped by the wind. Measuring some 60 m (200 ft) in length and 20 m (65 ft) in height, the hybrid creature may have pharaoh Chephren's face as the living image of the sun god, and stands guardian before the necropolis of Giza. From the Eighteenth Dynasty, the Sphinx was identified with the god Harmachis, a syncretistic deity that contained the triple form of the sun god during its daily route: Khepri in the morning, Re at noon and Atum in the evening.

Over the course of the centuries, the desert sands slowly covered up the Sphinx, which may be why Herodotus makes no reference to it in his history and description of Egypt. It was a Genoan naval captain – Giovanni Caviglia – in 1816, who first began the task of clearing away the sand. Caviglia was probably not motivated by entirely scientific considerations: he may have been drawn by the mysterious stories recounted by Arab

historians, including the renowned el-Makrizi, to the effect that a secret cavity existed in the monument, containing no less an object than the elusive cup of Solomon. In any case, Caviglia was responsible for a series of interesting observations concerning the monument, of which he also found a number of scattered components, including a part of the beard that once adorned its chin, which was taken to the British Museum.

The great Egyptologists of the last century, such as Auguste Mariette, and his successor, Gaston Maspero, took interest in the Sphinx, but it was the work undertaken between 1925 and 1936 by the Egyptologists Emile Baraize and Selim Hassan, that gave the Sphinx its current familiar appearance.

135 (above) The Sphinx was a masculine entity, a manifestation of the sun god and the depiction of the deified pharaoh. From the Eighteenth Dynasty onwards the Sphinx was assimilated with Harmachis, or 'Horus on the Horizon'.

136–137 (overleaf) Giant guardian of the necropolis of Giza, the Great Sphinx has always been thought of as mysterious as the pyramids, its gaze stretching away through space and time.

SAQQARA, THE NECROPOLIS OF MEMPHIS

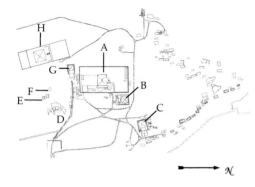

A Funerary complex of Djoser
B Pyramid of Userkaf
C Pyramid of Teti
D Monastery of Saint Jeremiah
E Tomb of Horemheb
F Tomb of Maya
G Pyramid of Unas
H Funerary complex of Horus Sekhemkhet

138 In the pyramid of Unas, the last king of the Fifth Dynasty, the walls of the interior chambers were covered for the first time with lengthy hieroglyphic inscriptions containing invocations and magic spells. These were the Pyramid Texts, which were intended to aid the pharaoh's soul in overcoming the many difficulties and eliminating the malevolent forces that it would encounter in the Afterworld, in order to be joined once again with the sun god Re. These magic texts then evolved into the Coffin Texts, painted on coffins, and, finally, in the New Kingdom, into the Book of the Dead.

To the south of Giza lies the immense necropolis of Saqqara, the largest of all the cemeteries linked to the capital, Memphis. Saqqara is dominated by the great step pyramid of Djoser, dating from the beginning of the Third Dynasty (around 2658 BC), the first known example of a pyramid in Egypt. Djoser's pyramid was designed by the great architect Imhotep, who was later deified as a magician and healer, and identified by the Greeks with the god of medicine, Asclepius. Imhotep first built a large mastaba, which he then raised by adding five superimposed levels, decreasing in size, until a pyramid of six steps was formed. In philosophical and religious terms, the pyramid may have represented a stairway for the king to ascend to heaven.

The pyramid was surrounded by a vast enclosure containing other buildings devoted to the cult of the pharaoh, including the funerary temple, dedicated to the worship of the deceased emperor, and the buildings used for the celebration of the *sed* festival (or 'jubilee'), which took place in the thirtieth year of a pharaoh's reign. This ritual, the origins of which probably date to the Predynastic era, was designed to regenerate the power of the king who, during the ceremonies, travelled along an established ritual route.

In the necropolis of Saqqara, there are 15 royal pyramids, the most important of which are those built by Userkaf, founder of the Fifth Dynasty (whose sun temple stands at Abusir), Unas (Fifth Dynasty) and Teti (Sixth Dynasty). The pyramid of Unas is the first to have hieroglyphic inscriptions covering the inside walls. These are the Pyramid Texts, a compilation of magical formulas intended to guide the pharaoh through the Afterworld, triumphing over all obstacles.

138–139 The Step Pyramid of Djoser at Saqqara. With the advent of the Third Dynasty, the tomb of the pharaoh also became the symbol of his divinity and of his celestial power that extended beyond death, benefiting the entire land. Imhotep, the celebrated architect of Djoser, expressed these concepts by raising a simple mastaba into a series of superimposed mastabas of decreasing size, thus forming a step pyramid, symbolizing a stairway reaching up to heaven to allow the ascent of the pharaoh's soul.

139 (left) The Fifth-Dynasty complex of Abusir is located to the north of Saqqara, and includes, besides the tombs of private citizens and the remains of the sun temple of Userkaf, the three pyramids of Sahure, Nyuserre and Neferirkare. The techniques and materials used in their construction resulted in structures that were neither particularly strong nor resistant, and which have decayed considerably over time. At the turn of the century they were studied extensively by the Egyptologist J.L. Burckhardt.

The earliest use of the necropolis of Saqqara pre-dates the time of the pyramids. The oldest tombs belong to the era of the pharaoh Aha (First Dynasty), the successor to Narmer, founder of Memphis and unifier of Egypt. The great mastabas of the First Dynasty, located to the north of the pyramid of Djoser, belonged to high officials from Memphis, while the rulers in this period had themselves buried in the royal cemetery of the city of Abydos. It was only in the Second Dynasty that the pharaohs, probably beginning with Re-neb and Nynetjer, were buried at Saqqara. Just as in life the pharaoh was surrounded by courtiers, in death Old Kingdom royal tombs were encircled with the tombs of high officials and their families. Over 250 underground burial chambers have been discovered, mostly dating to a period between the Third and the Sixth Dynasties, between 2658 and 2150 BC. These are sumptuous tombs, in some cases enormous in size and lavishly decorated with reliefs, originally painted, depicting the activity of the deceased which provide a glimpse of everyday life as it was experienced five thousand years ago, in the shadow of the pyramids.

Another group of tombs belongs to the New Kingdom, the most important of which date from the reign of Amenophis III, and especially from the time that elapsed between the reign of Tutankhamun and that of Ramesses II. Excavations conducted in the areas of the necropolis occupied by the New Kingdom tombs have yielded spectacular results in recent years; of particular significance are the discoveries of the tomb of the mysterious Aperia or Aper-el, the vizier of Amenophis III, whom some scholars have identified with the Biblical figure of Joseph; the private tomb of Horemheb (who later became pharaoh and who was therefore buried in the Valley of the Kings); and that of Maya, treasurer under Tutankhamun. One thing is certain: a great many tombs await discovery, as shown in April 1993, when a new tomb (perhaps the first in a new sector of the necropolis) was found, which belonged to a high official of the reign of Ramesses II. Activity in the necropolis of Saqqara did not cease with the end of the New Kingdom – it continued through the Twenty-Sixth, Twenty-Seventh and Thirtieth Dynasty, right up to the Graeco-Roman era.

The period between the Twenty-Sixth and the Thirtieth Dynasty was when the largest galleries were dug for the Serapeum, the famous necropolis of the sacred bulls of Apis. The name Serapeum derives from the term Usir-Apis, the 'deceased Apis', later linked to the Graeco-Egyptian god Serapis, though the cult of the Apis bull of Memphis dates from the Predynastic Period. Apis was linked to the concept of fertility and became associated with the important creator god of Memphis, Ptah. The immense underground structure, the excavation of which began under the rule of Ramesses II, contains 24 huge sarcophagi of sacred bulls, the largest of which weighs 70 tons.

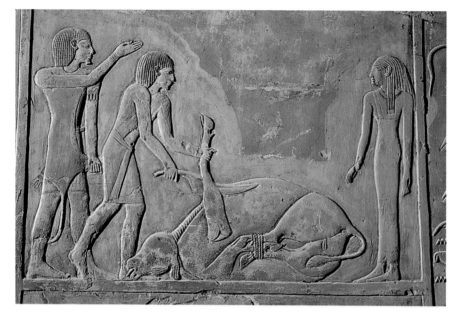

141 (top) A scene of ritual slaughter in a relief carved in one of the tombs of private citizens at Saqqara, dating to the Fifth Dynasty.

141 (centre) Relief depicting a funerary procession, found in one of the tombs of private citizens at Saqqara, dating to the Fifth Dynasty. In this detail, three servants carry foodstuffs and animals for the benefit of the deceased.

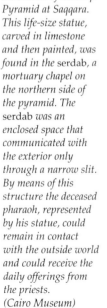

140 (opposite) Djoser, the builder of the Step Pyramid at Saqqara. This life-size statue, carved in limestone and then painted, was found in the serdab, a mortuary chapel on the northern side of the pyramid. The serdab was an enclosed space that communicated with the exterior only through a narrow slit. By means of this structure the deceased pharaoh, represented by his statue, could remain in contact with the outside world and could receive the daily offerings from the priests. (Cairo Museum)

141 (bottom) In the main chapel of the mastaba of Ti, a high official who lived during the Fifth Dynasty, a relief depicts in great detail the various phases of the construction of a wooden boat. This is a unique document, of exceptional importance for the study of the naval technology of the Old Kingdom.

A Palace of Apries
B Small temple
C Northern enclosure
D Mit Rahina
E Pond
F Enclosure of the temple of Ptah
G Kom el-Fakry
H Kom el-Rabiya
I Temple of Hathor
J Small temple of Ptah
K Colossus
L Alabaster sphinx
M Temple of Merneptah
N Palace of Merneptah
O Kom el-Qalaa
P Kom el-Arbayn
Q Kom el-Nawa

MEMPHIS, THE FIRST CAPITAL

Memphis was founded by Narmer in the region known as *Mekhattawi*, or 'that which binds the Two Lands', which at the time marked the boundary between Upper and Lower Egypt, right at the tip of the Nile Delta. The city became the great capital of Egypt during the Early Dynastic and Old Kingdom periods.

In antiquity it was called *Ineb-hedj*, or 'White Walls', referring – according to Herodotus – to the construction of a dam to protect the town from the Nile floods. It later took the name of *Ankh-tawi*, or 'the Life of the Two Lands'. One of the temples of Memphis dedicated to Hut-Ka-Ptah may have been the origin of the word *Aigyptos*, which the Greeks used for the country as a whole – Egypt.

Memphis extended over a vast area in antiquity, but not a great deal of the city survives. The few visible ruins are scattered amidst the palms near the village of Mit Rahina. Much of the city and its buildings remain unexplored.

142 (above) A colossal statue of Ramesses II at Memphis. Though unfinished, the statue, carved from a block of limestone, still measures about 10 m (33 ft) long. This magnificent piece of sculpture, found in 1820 by the Italian traveller Giovanni Caviglia, was donated by Mohammad Ali to the British Museum. However, the English were daunted by the task of transporting it and today it reposes in a small museum in the archaeological zone of Memphis.

143 (right) Memphis continued to serve as a major economic and trading capital during the New Kingdom. Although a large portion of the city, which extended over a vast area, is still buried under farmland or covered by buildings and homes of the small village of Mit Rahina, about a mile from Saqqara, it is possible to see the ruins of religious buildings, such as the temple of Ptah, the leading deity of Memphis, and a number of statues. The most noteworthy among them is this alabaster sphinx. Thought to date from the reign of Ramesses II, it is 8 m (26 ft) long and 4 m (13 ft) tall, weighing around 90 tons – perhaps the largest mobiliary work of art discovered.

DAHSHUR AND MEIDUM: DAWNING OF THE AGE OF TRUE PYRAMIDS

144 *The interior structure of the pyramid of Meidum is drawn here according to the studies of Flinders Petrie and Borchardt. 1 Outer sheath (Phase III) from the reign of Snefru. 2 Enlargement of the pyramid by increasing the number of steps (Phase II). 3 Original structure of the pyramid with seven steps (Phase I). 4 Entrance, located on the north side of the pyramid.*

5 *Burial chamber: the first ever in the body of a pyramid. Maspero penetrated the pyramid in 1882, but he found no trace of a sarcophagus.*

Dahshur and Meidum, situated a few miles south of Saqqara, are of particular significance because they are the sites of the earliest examples of geometrically true pyramids. Built between the end of the Third Dynasty and the beginning of the Fourth, they clearly represent a development on the Step Pyramid of Saqqara. At Meidum, the pharaoh Huni, a successor of Djoser and the last ruler of the Third Dynasty, built a step pyramid not unlike the one at Saqqara. Subsequently this was covered with a casing of limestone slabs, which gave the structure the appearance of a true pyramid, thus marking the point of transition between the two architectural forms. This change may also have marked a shift in the technological concepts of the era. If the step pyramid symbolically represented a stairway that the king's soul could climb up to reach heaven, this celestial ascent could now take place along the steep sides of the true

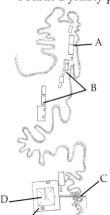

144–145 *At Meidum the prototype of the true pyramid was built. The last pharaoh of the Third Dynasty, Huni, constructed an imposing step pyramid which was subsequently covered with limestone slabs by Snefru, the first ruler of the Fourth Dynasty. The monument was thus given the appearance of a true pyramid. The*

experiment was not a great success, however. The outer sheath had no solid support at its base and came away from the older part of the structure, the step pyramid itself. Thus, the walls slipped downwards and a partial collapse exposed the central core of the building, giving it its current appearance.

pyramid, a purer form and a concrete materialization in stone of the nurturing rays of the sun god Re, with whom the soul of the pharaoh would be reunited. The first systematic study of the pyramid of Meidum was the work of the British Egyptologist Flinders Petrie, between 1888 and 1891, which brought to light a number of structures clearly associated with Fourth-Dynasty pyramids, both the

A Roman necropolis
B Northern necropolis
C Mastabas
D Pyramid of Snefru and Huni
E Satellite pyramids
F Southern necropolis

causeways and funerary temples. The causeway was oriented along an east–west axis, and ended at an enclosure wall which surrounded the pyramid. On the eastern side of the pyramid – but separated from the pyramid by a courtyard – was a chapel for offerings, an embryonic form of the funerary temple with a very simple structure consisting of

Snefru built two more pyramids at Dahshur, some miles north of Meidum. The first is known as the 'rhomboid pyramid', or the 'southern pyramid of Dahshur', while the other is known as the 'northern pyramid of Dahshur'. During the construction of the first, which in the initial plans was only slightly smaller than the pyramid of Cheops, the architects noted some

146 (below) The charming 'geese of Meidum' were found in a private tomb at Meidum – the mastaba of Nefermaat and his wife Atet. The work dates from early in the reign of Snefru, of the Fourth Dynasty. The birds were painted

on the plaster of a wall of a corridor in the tomb, built with unbaked bricks. They are a delightful expression of the technical virtuosity and highly developed sensitivity of the artists of the era. (Cairo Museum)

two rooms the innermost of which contained two plain stelae and a central altar. On the northern side of the pyramid an entrance gave on to a corridor that led to the burial chamber, the first time this chamber was inside the pyramid itself. To the south, between the pyramid and the enclosure wall, was a satellite pyramid.

Research has shown that the pyramid of Meidum was built in three successive phases. The original pyramid was made up of seven superimposed levels (Phase I). This was subsequently enlarged with a new casing, probably increasing the number of steps to eight (Phase II). In the final phase (Phase III), dating to the reign of Snefru, the first pharaoh of the Fourth Dynasty, the angle between the riser and the ledge of each step was filled in with material from other constructions, and a final casing was applied, consisting of smooth limestone slabs, giving the step pyramid the appearance of a true pyramid. The chapel for offerings on the east side of the pyramid also dates from this period. However, Snefru's modifications did not prove successful, because over time the outer covering of the pyramid slid down over the underlying layers of material, giving the construction the curious shape that it has today.

signs of collapse in the vaults of the inner chambers. The decision was therefore made to lighten the load the vaults supported by modifying the incline of the pyramid's faces – a solution which gave this pyramid its odd, rhomboid shape. It was only with the construction of the second, northern, pyramid of Dahshur that the architects succeeded in building a perfect true pyramid.

147 (right) The tomb of prince Rahotep, the son of Snefru and a priest of Heliopolis, and of his wife, Nofret, yielded these two splendid statues, made of painted limestone, depicting the deceased couple. The liveliness of the colours and the skill of the sculptors in

carving the figures confer on them such a lifelike appearance that when they were discovered during the last century, during the excavations of the Egyptologist Auguste Mariette, the founder of the Cairo Museum, the labourers fled in terror. (Cairo Museum)

146 The pyramid complex of Meidum as it might have looked during the rule of Snefru, consisting of: the funerary chapel on

the eastern side (a); the enclosure wall (b); the causeway (c); the valley temple (d); a satellite pyramid (e); and a mastaba (f).

THE FAIYUM, BETWEEN OASIS AND DESERT

The Faiyum, which is often incorrectly described as an oasis, is in fact a green and fertile region in the form of a vast and roughly circular depression, about 60 km (37 miles) east to west. In the northwest corner is Lake Qarun, which the ancients referred to as Lake *Moeris* and whose Coptic name, *Peiom*, is the source of the modern name Faiyum. The lake is linked to the Nile by means of a canal called Bahr Yussuf, or 'Joseph's Canal'.

The ancient Egyptians called the Faiyum *Mer-wer* – 'the Great Lake' – though it was actually an enormous marsh with an abundance of animal life and luxuriant vegetation. The region took on particular importance during the Twelfth Dynasty (when the capital was transferred to el-Lisht), and during the Ptolemaic period, when major reclamation projects were undertaken by Ptolemy Philadelphus, and again later, during Roman times.

The capital of the region is the city of Medinet el-Faiyum (population 100,000), which corresponds to the Ptolemaic city of Arsinoe, also called Crocodilopolis, a reference to the local custom of worshipping crocodiles, in honour of the crocodile-god Sobek. Numerous archaeological relics in the Faiyum date from the Greek and Roman periods, such as the ruins of the city of Karanis (near modern-day Kom Aushim) with a temple dedicated to the local gods, and the city of Dionysias, near the village of Qasr Qarun, at the westernmost point of the lakeshore, where the temple is still in excellent condition. Important relics also survive from the Middle Kingdom, such as the temple of Medinet Madi, the ancient city of Narmouthis. Here, the pharaoh Amenemhat III built a temple dedicated to the cobra-goddess Renenutet and to the crocodile-god Sobek, which was expanded during Ptolemaic and Roman times. Also dating to the Middle Kingdom are the mud-brick pyramids of the kings of the Twelfth Dynasty, situated at the southernmost end of the Faiyum: el-Lahun and Hawara.

The pyramid of el-Lahun was built by Sesostris II on a rocky foundation at the point at which the Bahr Yussuf enters the Faiyum, while the pyramid of Hawara, and the immense funerary temple, known in antiquity as the 'labyrinth' because it was said to have had three thousand rooms, were built by Amenemhat III.

148–149 The extensive temple of Amenemhat III (the sixth pharaoh of the Twelfth Dynasty) at Medinet Madi, approached by a long dromos of lion-headed sphinxes, lies partially buried amidst the desert sands in the southern portion of the Faiyum region. The temple of Medinet Madi, the site of the ancient city of Gia, called Narmouthis in Graeco-Roman times, was excavated and studied by a mission led by the Milanese papyrologist Achille Vogliano, between 1934 and 1939. This is the only well-preserved building for worship dating from the Middle Kingdom known in Egypt. Originally the temple was dedicated to the cobra-goddess, called Renenutet, the protectress of crops and harvests, and to the crocodile-god Sobek, who was particularly venerated in this region. The first temple was later expanded, during the Ptolemaic era, and dedicated to the worship of the pharaoh Amenemhat III, who had been deified.

A Lake Qarun
B Temple of Qasr el-
  Sagha
C Dimai (Soknopalou
  Nesos)
D Karanis
E Medinet el-Faiyum
F Khelua
G Medinet Madi
H Temple of Qasr
  Qarun
I Pyramid of Meidum
J Pyramid of Hawara
K Pyramid of el-Lahun

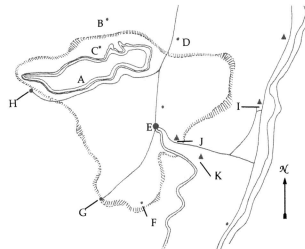

AMARNA, CAPITAL OF THE HERETIC PHARAOH

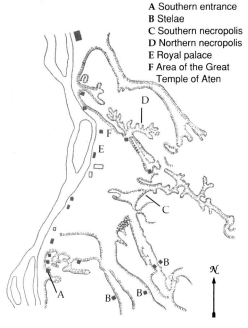

A Southern entrance
B Stelae
C Southern necropolis
D Northern necropolis
E Royal palace
F Area of the Great
Temple of Aten

N

At Tell el-Amarna, close to the modern village of Abu Qurqas, on the right bank of the Nile midway between Memphis and Thebes, stand the ruins of Akhetaten ('the horizon of Aten'), the short-lived but enormous capital built by the heretic pharaoh Amenophis IV – Akhenaten. The entire city was built at breakneck speed on a huge alluvial plain, bordered to the east by the mountains. The boundaries of the city itself were marked out by a series of stelae called 'boundary stelae'. Buildings in the city included a temple dedicated to Aten, the royal palace, the pharaoh's private residence and the homes of various officials and dignitaries. In 1887 the royal archives were discovered – a vast number of clay tablets covered with cuneiform writing, constituting the official correspondence between the pharaoh and the kings and governors in other lands of the Middle East.

Abandoned just 15 years after its construction, Akhetaten was used as a quarry for building materials and was never rebuilt – today there is nothing but an expanse of scarcely visible ruins scattered over a huge area.

The desolate and deserted appearance of the plain of el-Amarna should not deceive the modern visitor, however. In the days of Akhenaten, this was a vast garden, dotted with plants, flowers, splendid palaces with magnificent painted decorations depicting natural subjects and even a lake. The necropolis consists of 25 rock-cut tombs dug into the mountain, with wall paintings that testify to the profound artistic revolution that was begun and completed under the rule of Akhenaten, in a style now known as 'Amarna art'.

150 (below) Akhenaten marked the boundaries of his new capital Akhetaten – modern el-Amarna in Middle Egypt – with a series of 14 stelae, each of which was carved with a representation of the royal family worshipping before Aten, and a lengthy inscription containing formulas for prayers to the sun god.

150–151 (right) Amenophis IV, who changed his name to Akhenaten, meaning 'He Who Is Pleasing to Aten', established the worship of a single deity, Aten, the Sun Disk. In the fourth year of his reign the pharaoh also founded a new capital in Middle Egypt, called Akhetaten, or 'the Horizon of Aten' (now el-Amarna). During his reign, in parallel with his radical religious ideas, new artistic directions developed, contrasting sharply with previous conventions. The resulting style, now known as 'Amarna art', is marked by a sensuality and a realism previously unknown. In accordance with the new artistic canons, the features of the pharaoh's face were intentionally deformed and elongated, perhaps to express an intense spirituality. This statue was found at Karnak, in the temple of Aten, which Akhenaten had ordered built outside the eastern side of the enclosure wall of the great temple of Amun. It formed part of a series of Osirian colossi that stood before 28 pillars in the courtyard of the temple. (Museum of Luxor)

152 (left) An unfinished quartzite bust of Queen Nefertiti, the wife of Akhenaten, found during excavations at el-Amarna carried out by the Egypt Exploration Society in 1932. There is evident an effort by the artist to express a purity of line and beauty that contrasts sharply with the cruder realism of other works of the period. The marriage of Akhenaten and Nefertiti produced six princesses, including Ankhesenamun, who later married her half-brother Tutankhamun. (Cairo Museum)

153 (right) The heretic pharaoh Akhenaten in the act of making an offering. This painted limestone statuette, found at el-Amarna in 1911, shows the pharaoh wearing a dark blue Khepresh crown and, though the features of his face have been softened, the typical Amarna style is apparent. The face is sharp, the ears are disproportionately large and the lobes are perforated, and – in contrast with the usual conventions of statuary – the king is not portrayed striding with one leg forward. (Cairo Museum)

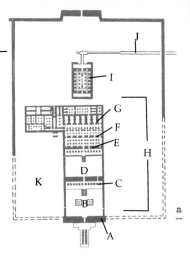

ABYDOS, THE CITY OF OSIRIS

*154 (above) Abydos
was one of the most
important religious
centres of ancient
Egypt. Since it was
believed to be one of
the sites of the tomb of
Osiris, the Lord of the
Underworld, many
people had small
cenotaphs built there,
so that they could take
part in the resurrection
of Osiris. Beginning
in the Middle
Kingdom, but
especially during the
Eighteenth and the*

*Nineteenth Dynasties,
the pharaohs had both
funerary temples and
cenotaphs built there,
including Sethos I.
His cenotaph – the
Osireion – is a
strange construction,
located behind the
funerary temple, and
is unique in Egypt. It
represents the
architectural
realization of the
cosmogonic concept of
time, and was a
simulacrum of the
tomb of Osiris.*

From at least the Early Dynastic
Period, Abydos was a religious centre
linked to the worship of the dead.
Originally a local god called
Khentamentiu was venerated, whose
name meant 'Foremost of the
Westerners', that is the Lord of the
Dead. Later, in the Old Kingdom, this
god was identified with the figure of
Osiris, and the name of the ancient
god become one of Osiris' attributes.
Abydos was believed to be one of the
sites of Osiris' tomb and was therefore
considered a 'holy city', the
destination for great pilgrimages. All
the pharaohs of the First Dynasty and
two of the Second were buried at
Abydos and from the Middle
Kingdom, certain pharaohs had
cenotaphs built here, in order to
participate symbolically in the
resurrection of Osiris.

Sethos I had two monuments built at
Abydos: a funerary temple and a
cenotaph. The temple, described by
Strabo, who called it the *Memnonium*,
was dedicated to Sethos I and to six
other deities (Osiris, Isis, Horus, Ptah,
Re-Harakhty and Amun-Re); the
cenotaph, known as the *Osireion*,
stands behind the temple, and its
structure (resembling a tomb) was
meant to symbolize the primordial
waters, with the primaeval mound in
the centre from which the earth took
shape.

Its walls are adorned with magical
inscriptions and cosmogonical
(explaining the origins and creation of
the universe) and astronomical
paintings. Ramesses II, who
completed the decoration of his
father's temple, also had a funerary
temple built for himself at Abydos,
of less impressive dimensions and
unfortunately less well preserved.

*154 (left) The List of
Kings, in the temple
of Sethos I at Abydos,
shows Sethos I and
his son, the future
Ramesses II, in the
act of burning incense
before cartouches
which represent 76
kings of Egypt who
had preceded them.*

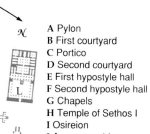

A Pylon
B First courtyard
C Portico
D Second courtyard
E First hypostyle hall
F Second hypostyle hall
G Chapels
H Temple of Sethos I
I Osireion
J Access corridor
K Area of storehouses
L Temple of Ramesses

154–155 Ramesses II also had a funerary temple built for himself at Abydos, not far from that of his father. The temple was decorated with magnificent painted reliefs which can still be seen. Above: a depiction of two of the tutelary deities of the nomes of Egypt; below: Ramesses II holds a sekhem-sceptre in his right hand while standing before an offering table.

156 (left) The sacred lake of the temple of Dendera, situated to the southwest of the main building, was intended for use both in the ablutions of the priests who served in the temple and . probably also in the mystery ceremonies connected with the death and resurrection of Osiris.

DENDERA, DOMAIN OF HATHOR

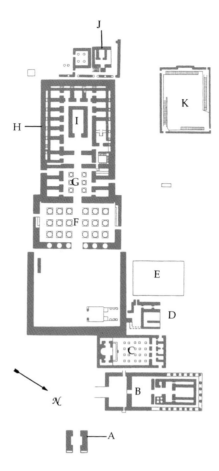

A Portal of Domitian and Trajan
B Roman mammisi
C Christian basilica
D Mammisi of the Thirtieth Dynasty and Ptolemaic Period
E Sanatorium
F Outer hypostyle hall
G Second hypostyle hall
H Great temple of Hathor
I Sanctuary
J Temple of the Birth of Isis
K Sacred Lake

Dendera was the capital of the sixth nome of Upper Egypt, and its necropolis contains tombs ranging in date from the Early Dynastic Period to the end of the Old Kingdom. The principal monument of Dendera is the temple dedicated to the goddess Hathor, of Graeco-Roman date. The temple is remarkably well preserved, with deep crypts set into the outer wall, and is decorated with elaborate reliefs. On the roof of the building are a number of chapels dedicated to Osiris as it was believed that Dendera was one of this god's tombs.

On the ceiling of one chapel was the renowned Zodiac (today replaced by a copy) which was removed by French troops during Napoleon's Egyptian expedition and taken to the Louvre. In front of the large building to the right of the entrance stood two *mammisi* (birth-house), small temples celebrating the birth of Ihy, son of the goddess Hathor. The first *mammisi* was begun under Pharaoh Nectanebo I (Thirtieth Dynasty) and completed during Ptolemaic times, while the second is Roman. To the south of the temple of Hathor, next to the sacred lake, is another little Roman temple from Augustan times, known as the 'Temple of the Birth of Isis'.

156–157 (above) The temple of Dendera, ancient Iunet, with the portal of Domitian and Trajan, the Roman mammisi (birth-house), its less imposing counterpart from the Thirtieth Dynasty, and a sanatorium, where invalids were treated, following instructions from the goddess Hathor received in dreams. In the mammisi *the maternity of Hathor, to whom the temple was dedicated, was celebrated. The cult of the pharaoh, who was identified with the god to whom the goddess had given birth, was also practised. Hathor was one of the most ancient Egyptian deities, and she was depicted in the form of a cow or a woman with the ears of a cow.*

157 (right) The stately hypostyle hall of the temple of Hathor at Dendera. In this masterpiece of the architecture of the Ptolemaic period, the ceiling is supported by 18 columns decorated with what are called Hathor-headed capitals, which depict the goddess in the shape of a woman with the ears of a cow. The temple was built in the first century BC, at the time of Ptolemy XII Neos Dionysos, and its *decoration was completed in the first century AD, in the reigns of Augustus and Nero. At Dendera, a triad, composed of Hathor, Horus of Edfu and their son Ihy, was worshipped. The most important festival in the temple was known as the 'Feast of the Good Union', when Hathor of Dendera visited Horus of Edfu in a great river procession that touched at all of the most important sanctuaries along the Nile.*

THEBES, GLORY OF AMUN

The ancient *Waset*, the city that the Greeks called Thebes, was the centre of the worship of Amun, the 'Hidden One', the king of the gods. To the glory of Amun, on the eastern bank of the Nile at Karnak, the greatest temple of them all was built – *Ipet-isut*, or the 'Most Select of Places' – and for sixteen centuries, every pharaoh wished to leave his imprint on it, enlarging or embellishing the buildings belonging to the temple.

Each year, during the 'Festival of Opet', the sacred image of the god Amun sailed down the Nile and paid a visit to the temple of Luxor, known as *Ipet-resit*, or the 'Private-chambers to the South'. In this way, the god celebrated his marriage with the queen, thus assuring the divine descent of royal power and its regeneration.

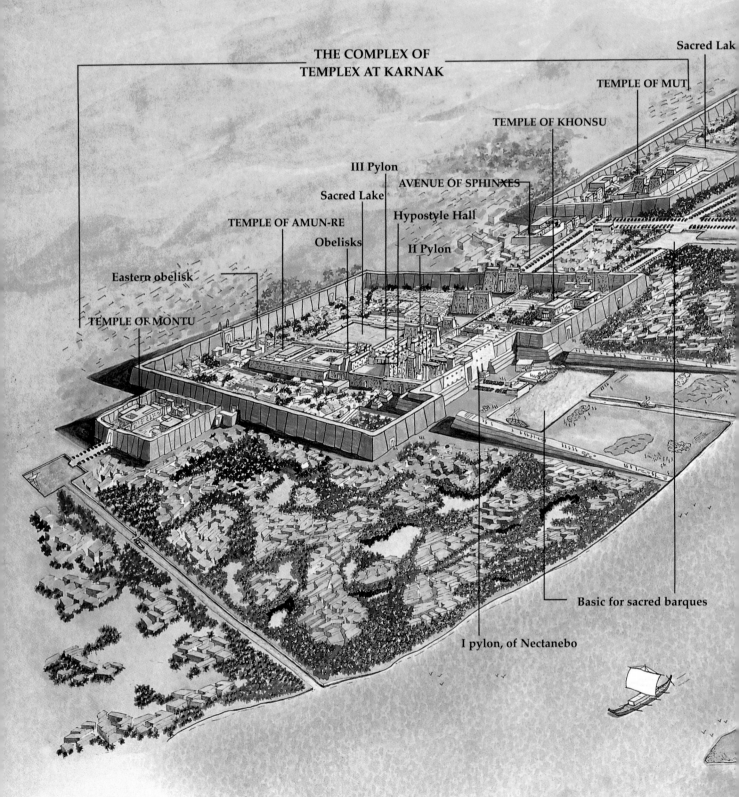

THE COMPLEX OF
TEMPLEX AT KARNAK

Sacred Lak

TEMPLE OF MUT

TEMPLE OF KHONSU

III Pylon

AVENUE OF SPHINXES

Sacred Lake

Hypostyle Hall

TEMPLE OF AMUN-RE

II Pylon

Obelisks

Eastern obelisk

TEMPLE OF MONTU

Basic for sacred barques

I pylon, of Nectanebo

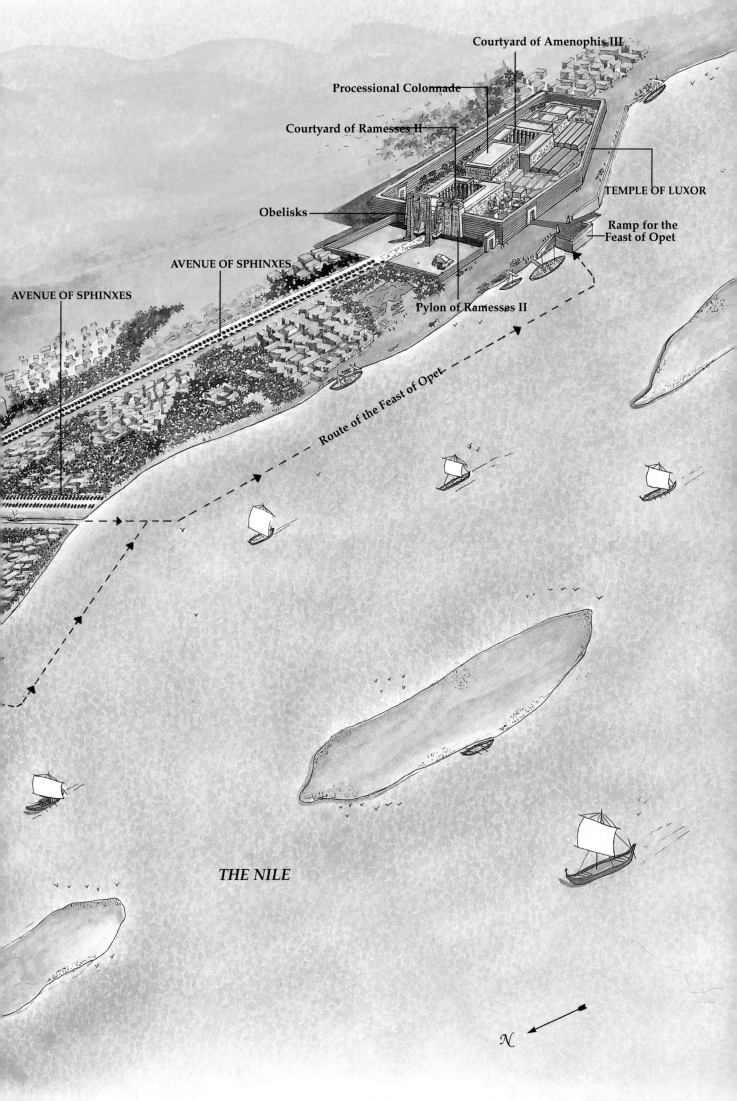

Courtyard of Amenophis III

Processional Colonnade

Courtyard of Ramesses II

TEMPLE OF LUXOR

Obelisks

Ramp for the
Feast of Opet

AVENUE OF SPHINXES

AVENUE OF SPHINXES

Pylon of Ramesses II

Route of the Feast of Opet

THE NILE

N

WESTERN THEBES, THE KINGDOM OF OSIRIS

On the western bank of the Nile, dominated by the Sacred Peak, devoted to the goddess, Meretseger, 'She Who Loves Silence', stretched the great necropolises of Thebes, the final resting places for all eternity of kings and royal spouses, of princes and princesses, of functionaries and courtiers. Here, between the Nile and the mountain, every pharaoh ordered the contruction of a 'Temple of Millions of Years', for the celebration of his cult. Each year, the god Amun paid a visit, in solemn procession, on the occasion of the 'Beautiful Feast of the Valley'.

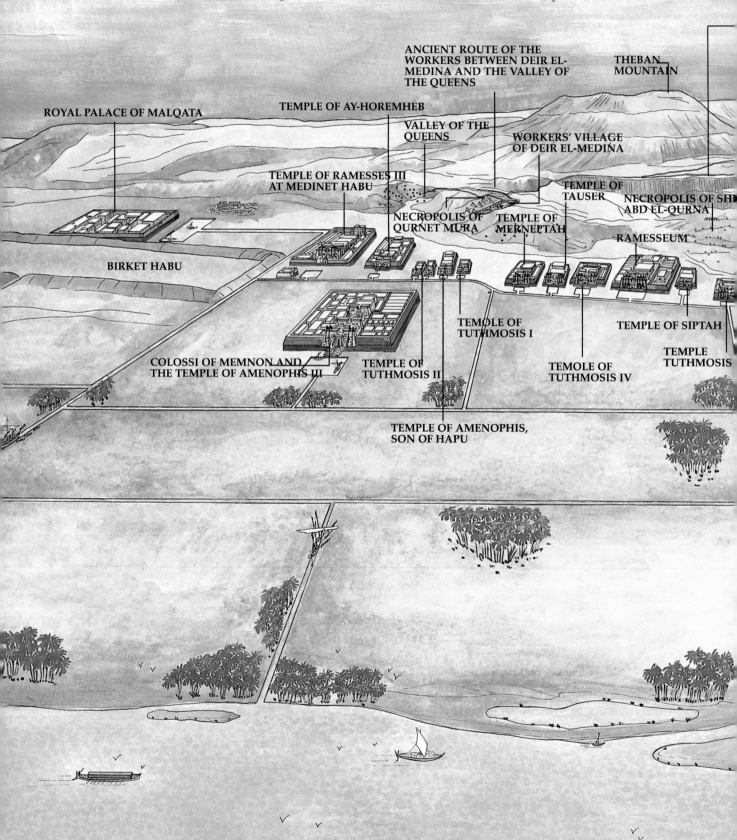

ANCIENT ROUTE OF THE WORKERS BETWEEN DEIR EL-MEDINA AND THE VALLEY OF THE QUEENS

THEBAN MOUNTAIN

ROYAL PALACE OF MALQATA

TEMPLE OF AY-HOREMHEB

VALLEY OF THE QUEENS

WORKERS' VILLAGE OF DEIR EL-MEDINA

TEMPLE OF RAMESSES III AT MEDINET HABU

TEMPLE OF TAUSER

NECROPOLIS OF SH ABD EL-QURNA

NECROPOLIS OF QURNET MURA

TEMPLE OF MERNEPTAH

RAMESSEUM

BIRKET HABU

TEMPLE OF TUTHMOSIS I

TEMPLE OF SIPTAH

TEMPLE TUTHMOSIS

COLOSSI OF MEMNON AND THE TEMPLE OF AMENOPHIS III

TEMPLE OF TUTHMOSIS II

TEMOLE OF TUTHMOSIS IV

TEMPLE OF AMENOPHIS, SON OF HAPU

THE NILE

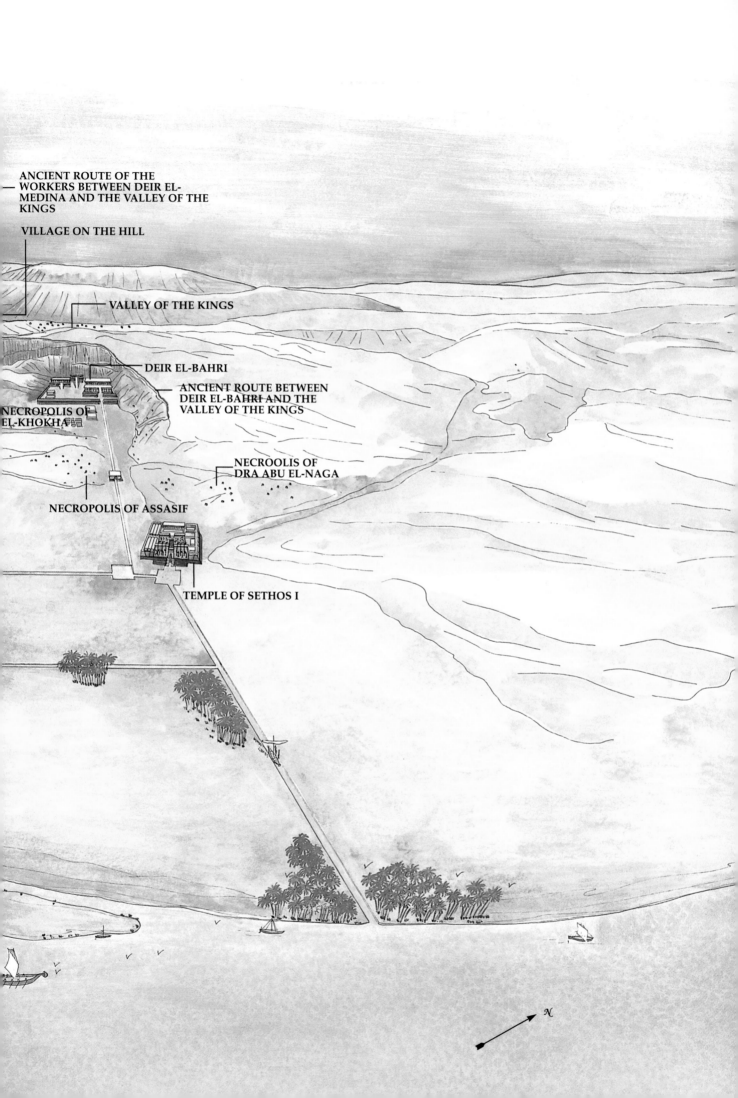

ANCIENT ROUTE OF THE
WORKERS BETWEEN DEIR EL-
MEDINA AND THE VALLEY OF THE
KINGS

VILLAGE ON THE HILL

VALLEY OF THE KINGS

DEIR EL-BAHRI

ANCIENT ROUTE BETWEEN
DEIR EL-BAHRI AND THE
VALLEY OF THE KINGS

NECROPOLIS OF
EL-KHOKHA

NECROOLIS OF
DRA ABU EL-NAGA

NECROPOLIS OF ASSASIF

TEMPLE OF SETHOS I

N

162–163 The avenue
(dromos in Greek)
lined with human-
headed sphinxes
leading up to the
temple of Luxor. It
was built during the
reign of Nectanebo I
(380–362 BC) and is
around 200 m (660 ft)
long.

LUXOR AND KARNAK, THE ANCIENT THEBES

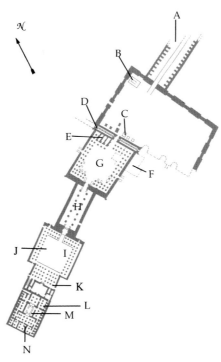

A Dromos of Sphinxes
 of Nectanebo I
B Chapel of Serapis
C Obelisk
D Pylon of Ramesses II
E Chapel of Hatshepsut
F Mosque
G Courtyard of
 Ramesses II
H Great colonnade
I Courtyard of
 Amenophis III
J Location of the cache
K Hypostyle atrium
L Hall of birth
M Chapel of the Barque
 of Alexander
N Sanctuary of
 Amenophis III

Modern Luxor is a populous town on the right bank of the Nile, where ancient Thebes, the city described by Homer as 'Thebes of the hundred gates', once stood. The name Luxor comes from the Arabic word *el-Uqsur*, the plural of *el-Qasr*, meaning encampment or fortification, with reference to the two military camps built here in Roman times. Thebes, which the ancient Egyptians called *Waset*, extended over the area between modern Karnak and Luxor. In this vast city (at its height it had more than a million inhabitants), at one time capital of an empire that extended from the Euphrates to Upper Nubia, the god Amun was worshipped, and the heart of the Amun cult lay in the great temple of Karnak.

Once a year, on the occasion of the Festival of Opet, in the second and third month of the flood season, a solemn procession would transport the sacred barque of the god from the temple of Karnak to the temple of Luxor, called *Ipet-resit*, or 'Private Chambers to the South (of Amun)'.

The temple of Luxor, some 260 m (850 ft) long today, was built by Amenophis III on the foundations of a previous religious structure, dating from the time of Queen Hatshepsut. The queen had also ordered the construction of six kiosks, at the stopping points of the sacred barque of Amun, along the original Eighteenth-Dynasty *dromos*, the sacred avenue that connected the temple of Luxor with the temple of Karnak. From the Eighteenth Dynasty on, the effigies of the sacred barques of Amun, Mut and Khonsu were sailed to the temple of Luxor along the course of the Nile. At the Festival of Opet, Amun of Karnak paid a visit to Amun

164 (below) The temple of Luxor seen from the south. The succession of elements in this complex temple is clearly visible. The sanctuary of Amenophis III is followed by a complex of antechambers, then the hypostyle hall, the great courtyard of Amenophis III, the colonnade, and, lastly, the courtyard and pylon of Ramesses II. The appearance of the temple during the reign of Hatshepsut is not known, but Amenophis III built the most ancient part of the temple to the south upon a raised platform, later adding a courtyard to the north, and beginning work on the impressive colonnade of 14 columns.

of Luxor, also known as *Amun-em-ipet*, meaning 'Amun-Who-Is-In-His-Harem', revitalizing the Amun of Luxor. One of the glories of the temple of Luxor is a majestic colonnade dating to the reign of Amenophis III, with 14 columns with papyrus-shaped capitals standing 18 m (60 ft) tall (and almost 10 m (33 ft) in circumference). The colonnade is enclosed on both sides by a masonry curtain wall, with reliefs depicting various phases of the Festival of Opet, completed and decorated during the reigns of Tutankhamun and Horemheb. A magnificent courtyard followed, lined with a double row of columns, and bordered to the south by the hypostyle hall. From here, the visitor passes on to the inner section of the temple, where there is a series of four antechambers and ancillary rooms, and the sanctuary of the sacred barque, situated in the innermost room. The chapel was rebuilt by Alexander the Great.

The temple was enlarged by Ramesses II, who built the first pylon, decorated with reliefs depicting the battle of Qadesh in Syria (1274 BC), the first courtyard and, on the interior of the temple, a triple sanctuary for the barques of Amun, Mut and Khonsu – the Theban triad. The courtyard of Ramesses II, surrounded by a peristyle of 74 papyrus columns arranged in a double row and adorned with 16 statues of the pharaoh, incorporates a three-part chapel on the northern side, also dedicated to the Theban triad and dating to Hatshepsut's reign; on the eastern side of the courtyard a Byzantine church was built in the sixth century AD, and on top of that, during the reign of the Ayyubid sultans (thirteenth century AD), the mosque

165 (opposite) Aerial view of the temple of Luxor and the avenue of sphinxes that connected the temples of Luxor and Karnak, 3 km (2 miles) apart. From the fourth to the sixth century AD, the entire temple of Luxor was incorporated into a Roman military camp, or castrum. In the late sixth century, a Byzantine church was built in the courtyard of Ramesses II, and then in the thirteenth century the mosque of Abu el-Haggag was built on top of the church. The mosque is still in use today. The height of the mosque entrance is an indicator of the level of the sand before modern excavations.

of Abu el-Haggag was built, which is still used today. Also dating to the reign of Ramesses II are two large obelisks that once stood before the first pylon (a word derived from the Greek meaning 'gateway') and which were given to France by the Pasha of Egypt, Mohammad Ali, in 1819. The western obelisk, more than 21 m (70 ft) tall and weighing 210 tons, was removed by the French in 1836 and erected in Paris in the Place de la Concorde. All claims to ownership over the second obelisk, which remained in its position in Egypt, were renounced by France in 1980.

The ceremonies that took place in the temple of Luxor were of great importance and their religious symbolisim was complex. During the Festival of Opet, the feast of the royal jubilee, the divine rebirth of the pharaoh, son of Amun, was celebrated, reaffirming in this way his

power. In the dim light of the 'hall of divine birth', Amun, who on this occasion took the form of the pharaoh, would meet the queen. Thoth, the ibis-headed god would announce to her an imminent birth. Amun would then order Khnum, the 'Divine Potter', to shape a baby boy on his potter's wheel, and his *ka*, or 'spirit double', which would represent the child's divine and immortal spirit. The queen, assisted by Hathor, Isis and Nephthys, would give birth to the divine son, offspring of pharaoh and gods, recognized by his father Amun. To Amun, the divine son would make offerings of incense and fresh flowers, receiving in exchange his divine nature, his youth and the promise of long life. He would then be crowned as the legitimate sovereign of the Two Lands. The pharaoh, thus regenerated and reconfirmed in his royal position, could ensure the prosperity of his people for another year. The temple of Luxor also served as a shrine for the worship of the divine and immortal portion of the pharaoh, the royal *ka*, symbol of legitimacy of the pharaoh's power, which was universal and not restricted to any individual pharaoh. This concept lasted for over seventeen centuries, which explains why Alexander the Great – whose legitimacy as the sovereign of Egypt depended on his being recognized as the son of Amun – chose to rebuild the sanctuary of the god's barque.

According to Theban cosmogony, the temple of Luxor was also a recreation of the temple of Heliopolis, the site of origin of the Ogdoad, the collective name for the eight primordial deities, who were engendered by the demiurge and 'creator of the earth', the serpent Irta,

166–167 (above and opposite) Reliefs illustrating the Festival of Opet on the walls east and west of the great colonnade of Amenophis III. Various musicians accompany the procession of the sacred barques, while numerous oxen are prepared to be sacrificed, in order to pay homage to the gods and for the pleasure of the participants. During this festival, which was held once a year during the second and third months of the season of flooding, Amun of Karnak, accompanied by his spouse Mut and his son Khonsu, came to visit his 'Southern Chambers', or Ipet-resit, as the temple of Luxor was called, sailing up the Nile in a great procession.

also known as Kematef, who in turn created the world. According to myth, Kematef and the Ogdoad, once their mission was accomplished, were buried in a mythical tomb at Medinet Habu where, throughout the New Kingdom, Amun of Luxor would pay a visit every ten days in the 'Feast of the Tenth Day'. During the reign of Ramesses II, the procession did not enter the temple through the main entrance of the first courtyard, but through the western gate, overlooking the Nile, the eastern gate being reserved for the populace at large. The main entrance to the temple was used during the annual festival of Amun-Min-Kematef, which celebrated Amun in his capacity as the god of fertility. During the era of Nectanebo I the *dromos* linking Luxor to Karnak was adorned with hundreds of human-headed sphinxes, still visible in part. Under Roman rule, specifically during the reign of Emperor Diocletian, around AD 300, the southernmost part of the temple was dedicated to the emperor cult and the temple itself was incorporated into the *castrum* of the Roman garrison stationed in Luxor.

Excavations in the temple area, almost buried by sand and by houses of the residents of the village of Luxor, were begun in 1885 by Gaston Maspero, who restored the complex to its current state. In terms of purity of structural design and the elegance of its columns, the temple is one of the most remarkable architectural achievements of the New Kingdom.

One of the most important finds of recent years was made here, in the courtyard of Amenophis III. A cache of magnificent statues was found, of which the finest, of red quartzite, depicted the pharaoh himself.

168 (opposite) Two great colossi, depicting Ramesses II seated on his throne, watched over the entrance to the temple of Luxor. The head of the pharaoh in the foreground belonged to one of four other colossi which stood before the first pylon.

169 Ramesses II frequently usurped the monuments of his predecessors by having his name carved on them, as, for instance, on the two colossi of Amenophis III on either side of the passage that led from the first courtyard to the great colonnade.

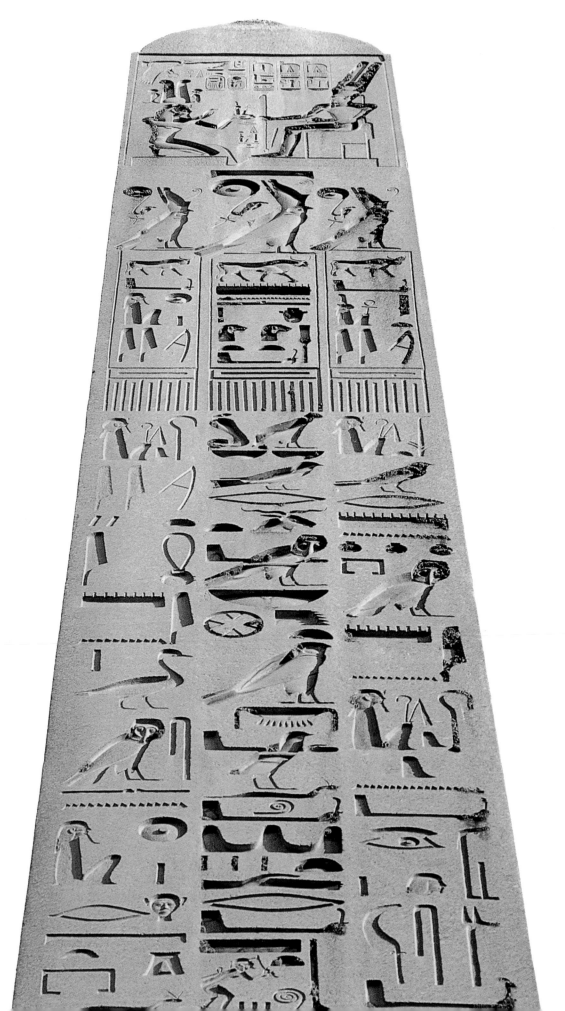

170 (left) The pink
granite obelisk in
front of the eastern
side of the pylon of the
temple of Luxor.
Each of its faces bears
three columns of
hieroglyphic text
commemorating the
rule of Ramesses II.

171 (above) The great
colonnade of the
temple of Luxor
consists of two rows of
seven columns with
capitals in the form of
open papyrus. The
colonnade connects the
courtyards of
Ramesses II and
Amenophis III.

172–173 Aerial view of the vast temple precinct of Amun-Re at Karnak, from the east. The complex of Karnak, known as Ipet-isut, was built in a number of different stages over a period of time spanning sixteen centuries, from the reign of Sesostris I during the Twelfth Dynasty that of Nectanebo I in the Thirtieth Dynasty. Unlike other Egyptian temples, Karnak, which can be read as a theological treatise in stone, runs along two separate axes – from east to west and from north to south – representations of the heavens and the earth, of divine power and royal power. The Sacred Lake, begun in the reign of Tuthmosis III but completed during the rule of the pharaoh Taharqa (Twenty-Fifth Dynasty, 690–664 BC), was filled with water symbolizing the powers of life of the primordial ocean. This basin also provided the fresh water needed for purification rituals, and a home for the sacred birds of the temple.

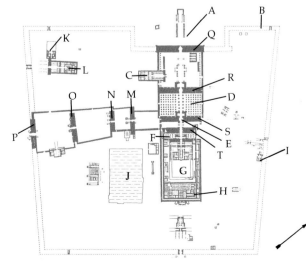

THE TEMPLES OF KARNAK, REALM OF AMUN

Just a few miles to the north of Luxor are the temples of Karnak, which form the largest and most complex example of ancient Egyptian religious architecture. At Karnak there are three main sacred areas, or precincts, each with its temple, dedicated to Montu, an ancient local warrior god, to Amun, the chief god of Thebes, and to the goddess Mut. Mut, along with her husband Amun and their son Khonsu, was a member of the Theban triad. The great temple of Amun was the most important element of the complex and was probably begun during the Middle Kingdom, but took on its impressive dimensions during the Eighteenth Dynasty.

Since nearly every pharaoh wished to enlarge or improve upon the temple – often destroying and reusing previous structures and buildings – the whole site is architecturally complicated. There are four courtyards, ten pylons, a sacred lake and a multitude of associated buildings.

The last pharaoh to carry out major construction on the temple, and who was responsible for its final appearance, was Nectanebo I, of the Thirtieth Dynasty. He ordered the construction of the enormous first pylon, approached by the avenue of ram-headed sphinxes (the ram was sacred to Amun), which still serves as the entrance to the temple. The temple of Amun has a two-fold orientation: an east–west axis and a north–south one. The east–west axis, incorporating the first to sixth pylons, corresponded to the trajectory of the sun: the solar and celestial axis. The north–south axis, incorporating the seventh to tenth pylons, ran parallel to the course of the Nile, and was the real and earthly axis. The first pylon leads into the first

A Avenue of ram-headed sphinxes
B Enclosure wall of Precinct of Amun
C Temple of Ramesses III
D Great hypostyle hall
E Obelisks
F Wadjit (small hypostyle hall)
G Courtyard of the Middle Kingdom
H Akhmenu
I Temple of Ptah
J Sacred Lake
K Temple of Opet
L Temple of Khonsu
M Seventh pylon
N Eighth pylon
O Ninth pylon
P Tenth pylon
Q First pylon (of Nectanebo I)
R Second pylon
S Third pylon
T Fourth pylon

174 (below) Detail of reliefs decorating the 'Botanical Garden' of Tuthmosis III (1479–1425 BC), with depictions of remarkable animals and exotic or fabulous plants.

courtyard, in which Sethos II and Ramesses III built two chapels where the procession of sacred barques paused.

When these two chapels were built, they stood outside the temple area. The eastern side of the first courtyard terminates with the second pylon. The gate is flanked by several colossal statues of Ramesses II, the largest of which, on the northern side, was usurped by Pinudjem I, High Priest at Thebes in the Twenty-First Dynasty. Once through the second pylon, the most impressive part of the temple is reached: the great hypostyle hall between the second and third pylons, with its 134 enormous columns, each more than 19 m (65 ft) tall, which

174 (right) View along the north–south axis of the temple of Amun, from the eighth pylon. In the background is the obelisk of Hatshepsut. The temple's two axes intersected at a precise location, in the area in front of the fourth pylon, marked by six obelisks.

symbolized the primordial swamp. The construction of this part of the temple took about a century; it was begun by Sethos I, continued by Ramesses II and completed by his successors. The third pylon, built by Amenophis III, leads to a remarkable space where the celestial axis intersected the terrestrial one, and this meeting was marked by the four obelisks of Tuthmosis I and Tuthmosis III (of which only one, of Tuthmosis I,

174–175 The first
pylon of the temple of
Karnak was built
during the reign of
Nectanebo I (Thirtieth
Dynasty) and was left
unfinished. On its
eastern façade are
eight channels,
designed to support
giant flagstaffs
bedecked with banners.
The construction of
the temple, begun in
the Middle Kingdom
period during the
reign of Sesostris I
(1960-1926 BC), took
sixteen hundred years
to complete.

175 (left) The
'Festival Hall' formed
part of the complex of
buildings known as
Akhmenu, built by
Tuthmosis III to the
east of the Middle
Kingdom courtyard,
probably on the
occasion of the jubilee
ceremonies linked to
the concept of renewal
of the royal power. The
twenty columns,
divided into two rows
of ten each, have a
slightly flared profile.

survives). Between the fourth and the fifth pylon (built during the reign of Tuthmosis I) there stands a transverse vestibule, called *Wadjit* in ancient Egyptian (the 'luxuriant'), originally adorned with columns – here Queen Hatshepsut ordered two obelisks to be erected, only one of which still stands. Beyond the sixth pylon is the chapel built by Philip Arrhidaeus (323–317 BC), the half-brother of Alexander the Great, and then the great courtyard dating from the Middle Kingdom. On the eastern side of this is the *Akhmenu*, a building constructed by Tuthmosis III in which, apart from the 'Festival Hall', there was the so-called 'Botanical and Zoological Garden'. The 'Botanical Garden' is a complex of halls decorated with depictions of plants and animals, which either came from distant lands (mostly from Syria or Palestine, where the pharaoh conducted a number of military campaigns) or else had remarkable characteristics.

A great deal of discussion has been devoted to the function of this area of the temple, unlike anything else found in Egypt; the most likely hypothesis is that ancient Egyptians desired to portray the great variety of specimens that could be found in nature, and show at the same time their place in the orderly system underlying the universe. Further east, outside the enclosure walls of the temple of Amun, are the ruins of the temple built by Amenophis IV, or Akhenaten, before he left Thebes for his new capital of Akhetaten at Amarna. Along the north–south axis is the so-called courtyard of the cache, where in 1901 a French archaeologist discovered a cache in which the priests of Amun – probably under the Ptolemies – had hidden no fewer than 17,000 bronze statuettes, and about 900 large stone statues.

176 (above) The god Amun-Re was the chief deity worshipped at Karnak and formed part of the Theban triad, along with his bride Mut and his son Khonsu.

176 (below) One of the numerous ram-headed sphinxes (or criosphinxes), creatures that were sacred to the god Amun, that lined the access avenue to the first pylon.

177 (right) The imposing bulk of the second pylon marks the western boundary of the great hypostyle hall. Built by Horemheb, who made much use of materials quarried from the temple of Akhenaten (located outside and to the east of the precinct of Amun), the second pylon was the actual façade of the temple of Karnak.

178 A series of Osiris colossi lines the wayside chapel built by Ramesses III at the southeast corner of the area before the second pylon. The chapel was designed to accommodate the barques of the Theban triad during a pause in the great religious processions.

179 (right) The papyrus-shaped capitals of 122 of the columns supporting the enormous architraves of the hypostyle hall of Karnak, built during the reign of Sethos I (northern wing) and Ramesses II (southern wing). This forest of columns, probably the most spectacular feature of the entire temple, may have symbolized the primordial swamp.

The courtyard of the cache is bordered to the south by the seventh pylon, alongside which is the Sacred Lake, a representation of the Primordial Ocean out of which the world was created. The waters of the lake, in which the sacred geese of Amun swam, were fed by the Nile, and were used both for the ritual ablutions of the priests and for sailing the sacred barques. The north–south axis is continued by the eighth and the ninth pylons. The ninth pylon was built at the orders of Horemheb, reusing the magnificent decorated stone blocks from the temple of Aten. A joint French–Egyptian team has been working on this structure since 1965, reassembling it after the necessary reinforcements have been made.

To the west of the ninth pylon stands the temple of Khonsu, who was venerated together with his parents Amun and Mut as the Theban triad. The tenth pylon overlooks the temple's outer enclosure wall, where a *dromos* of ram-headed sphinxes – criosphinxes – once linked the temple of Amun to the temple of Mut; a second *dromos* of human-headed sphinxes linked Karnak to Luxor.

It is difficult today to imagine the power and wealth of the temple of Amun at the peak of its importance and splendour. Suffice it to say that the estate of the clergy of Amun, continually enriched by lavish offerings to the god, of whom the priests were considered to be the guardians, rivalled (and in some cases exceeded) the estate of the pharaoh himself. According to the Harris Papyrus, a total of more than 20,000 individuals laboured in some way for the temple.

180–181 The line of the north–south axis of the temple of Amun with the eighth pylon and the obelisk of Hatshepsut in the background. Next to it is the smaller obelisk of Tuthmosis I. The north–south axis, including four pylons, from the seventh to the tenth, runs parallel with the course of the Nile. The obelisks marked the intersection of the temple's two axes.

182–183 (overleaf) A relief showing the transportation of the sacred barques on the outer side of the southern wall of the way-side chapel of Philip Arrhidaeus (323–317 BC). This building copied a previously existing chapel dating to the reign of Tuthmosis III (Eighteenth Dynasty, 1479–1425 BC). Once a year, during the Feast of Opet, the barques of Amun-Re, Mut and Khonsu would sail down the Nile, from Karnak to Ipet-resit, the temple of Luxor. Here, the union of Amun with the queen was celebrated, and the queen would give birth to a child, thus confirming the divine origin of the pharaoh.

BIBAN EL-MULUK, THE VALLEY OF THE KINGS

The Valley of the Kings is called Biban el-Muluk in Arabic, a name meaning 'the Gates of the Kings', clearly a reference to the entrances of the numerous tombs that, even in ancient times, could be seen in the mountainsides. The valley forms a deep rift in the limestone mass of the mountain of Thebes. A western branch is called the West Valley, or Valley of the Apes, where two pharaohs had tombs dug – Amenophis III and Ay. The mountain called el-Qurn ('the Horn'), also known as the Theban Peak, dominates the valley. Its triangular shape is evocative of a pyramid, a monument that marked royal tombs during the Old Kingdom. Perhaps it was the presence of this natural feature, the Theban Peak (later linked to the serpent-goddess Meretseger), that led the first pharaohs, in the Eighteenth Dynasty, to choose this spectacular site, scorched by the desert sun, as their final and eternal resting place. One of its main advantages was that it was extremely difficult to get to, and was therefore easy to protect. Amosis (the first pharaoh of the Eighteenth Dynasty) may have been the first to choose this place, though his tomb has never been found. Or it may have been his son, Amenophis I, who had the idea, but the first pharaoh whom we can certainly say was buried in the valley was Tuthmosis I.

The precise site of a pharaoh's tomb was selected in the early years of his reign. The architectural plans were drawn up and labourers – some 60 men divided into two teams – living in the nearby village of Deir el-Medina were hired. Work began immediately and continued for a period which varied according to the length of the

184 *The burial chamber of the tomb of Ramesses IV (KV no. 2) is painted with a number of scenes from the Book of Gates. In the centre of the chamber is a large granite sarcophagus, nearly 3 m (10 ft) tall, decorated with scenes from the Underworld. The tomb is 66 m (216 ft) in length and has a fairly simple plan: a long corridor runs directly into the* chamber of the sarcophagus, which is preceded by a small antechamber. This is the only tomb for which an architectural plan from the time of its construction survives. A papyrus, in the collections of the Egyptian Museum of Turin, which may have belonged to one of the royal architects, clearly shows the layout of this tomb.

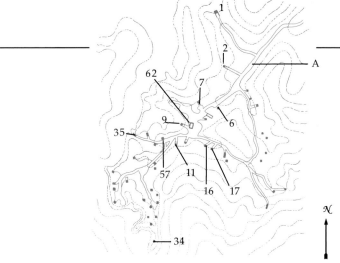

A Chief wadi
1 Tomb of Ramesses VII
2 Tomb of Ramesses IV
6 Tomb of Ramesses IX
7 Tomb of Ramesses II
9 Tomb of Ramesses VI
11 Tomb of Ramesses III
16 Tomb of Ramesses I
17 Tomb of Sethos I
34 Tomb of Tuthmosis III
35 Tomb of Amenophis II
57 Tomb of Horemheb
62 Tomb of Tutankhamun

185 Aerial view, taken from a balloon, of the Valley of the Kings, known in antiquity as Ta-sekhet-aat, or 'Great Field'. The valley is a deep rift in limestone rocks, dominated by the Theban Peak – called el-Qurn in Arabic – which is sacred to the cobra-goddess Meretseger, whose name means 'She Who Loves Silence.' It was perhaps the pyramidal shape of this mountain that singled the valley out as the ideal site for the royal necropolis, possibly during the reigns of Tuthmosis I and Hatshepsut who are the first rulers known to have had their tombs dug here. A toal of 62 tombs has so far been recorded in the valley. Some of them are undecorated, others are unfinished, clearly abandoned because of the precarious condition of the rock. The style of decoration varies according to the period, but the subject is inevitably linked to religious topics and derived from the great funerary texts: the Book of Amduat, the Book of the Dead, the Book of Gates and the Book of Caverns.

185

pharaoh's reign – from a few months to a few years. The Valley of the Kings served as the royal necropolis for the rest of the Eighteenth Dynasty, all of the Nineteenth Dynasty and the Twentieth Dynasty, up to the time of Ramesses IX, the last pharaoh to be buried there. The road that now runs along the bottom of the valley follows the route used in antiquity for transporting the royal sarcophagi to their eternal resting place.

Once the pharaoh had been buried, there was no further reason to return to the valley as the royal cult was practised in the 'Temples of Millions of Years', built between the valley and the Nile. The labourers who worked on the the tombs in the necropolis travelled to the site along a more direct route, which can still be used today. Contrary to what is generally believed, the entrances to the tombs were not hidden but were open to plain view, and the police force of the

necropolis regularly inspected them, making sure that the seals were intact, and patrolling the access route to the Valley. All these precautions, however, were in vain, as we learn from a number of papyri. As early as the Twentieth Dynasty a number of tombs had been plundered and by the Twenty-First Dynasty the situation was so serious that almost every tomb had been looted. The priests then moved the bodies of many pharaohs (including Ramesses II) to a secret hiding place, the famous cache of Deir el-Bahri.

The Valley of the Kings was forgotten for many centuries, until the era of the Ptolemies when the first Greek and Roman 'tourists' arrived. The historian Diodorus Siculus, who came to Egypt in 57 BC, wrote: 'It is said that these are the tombs of ancient rulers – they are splendid and the descendants of these kings have no chance of producing anything more beautiful'.

186 A detail of the northern sky, from the astronomical ceiling in the tomb of Sethos I (KV no. 17). These astronomical depictions, which group the stars in different formations from the traditional Babylonian system, which is the basis of the modern one, have never been entirely explained.

186–187 The northern wall of the chamber of the sarcophagus in the tomb of Sethos I: the winged goddess Nephthys and the Second and the Third Hours of the Book of Amduat are depicted,

along with the barque of Re, sailing across the waters of the underworld, accompanied by a procession of other boats. Osiris, the lord of the world beyond, appears numerous times.

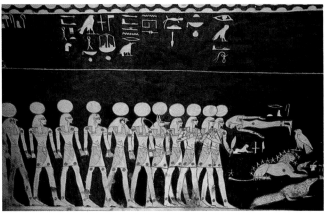

187 (left)
The constellations of the northern sky adorn the eastern side of the vault of the tomb of Sethos I. This astronomical ceiling, which includes depictions of stars and constellations, some of which have been identified as Orion or Sirius, was designed not only to allow the royal ba to pass into heaven, but also served the purpose of associating the body of the pharaoh with the firmament.

THE TOMB OF SETHOS I, THE GREATEST DISCOVERY OF THE TITAN OF PADUA

After many days of exhausting labour removing a huge amount of rubble, guided by his remarkable intuition, on 18 October 1817 Giovanni Battista Belzoni, the Titan of Padua, discovered the largest and most beautiful tomb in the Valley of the Kings. It belonged to Sethos I, father of Ramesses II, who reigned from 1294 to 1279 BC. The tomb was immense, over 100 m (330 ft) long, extendingin a complex series of stairways, hallways and chambers, decorated with splendid reliefs but haunted by a desolating sense of emptiness, despoiled of every treasure, probably in pharaonic times, and then forgotten. In the burial chamber alone, with the vault of the ceiling painted with the celestial constellations, stood a splendid alabaster sarcophagus which Belzoni transported back to England. It was bought by the collector Sir John Soane and still stands in the Soane Museum in London.

1 The Litany of Re. An anthology of religious texts in which the god Re is first invoked under 75 different manifestations; the pharaoh then goes on to identify himself with Re and with other gods.

2 Book of Amduat: fourth and fifth hour.

3 Wall that closed the entrance to the tomb; opened by Belzoni.

4 Shafts were found in many tombs in the Valley of the Kings, where they probably served a ritual purpose rather than any practical function. They may have been connected both with the concept of the regenerating power of water, the primordial element from which the world sprang, and with an evocation of the underworld kingdom of Osiris. The pharaoh was assimilated with this god, thus rejoining the sun god Re.

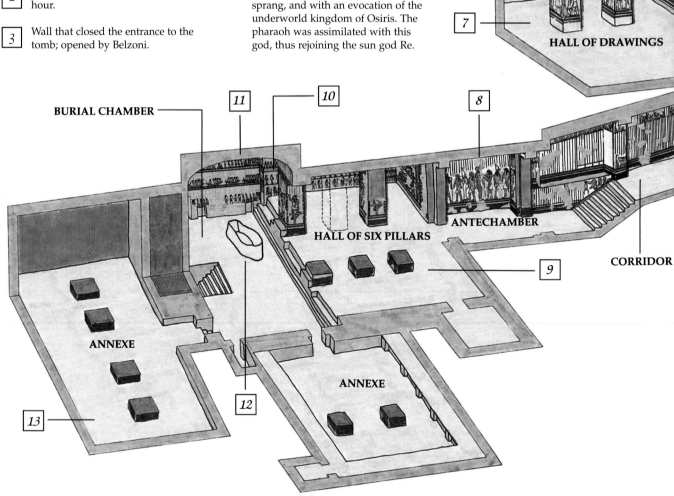

7 HALL OF DRAWINGS

BURIAL CHAMBER

11

10

8

HALL OF SIX PILLARS

ANTECHAMBER

CORRIDOR

9

ANNEXE

ANNEXE

12

13

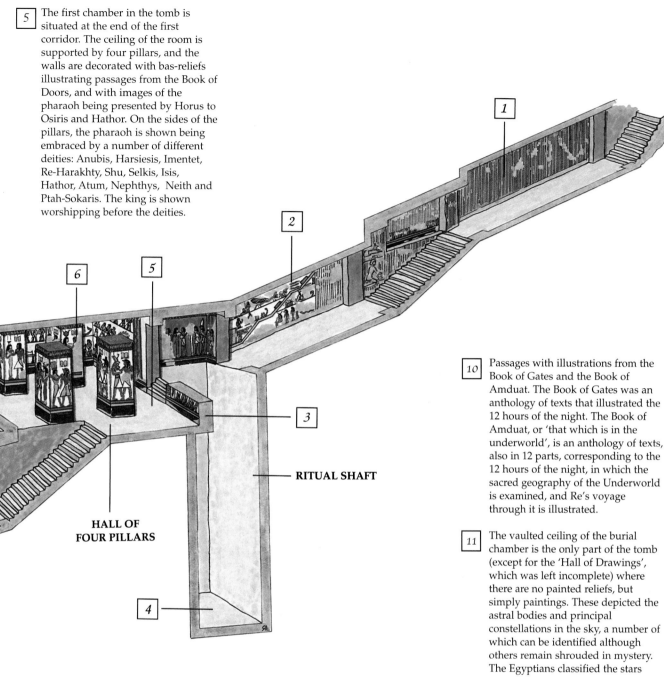

5 The first chamber in the tomb is situated at the end of the first corridor. The ceiling of the room is supported by four pillars, and the walls are decorated with bas-reliefs illustrating passages from the Book of Doors, and with images of the pharaoh being presented by Horus to Osiris and Hathor. On the sides of the pillars, the pharaoh is shown being embraced by a number of different deities: Anubis, Harsiesis, Imentet, Re-Harakhty, Shu, Selkis, Isis, Hathor, Atum, Nephthys, Neith and Ptah-Sokaris. The king is shown worshipping before the deities.

6

5

2

1

3

RITUAL SHAFT

HALL OF FOUR PILLARS

4

10 Passages with illustrations from the Book of Gates and the Book of Amduat. The Book of Gates was an anthology of texts that illustrated the 12 hours of the night. The Book of Amduat, or 'that which is in the underworld', is an anthology of texts, also in 12 parts, corresponding to the 12 hours of the night, in which the sacred geography of the Underworld is examined, and Re's voyage through it is illustrated.

11 The vaulted ceiling of the burial chamber is the only part of the tomb (except for the 'Hall of Drawings', which was left incomplete) where there are no painted reliefs, but simply paintings. These depicted the astral bodies and principal constellations in the sky, a number of which can be identified although others remain shrouded in mystery. The Egyptians classified the stars according to a system that was different from the Babylonian system, which is the basis of that still in use today. Portraying the heavens directly above the sarcophagus was intended to allow the soul of the pharaoh to hover magically among the deathless stars.

12 Only one major artifact remained in the tomb – the marvellous and finely carved solid alabaster sarcophagus, with passages from the Book of Gates. This sarcophagus was later transported to England where it was was purchased by the well-known antiquarian and collector, John Soane, and is still on display in his museum in London. The mummy of Sethos I was uncovered by Maspero in 1881 in the celebrated Deir el-Bahri cache.

13 Annexe without decorations, and partially collapsed.

6 On the pillars the pharaoh is shown in the presence of a number of deities.

7 Hall of Drawings. An unfinished room in which there were only sketches and uncoloured drawings on the walls – no reliefs – illustrating the ninth, tenth and eleventh hours of the Book of Amduat. An analysis of the walls has revealed the techniques of the ancient artists. The walls were smoothed with a layer of fine plaster, made of sand and gypsum, and then painted with liquid plaster. The artists used a piece of black charcoal to outline the images, which were then corrected in red; next, the sculptors moulded in low relief the figures that had been sketched. Finally, the reliefs were painted.

8 Belzoni called this room – which gives on the the hall with six pillars – the 'Hall of Beauties' because of the exquisite style of the wall decorations, depicting the pharaoh in the presence of a number of deities.

9 The Hall of Six Pillars: the pillars are decorated with depictions of Osiris, Harsiesis, Re-Harakhty, Anubis, Shu, Geb, Horus, Iunmutef, Ptah-Sokaris and the souls of Pe and Nekhen. This room is in effect the upper section of the burial chamber, from which it is separated only by a difference of level. The walls are decorated with scenes from the Book of Doors and the Book of the Celestial Cow, an anthology of texts connected with the Book of Gates.

190 (above) A scene
from the Book of
Gates, in the burial
chamber of Ramesses I,
the first pharaoh of the
Nineteenth Dynasty
(KV no. 16). This
tomb, one of the
smallest in the entire
Valley of the Kings,
because of the
extremely brief reign
of the pharaoh, is
decorated only in the
chamber of the
sarcophagus, with
extremely vivid and
brightly coloured
scenes that stand out
against the light grey
background.

191 (right) In the
burial chamber of
Ramesses I (KV no.
16), Osiris, Lord of the
Underworld, is shown
holding the heqa-
sceptre and the
nekhakha-flail, classic
attributes of this god.

Silence again enveloped this sacred
site until the arrival of a Jesuit named
Claude Sicard, who identified the site
of ancient Thebes and rediscovered
the tombs of the Valley of the Kings,
between 1708 and 1712. Many other
travellers followed in his footsteps,
and some of them made important
studies and discoveries. A Scot named
James Bruce found the tomb of
Ramesses III in 1768. The scholars
who formed part of the Napoleonic
expedition of 1798 made the first
scientific survey of the Valley.
Giovanni Battista Belzoni found the
tomb of Sethos I, the father of
Ramesses II, in 1817. A Frenchman,
Victor Loret, found the tomb of
Amenophis II in 1898. Then, in 1922,
the English archaeologist Howard
Carter found the tomb of
Tutankhamun. Of the 62 known tombs
in the Valley of the Kings only about
20 housed the body of a pharaoh.
Many were abandoned before
construction was complete because
the labourers encountered unsuitable
rock. Others contained the bodies of
different members of the royal family.

The wall paintings and decorations
were not concerned with scenes of
everyday life, nor episodes from
history or the life of the ruler, but
solely with the Afterworld and the
voyage that the pharaoh would have
to undertake, passing a number of
tests and ordeals, before attaining the
realm of Osiris. The texts painted on
the walls, from the Book of the Dead,
the Book of Amduat, the Book of
Gates and the Book of Caverns, were
usually accompanied by illustrations
that served as commentary. The texts
provided the dead with the crucial
knowledge of the magic formulas that
were essential in overcoming the
difficulties that would beset them.

192 (above) On one of the pillars of the chamber containing the sarcophagus in the tomb of Tuthmosis III (KV no. 34) is a depiction of the pharaoh grasping a sceptre and a ceremonial mace, followed by his wives and his daughters. This scene is preceded by a depiction of the pharaoh being suckled by the goddess Isis in the form of an animated sycamore tree, and a brief text says: 'Menkheperre is suckled by his mother Isis'. The throne name of Tuthmosis III was Menkheperre.

192 (below) Passages from the Book of Amduat, written in cursive hieroglyphs on the walls of the sarcophagus chamber of the tomb of Tuthmosis III. The Book of Amduat, or 'That Which Is in the Underworld', was extensively illustrated in this tomb. It was one of the great funerary texts, outlining the sacred geography of the world beyond.

192–193 The massive sarcophagus of Tuthmosis III, made of reddish quartzite, takes pride of place in the pharaoh's burial chamber. Both sarcophagus and burial chamber have an oval shape, echoing that of a cartouche.

The walls of the chamber are painted in sober shades with only a few variations of hue and there are no reliefs. Texts and illustrations are scenes from the Book of Amduat, telling the story of the sun's journeys through the Underworld. They are transcribed into cursive hieroglyphs, and this, together with the subdued colours, gives the impression that the burial chamber is lined with an unrolled papyrus. This tomb was discovered in 1898 by Victor Loret, who succeeded Gaston Maspero as the director of the Egyptian Antiquities Service. Unfortunately, when the discovery was made, the burial chamber had already been plundered and the cover of the sarcophagus lay shattered on the floor. The mummy of the pharaoh Tuthmosis III had been discovered, however, several years earlier, in 1881, in the renowned cache of royal mummies at Deir el-Bahri.

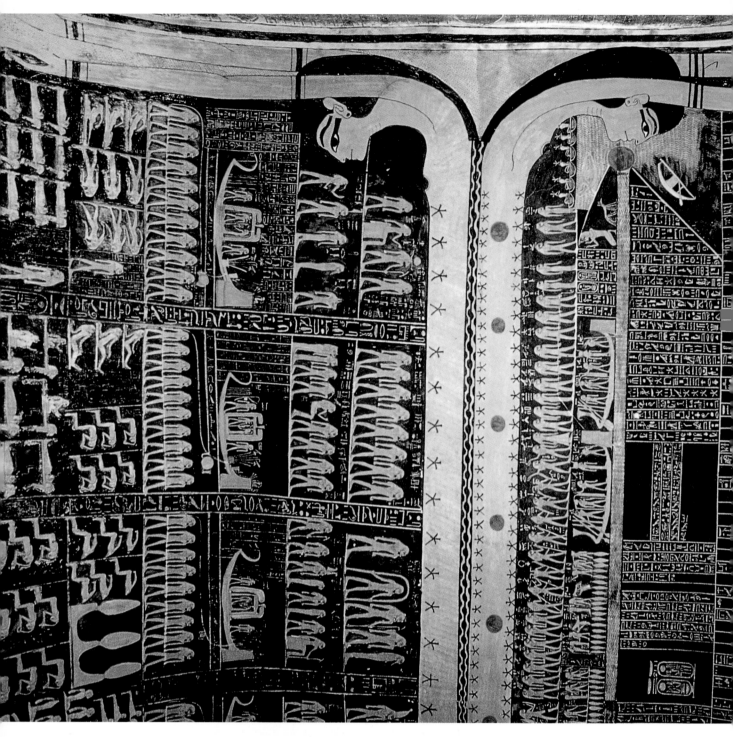

194 (left) The eastern wall of the chamber of the sarcophagus of the tomb of Ramesses VI (KV no. 9) is decorated with texts from the Book of the Earth, linked to the theme of the creation of the sun disk. The Book of the Earth (which is also known as the Book of Aker) is a compendium of texts dealing with the night journey of the sun god into the Afterworld.

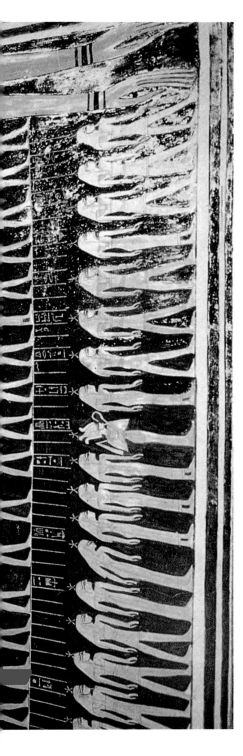

194–195 (left) The astronomical ceiling in the tomb of Ramesses VI (KV no. 9), with depictions of scenes from the Book of the Day and the Book of the Night. The sky-goddess Nut, the incarnation of the heavenly firmament, is shown curved into an arch to emulate the celestial vault, both in the right half of the ceiling, and also in the left half. Nut is shown swallowing the sun in the evening and renewing it in the morning. This goddess therefore acquired a life-giving and regenerative role, in her capacity of 'Lady of the Heavens and of the Stars', but also – and primarily – through her role as the 'Mother of the Sun'. As the deceased pharaoh was associated with the sun deity, he shared in the sun's rebirth, through Nut, who also had another function, that of a protective goddess, warding off evil from the deceased.

195 (above, right) Detail of paintings in Ramesses VI's burial chamber illustrating passages from the Book of the Earth (or the Book of Aker).

195 (below right) Detail from the Book of the Earth on the north wall of Ramesses VI's burial chamber: the sun disk has been raised from the depths of the Underworld in the arms of the goddess Nut, 'Lady of the Heavens and of the Stars, Mother of the Sun'. Nut controls the movement of the stars and each day gives the gift of life to the sun, and in this way renews the process of creation of the earth.

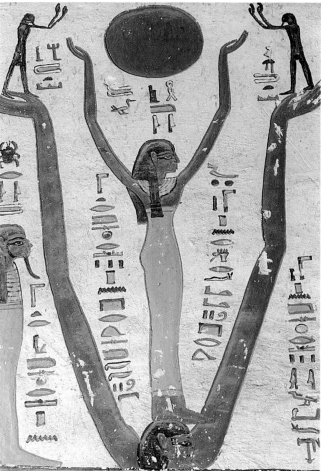

A Stairway
B First door
C Corridor
D Second door
E Antechamber
F Burial Chamber
G Treasury
H Annexe

TUTANKHAMUN, THE TOMB REDISCOVERED

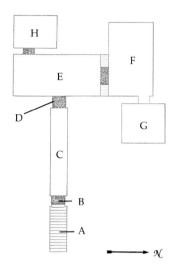

196 (below left) The superb third coffin (no. 255) of Tutankhamun, made of solid gold, weighs 110.4 kg (243 lbs) and is 188 cm (74 in) in length. This coffin contained the mummy of the young pharaoh, covered by the famous mask. It was placed within a second coffin (no. 254), made of wood covered in gold foil, which in turn was set within the first, outermost, coffin, also made of wood covered in gold foil (no. 253). All three coffins showed the pharaoh in the same position, with his arms crossed over his chest and his hands grasping the royal attributes: the heqa-sceptre and the nekhakha-flail. The entire set of three coffins was contained within a large quartzite sarcophagus (no. 240), which can still be seen in the tomb, with the outermost within it. (Cairo Museum)

196–197 The burial chamber of the tomb of Tutankhamun is the only room in the entire structure that is decorated. When discovered it was almost entirely filled by the shrines made of gilded wood; it now contains only the large quartzite sarcophagus and the outermost coffin with the mummy of the king. Three images of Tutankhamun decorate the wall behind. On the right, the pharaoh is depicted as Osiris during the ceremony of the 'Opening of the Mouth', with Pharaoh Ay, Tutankhamun's successor, officiating. In the centre, Tutankhamun is shown, dressed in the garb of the living, in the presence of the goddess Nut, the mistress of the heavens. In the third scene, Tutankhamun is shown wearing the nemes; followed by his ka he presents himself before Osiris.

When the Burial Chamber of the tomb of Tutankhamun was officially opened, on 17 February 1923, after the Antechamber had been emptied, more than two months had passed since that famous evening of 26 November 1922 when Carter, Lord Carnarvon, his daughter Lady Evelyn, and Arthur Callender entered the tomb, almost furtively, for the first time.
It had taken almost fifty days to empty the Antechamber; the time required to dismantle and remove the contents of the Burial Chamber, including the gilded wooden shrines and the sarcophagus was to be far greater, and the work was not completed until November 1930, eight years after the original discovery. Once freed of its contents, it became possible to examine with some care the wall paintings in the only decorated room in the entire tomb. The walls had a yellow background, almost the colour of gold, as if to underline the name that ancient Egyptians gave to the burial chamber – the 'Golden Room'.

The surface of the paintings was in an excellent state of preservation, even though it was speckled with innumerable tiny circular stains due to the development of colonies of micro-organisms. The decoration is quite simple and ordinary in style: the northern wall, seen on entering the room, features Tutankhamun in the centre, wearing the dress of the living, holding the sceptre and the ritual mace, before the goddess Nut, depicted in the act of performing the *nyny* ritual. This central scene is flanked by two others: on the right, Tutankhamun is shown dressed as Osiris in the presence of Pharaoh Ay, his successor. Ay, wearing the costume of the *sem*-priest and the distinctive skin of a panther, officiates at the rite of the 'Opening of the Mouth', through which the deceased is revived. On the left, Tutankhamun is shown with his head draped in the *nemes*, and, followed by his *ka*, standing before Osiris. On the adjacent western wall, are illustrations of passages taken from the Book of Amduat, showing the voyage of the sun barque through the 12 hours of the night, represented by 12 deities with the faces of baboons. The eastern wall illustrates the transport of the royal sarcophagus, set inside a shrine mounted on a sledge, drawn by 12 characters, of whom two are dressed differently from the others, indicating a superior social standing. The south wall was painted last, and is a scene of Tutankhamun, accompanied by Anubis, in the presence of the goddess Hathor. The centre of the room is now occupied by the quartzite sarcophagus containing the outermost coffin.

198 (below) Tutankhamun's mask, made of solid gold, was placed directly upon the pharaoh's mummy, and had the function of magically protecting him. This beautiful object weighs 10 kg (24 lbs) and is decorated with semiprecious stones (turquoise, cornelian and lapis lazuli) and coloured glass paste. The pharaoh is portrayed in a classical manner, with a ceremonial beard, a broad collar formed of twelve concentric rows consisting of inlays of turquoise, lapis lazuli, cornelian and amazonite. The traditional nemes headdress has yellow sripes of solid gold broken by bands of glass paste, coloured dark blue. On the forehead of the mask are a royal uraeus and a vulture's head, symbols of the two tutelary deities of Lower and Upper Egypt: Wadjet and Nekhbet. (Cairo Museum)

199 (right) The third coffin, of solid gold, which contained the mummy of Pharaoh Tutankhamun. When it was found it was almost entirely covered with a hardened layer of pitch, completely concealing its splendour, which was removed with solvents and a scalpel. Study of the mummy has shown that the pharaoh died aged about 18, and that he stood 162 cm (5ft 4 in) tall. (Cairo Museum)

200–201 Tutankhamun, whose birth name, was Tutankhaten, was probably the son of the heretic Pharaoh Amenophis IV (Akhenaten) and of his queen, Kiya. At a very early age he married his half-sister Ankhesenamun, the daughter of Amenophis IV and Queen Nefertiti. Tutankhamun (a name which means 'the living image of Amun') took the throne in 1333 BC, assuming the praenomen of Nebkheprure. He died around 1323 BC at the age of about 18. Tutankhamun was succeeded on the throne of Egypt by Ay, who reigned for four years, and by Horemheb, who was the last pharaoh of the Eighteenth Dynasty. (Cairo Museum)

202 One of the two life-sized statues which stood guard at the sealed door of the Burial Chamber, on the north side of the Antechamber. The two statues, almost identical except for their headgear, are made of wood, painted with black resin and overlaid with gold in parts. They depict the pharaoh, or rather the pharaoh's ka, in a striding pose and holding a mace in one hand and a long staff in the other. On the gilded triangular skirt, is written that this is the 'royal ka of Harakhty, the Osiris Nebkheprure, the Lord of the Two Lands, made just'.
(Cairo Museum)

203 *A very fine*
shabti *of*
Tutankhamun,
portrayed holding the
heqa-*sceptre and the*
nekhakha-*flail, and*
inscribed with a text
from Chapter 6 of the
Book of the Dead. This
passage specifies the
functions of these
mummiform
statuettes, made of
wood, terracotta,
faience or metal, and
in some cases left in
the tomb in their
hundreds. The shabtis
(a name that means
'answerers') were
intended to work in
the Afterlife in place of
the deceased, who
could command them
by reciting a special
spell. In the New
Kingdom especially
the shabtis *were*
considered as chattels,
not unlike slaves. In
Tutankhamun's tomb,
a staggering total of
413 shabtis *was*
found, arranged in 26
coffers placed in the
Annexe and in the
Treasury, but only 29
of them were inscribed
with the text of the
formula from the Book
of the Dead.
(Cairo Museum)

204 *Detail of the back-panel of Tutankhamun's royal Golden Throne, found in the Antechamber. The throne was made of wood covered with sheet gold, and adorned with semi-precious stones and coloured glass paste. His wife, Queen Ankhesenamun, whose head is adorned with two tall plumes and a sun disk, stands before the pharaoh, languidly seated on a throne; the queen places one hand on his shoulder while in her other she proffers a vase of scented unguents. The rays of the sun god Aten shine upon the royal couple and endow them with vital energy. The influence of Amarna art and religious conceptions can be clearly seen in the sensitivity and naturalism of this scene.*
(Cairo Museum)

205 *(right) A graceful statuette of gilded wood, depicting the goddess Selkis, one of the four protective deities of the outer canopy of the Canopic Shrine containing the viscera of the deceased pharaoh. The goddess is shown dressed in a long tunic, and her head is covered by a* khayt, *surmounted by a scorpion, a symbol that transcribes the goddess's name. The delicate depiction of the body and the face shows a powerful influence of Amarna art.*
(Cairo Museum)

206 (left) The goddess Isis extends her arms in a protective gesture across one of the walls of the outer canopy, made of gilded wood, of the spectacular Canopic Shrine of Tutankhamun. Within this was a series of smaller shrines, of gilded wood and calcite. This set of cases was found in the room off the Burial Chamber called the Treasury. Three other guardian deities protected the shrine: Nephthys, Selkis and Neith. Each of them was associated with one of the cardinal points of the compass. Within the canopic chest itself were four gold coffinettes, with the viscera of the pharaoh. (Cairo Museum)

207 The small wooden shrine covered with thick gold foil, set on a wooden sledge encased with silver-leaf, found in the Antechamber of the tomb. Originally it must have contained a gold statuette of the pharaoh, stolen during one of the two episodes of tomb-robbery which took place in antiquity. The walls of the shrine are covered with scenes executed with exquisite craftsmanship depicting scenes of hunting and everyday life, featuring the pharaoh and his wife, Ankhesenamun. (Cairo Museum)

208 Two of the many pectorals belonging to Tutankhamun. Top: the goddess Nekhbet, in the shape of a vulture, clutching two shenu-signs (powerful protective amulets) in her talons, found on the mummy of the pharaoh. Bottom: a winged scarab, the image of the sun god at dawn, as it pushes the sun disk Re ☉ upwards. The 🪲 kheper scarab stands upon a hieroglyphic sign ‖‖‖ that indicates a plural khepru and upon a neb ⌣ sign in such a way that the pectoral can be read as the praenomen of Tutankhamun, Nebkheprure. (Cairo Museum)

209 (right) A precious ointment-holder, made of gold, in the form of a double-cartouche, with tall plumes and a sun disk. Each face of the container has images of the pharaoh, showing him in different phases of his life (as a young prince, as an adult, as the deceased pharaoh, and as the pharaoh reborn), seated upon a neb sign, beneath a Re sun disk. The sequence of colours in the depictions of the pharaoh (orange, red, black and orange again) perhaps represents the solar cycle, thus constituting a small rebus which indicates the word kheper. Here too we can read the pharaoh's praenomen. (Cairo Museum)

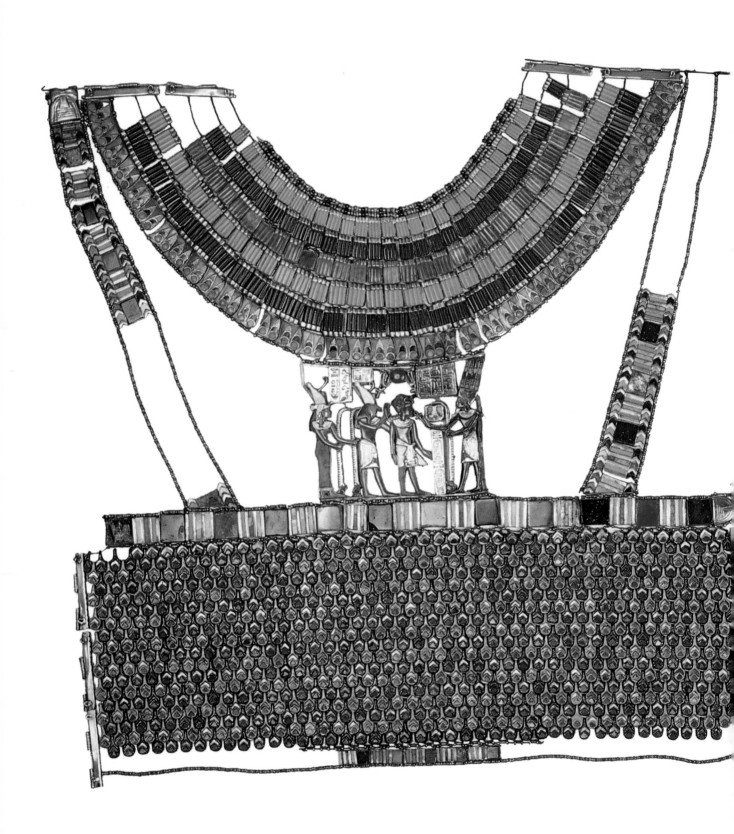

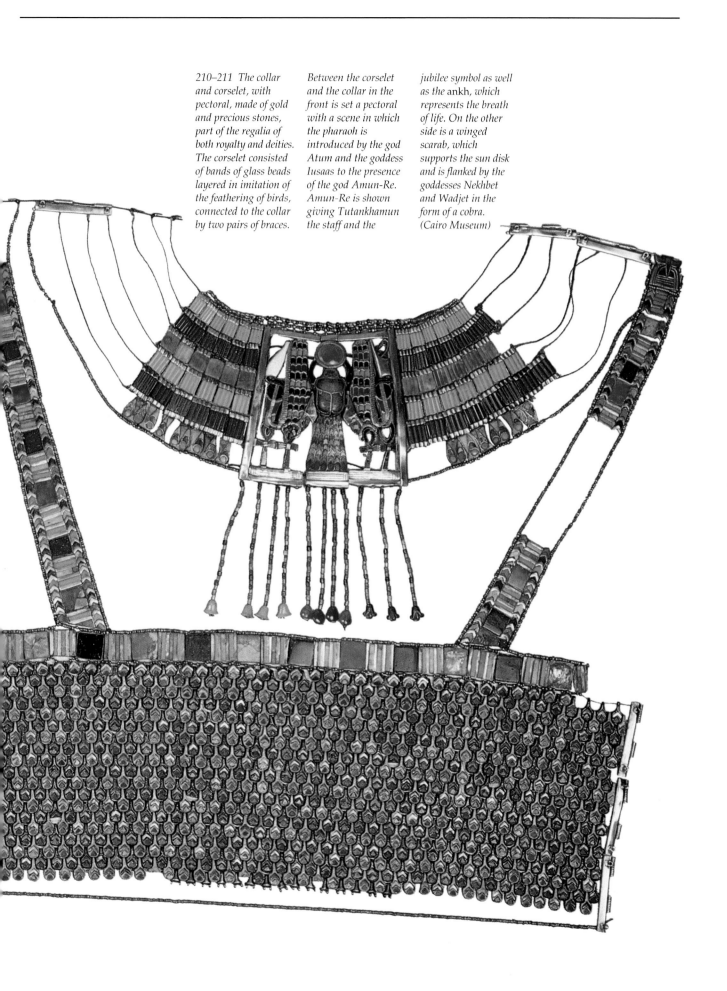

210–211 The collar and corselet, with pectoral, made of gold and precious stones, part of the regalia of both royalty and deities. The corselet consisted of bands of glass beads layered in imitation of the feathering of birds, connected to the collar by two pairs of braces.

Between the corselet and the collar in the front is set a pectoral with a scene in which the pharaoh is introduced by the god Atum and the goddess Iusaas to the presence of the god Amun-Re. Amun-Re is shown giving Tutankhamun the staff and the

jubilee symbol as well as the ankh, which represents the breath of life. On the other side is a winged scarab, which supports the sun disk and is flanked by the goddesses Nekhbet and Wadjet in the form of a cobra. (Cairo Museum)

212 *The golden amulet found at the neck of the mummy of Tutankhamun, depicting a winged* uraeus *(the sacred cobra that protected royalty) with a woman's head. The mummy of the pharaoh was adorned with around 150 jewels and amulets, which were not only for decoration, but also magically protected the deceased. (Cairo Museum)*

213 The golden fan discovered between the third and the fourth shrines in the Burial Chamber is decorated in an extremely fine manner. Here, the pharaoh is depicted in his chariot, returning triumphantly from the hunt. An inscription running vertically down the handle specified that the ostrich feathers in the fan had been acquired by the pharaoh himself 'in the desert to the east of Heliopolis'.

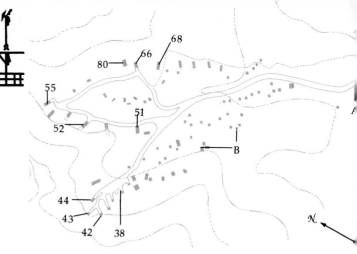

TA-SET-NEFERU, THE VALLEY OF THE QUEENS

38 Tomb of Sat-ra
42 Tomb of Pra-her-
   unemef
43 Tomb of Set-her-
   khepshef
44 Tomb of Khaemwaset
51 Tomb of Isis
52 Tomb of Tyti

55 Tomb of Amun
   (-her)-khepshef
66 Tomb of Nefertari
68 Tomb of Meritamun
80 Tomb of Tuya
A Chief wadi
B Shafts of the
   Eighteenth Dynasty

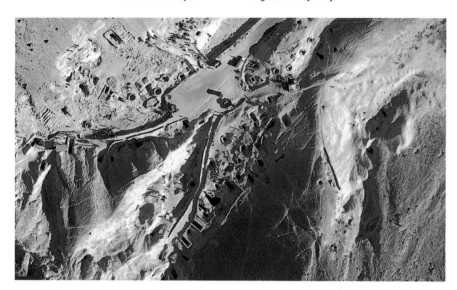

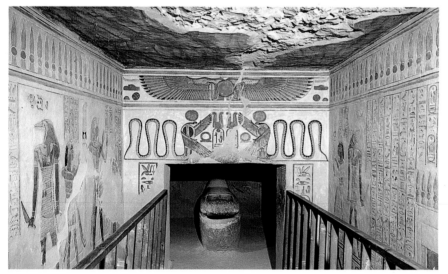

The Valley of the Queens, in Arabic Biban el-Harim, lies at the southernmost tip of the immense necropolis of ancient Thebes; the site, almost overlooked by travellers and explorers of the nineteenth century, was named by Jean François Champollion and by the Englishman John Gardner Wilkinson, who were the first to explore the Valley in the early decades of last century.

The ancient Egyptians called the valley *Ta-set-neferu*, 'the Place of the Children of the Pharaoh', and it contained over a hundred tombs, the first of which were dug in the Eighteenth Dynasty (around the sixteenth century BC). Originally intended as the final resting place for the princes and princesses of royal blood, later, beginning with the rule of Ramesses I, the wives of the pharaohs were also buried there.

The site was believed to be sacred, and it was therefore well suited to its function as a royal necropolis. As with the Valley of the Kings, its proximity to el-Qurn, the Theban Peak, the pyramid-shaped mountain sacred to the cobra goddess Meretseger, was one factor; another was the presence at the end of the valley of a waterfall and cave that possessed a structure and natural features suggestive of religious and funerary concepts.

214 (above) The Valley of the Queens is the southernmost of the necropolises of Thebes, and contains about 100 funerary shafts and tombs, from the Eighteenth, Nineteenth and Twentieth Dynasties. The ancient Egyptians called this place Ta-set-neferu, which –

according to the most recent and generally accepted translation – means 'the Place of the Children of the Pharaoh', clearly referring to the presence in this necropolis of not only the great royal spouses but also of princes, princesses and other members of the royal court.

214 (below) The tomb of Prince Amun (-her)-khepshef, the son of Ramesses III, discovered by the Missione Archeologica Italiana, led by Ernesto Schiaparelli, in 1904

(QV no. 55). Because of the quality of its perfectly preserved polychrome bas-reliefs, it is considered to be the finest tomb in the necropolis after that of Nefertari.

215 Portrait of Prince Khaemwaset, another son of Ramesses III buried in the Valley of the Queens. This tomb was also discovered by Schiaparelli (QV no. 44). The prince wears his hair in the style of the young, with his head shaved and his hair gathered in a single braid on the side, held with a pin used typically by young boys.

Nefertari and Her Tomb

Nefertari's tomb, with its spectacular wall paintings, is perhaps the most beautiful tomb in all Egypt. It was discovered by Ernesto Schiaparelli in 1904 in the Valley of the Queens. The tomb was closed to the public in the 1950s because of numerous serious problems that threatened the spectacular paintings. It was not until 1986, under a joint operation by the Egyptian Antiquities Organization and the Getty Conservation Institute, that emergency measures were taken to stabilize the condition of the paintings. In February 1988, the restoration proper began, following a number of multidisciplinary studies carried out by an international team of scientists. First of all the plaster was reinforced, then fragments of paint that had come loose from the walls were glued back on, and finally work began on cleaning the paintings and removing the old and badly executed restorations, replacing them with a mortar that was exactly the same as that used at the time of the pharaohs. In April 1992, the restoration of the tomb was completed, but in order to preserve the delicate paintings, the Egyptian authorities took the decision to close the tomb to the public once and for all.

Nefertari Meri-en-Mut (a name that means 'the Lovely One, Beloved of Mut') probably married the great pharaoh Ramesses II before he took the throne. It seems she was held in highest esteem and was the most important of all the pharaoh's numerous wives. Her status is confirmed by the fact that she was always in Ramesses's entourage, even during important voyages, such as the one to Nubia, during the 24th year of his reign (around 1255 BC) for the

216 *Queen Nefertari, seen here led by the goddess Isis into the presence of the god Khepri, with the head of a scarab, in the vestibule of her tomb (QV no. 66). The tomb of Nefertari was discovered by the Missione Archeologica Italiana, led by Ernesto Schiaparelli,* *in 1904. Recently, the tomb has been painstakingly restored in a joint operation carried out by the Getty Conservation Institute and the Egyptian Antiquities Organization, restoring the remarkable wall paintings to their original splendour.*

216–217 In the
vestibule of the
antechamber of her
tomb, Nefertari,
welcomed by the
goddesses Selkis (left)
and Neith (right) –
deities that had a
protective role in the
funerary cult – is led
by the goddess Isis and

the god Harsiesis into
the presence of the two
great sun deities. On
the left Isis presents
the queen to the
scarab-faced god
Khepri, who represents
the sun at its dawning,
while on the right
Harsiesis (a name that
is used to indicate

Horus, the son of Isis)
presents Nefertari
before the god Re-
Harakhty, the sun god
and sovereign of the
horizon, who is
protected by Hathor-
Imentet, a form of the
goddess Hathor linked
to the west and to the
funerary universe. The

brief texts that
accompany this scene
contain the words of
the gods who are shown
receiving Nefertari:
they state that they will
endow her with
'eternity', the 'form of
Re in the heavens' and
'life eternal, strength
and endurance'.

218 (above) The bull, seven celestial cows and the four rudders of the heavens, portrayed on the south wall of the first eastern side annexe are derived

from Chapter 148 of the Book of the Dead. This chapter is entitled 'Spell for Procuring Supplies for a Soul in the Kingdom of the Dead'.

218 (below) Nefertari recites the spells necessary to obtain the palette of the scribe before the god Thoth, the divine scribe endowed with magic powers; this ritual is prescribed in Chapter 94 of the Book of the Dead.

219 (right) Nefertari, standing before an offering table, proffers two ritual vases to the goddess Hathor, on the eastern wall of the stairway that leads into the burial chamber of her tomb.

224–225 The burial chamber of the tomb of Nefertari, with the four large pillars that support the ceiling. On the southern faces of the first two pillars are depictions of two forms of Horus which were connected in ancient times with funerary ritual and priestly functions: Horus-iun-mutef and Horus-nedj-itef.

When Schiaparelli discovered Nefertari's tomb and entered this room, he found only a few fragments of the sarcophagus and just scraps of the queen's mummy. Originally, the sarcophagus stood in the middle, between the pillars. The pieces are now conserved in the Egyptian Museum of Turin, Italy.

inauguration of the small temple of Abu Simbel, dedicated to the goddess Hathor and to Nefertari herself. On the façade of this temple the queen is shown as being the same size as the pharaoh himself, a graphic indication of her status since the wife of the pharaoh was usually shown at his side on a scale such that she was barely higher than his knee.

Nefertari's origins remain shrouded in mystery – a number of clues suggest that she came from the area around Thebes, and that she was in fact a relative of Pharaoh Ay, the last ruler of the Eighteenth Dynasty; she may have been Ay's daughter. Although she and Ramesses had five or six children, none of them succeeded to the throne. Ramesses' heir – Prince Merneptah – was Ramesses' son by the other Great Royal Bride, Queen Isis-Nofret, whose tomb has not yet been discovered.

NEFERTARI - 'THE LOVELY ONE BELOVED OF MUT': EASTERN SIDE OF THE TOMB

Ernesto Schiaparelli, director of the Egyptian Museum of Turin and the guiding spirit behind the Missione Archeologica Italiana, was hardly new to the thrill of discovery when, in autumn 1904, while digging in the Valley of the Queens, he found the tomb of the most celebrated queen of Egypt, Nefertari, the great royal wife of Ramesses II. This tomb, however, was different, even though it had been plundered and every object removed: its wall paintings, covering the entire tomb, are so perfect and beautiful that they remain unrivalled in all of Egypt. When the splendid paintings were

discovered they were already in poor condition, due to the infiltration of water and salts. Schiaparelli carried out an initial, provisional restoration but the situation worsened over the years, and the tomb was closed until a complete restoration could be carried out. This was begun in 1988 and completed in 1992, through the intervention of the Getty Conservation Institute in Los Angeles, and the Egyptian Antiquities Organization. In order to preserve this artistic jewel for future generations, the agencies responsible for the tomb decided against reopening it to the public.

1. Nefertari in the presence of the gods Osiris and Anubis.

2. Frieze with *uraei* and ostrich plumes. In the centre is a deity holding its hands over two symbols connected with the concept of eternity.

3. The goddess Neith: her name is shown by the emblem on her head.

4. The 'seven celestial cows' mentioned in chapter 148 of the Book of the Dead.

5. Nefertary making offerings to Osiris, Lord of the Underworld, and to Atum, the creator god of Heliopolis, considered a manifestation of Re.

6. A symbolic depiction of the triumph of the queen in the kingdom of the Afterlife, as illustrated in chapters 94 and 148 of the Book of the Dead.

7. Nefertari holds out vases containing offerings to Hathor and Selkis, while the goddess Maat spreads her wings in an attitude of protection.

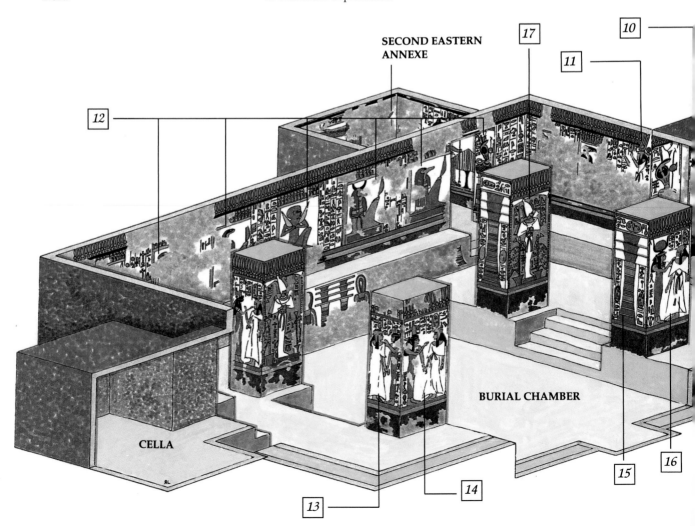

SECOND EASTERN ANNEXE

BURIAL CHAMBER

CELLA

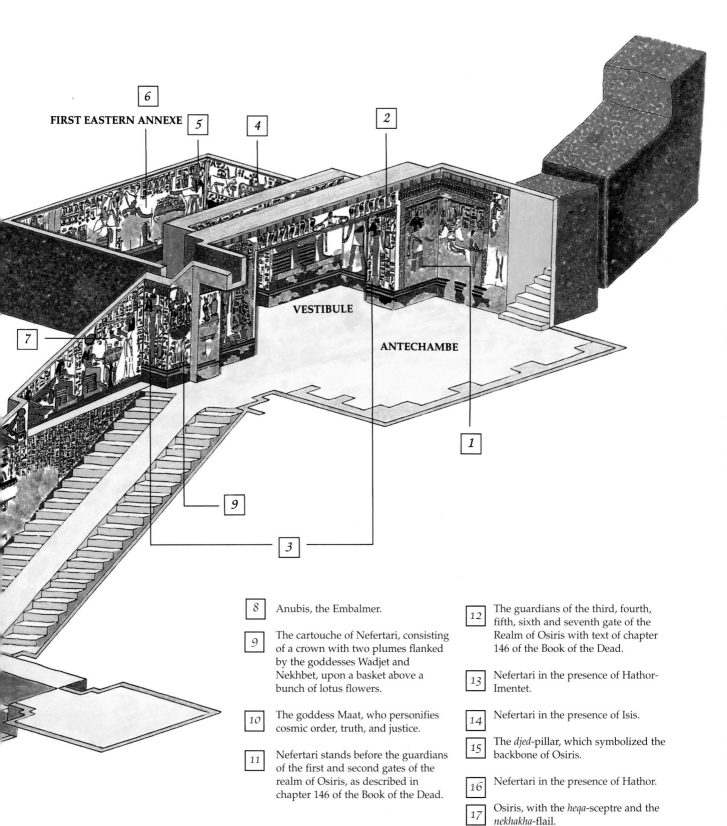

FIRST EASTERN ANNEXE

6

5

4

2

VESTIBULE

ANTECHAMBE

7

1

9

3

8   Anubis, the Embalmer.

9   The cartouche of Nefertari, consisting of a crown with two plumes flanked by the goddesses Wadjet and Nekhbet, upon a basket above a bunch of lotus flowers.

10   The goddess Maat, who personifies cosmic order, truth, and justice.

11   Nefertari stands before the guardians of the first and second gates of the realm of Osiris, as described in chapter 146 of the Book of the Dead.

12   The guardians of the third, fourth, fifth, sixth and seventh gate of the Realm of Osiris with text of chapter 146 of the Book of the Dead.

13   Nefertari in the presence of Hathor-Imentet.

14   Nefertari in the presence of Isis.

15   The *djed*-pillar, which symbolized the backbone of Osiris.

16   Nefertari in the presence of Hathor.

17   Osiris, with the *heqa*-sceptre and the *nekhakha*-flail.

𝒩

WESTERN SIDE OF THE TOMB

1 The entire tomb is designed as a spiritual voyage undertaken by the soul of the queen as she descended into the kingdom of the dead, where she was transformed. After a lengthy journey she returned to daylight and was assimilated with the sun god Re. the staiway symbolically represents the last stage of this process.

2 An animated *djed*-pillar depicts the backbone of Osiris, the lord of the underworld. The pillar has two arms, which hold he attributes typical of the god: the flaid and the *heqa*-sceptre.

3 On the walls of the Antechamber, in vertical registers, are passages from Chapter 17 of he Book of the Dead, containing magic spells necessary for the soul of the queen to return to daylight. The uppermost register formed a commentary on the text.

4 Double staircase with a central ramp down which the sarcophagus would travel.

5 Descending corridor, symbolizing the descent of the queen into the underworld.

6 Nefertari in the presence of the goddess Isis, who extends an *ankh* sign to her as a symbol of eternal life.

7 The chamber of the sarcophagus, with four pillars. On he walls of the western side are passages from Chapter 144 of the Book of the Dead, describing the underground world where Osiris reigns, and where the queen dwelt in preparation for her symbolic rebirth.

8 Nefertari in the presence of the god Anubis.

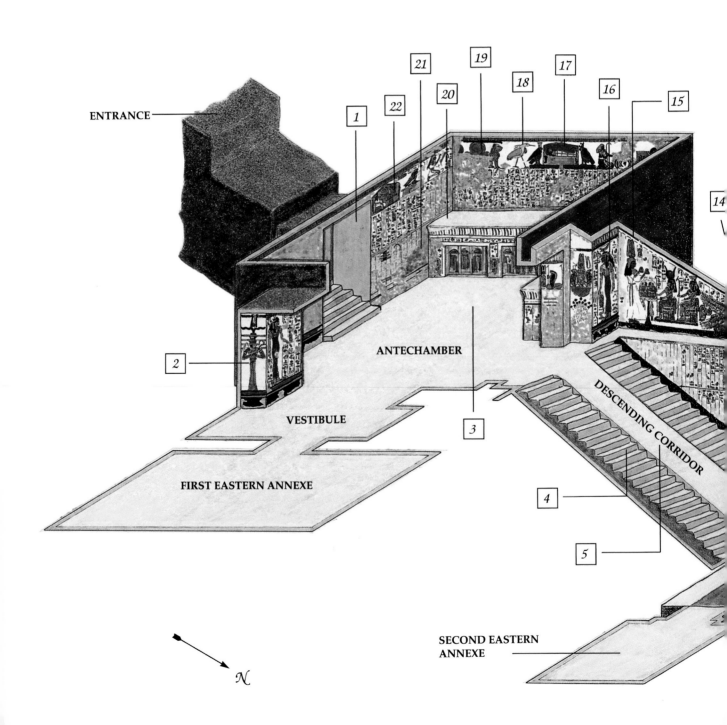

ENTRANCE

21 19 17
    18   16   15
22 20
1

14

2

ANTECHAMBER

VESTIBULE

3

DESCENDING CORRIDOR

FIRST EASTERN ANNEXE

4

5

N

SECOND EASTERN ANNEXE

9	Nefertari in the presence of Isis.

10	The god Osiris, Lord of the Underworld.

11	A frieze of plant stalks bound together with a cord.

12	The three guardians of the second gate of the kingdom of Osiris, described in Chapter 144 of the Book of the Dead, each with e specific role. Threatening in pose and gesture, two hold knives and the other a small tree branch.

13	Nefertari addresses, with the appropriate spells and phrases, the three guardians of the first gate of the Kingdom of Osiris. The soul of the deceased had to pass through numerous gates and doors before finally being allowed to enter the realm of Osiris. Chapters 144 and 146 of the Book of the Dead contained spells to aid the soul in this task.

14	The god Anubis, the Embalmer, turns to Nefertari, welcoming her to the Kingdom of the Dead.

15	Nefertari, before a lavish offering table, sets down two ritual vases containing offerings of wine intended for the goddesses Isis and Nephthys; behind them is the goddess Maat, her wings spread in an attitude of protection.

16	The goddess Selkis, her head adorned with a scorpion, a transcription of her name.

17	Isis and Nephthys, deities depicted in the form of two hawks, protect the queen's mummy.

18	The *bennu*-bird, a phoenix-like bird symbolizing resurrection.

19	Two lions flank the symbol of the *akhet*-horizon, denoting Atum, the creator god, father of the god Shu and the goddess Tefnut.

20	Ledge with a decorated cornice, probably intended for funerary furnishings.

21	Traces of the original decorations, made up of *djed*-pillars alternating with *tit*-knots.

22	The queen plays at *senet*, an early forerunner of the modern game of draughts.

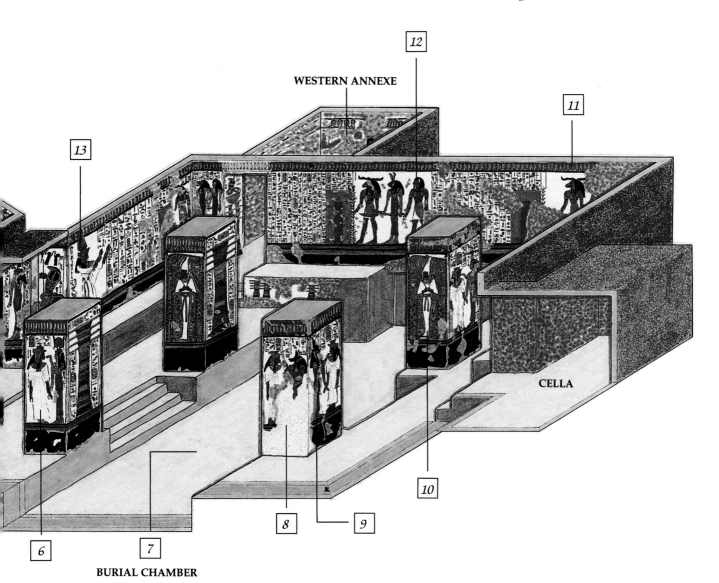

WESTERN ANNEXE

BURIAL CHAMBER

CELLA

226–227 Aerial view of the so-called 'Tombs of the Nobles' and the valley of Deir el-Bahri. The grand temple of Hatshepsut dominates the scene, and next to it is the natural amphitheatre where the famous cache of royal mummies was found. The tombs of private citizens, incorrectly termed the 'Tombs of the Nobles', are arranged in different necropolises (from north to south: the Intef cemetery, Dra Abu el-Naga, el-Khokha, Assasif, Sheikh Abd el-Qurna, Qurnet Murai and Deir el-Medina). Several hundred tombs are known, though only a tiny fraction are open to the public. The inhabitants of the village of Qurna have converted many of the tombs into dwellings.

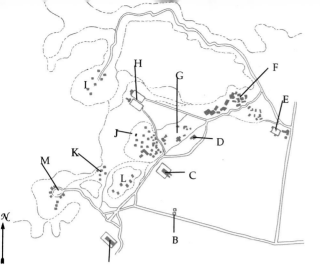

THE TOMBS
IN THE MOUNTAIN

The private tombs of the Theban necropolis, often inaccurately referred to as the 'Tombs of the Nobles', are grouped in different necropolises which extend though the Valley of the Queens and the Valley of the Kings: the Intef cemetery, Dra Abu el-Naga, el-Khokha, Assasif, Sheikh Abd el-Qurna, Qurnet Murai and Deir el-Medina. The majority of the several hundred tombs are decorated, but unlike the royal tombs, in which the subjects are exclusively taken from the major religious texts, such as the Book of the Dead and the Book of Gates, the paintings are usually scenes of everyday life or funerary rituals and ceremonies.

Generally the tombs consist of an outer courtyard, a chapel – the focus of the funerary cult – and an underground burial chamber connected to the chapel by a long sloping corridor. Sometimes the entrance was marked by a small pyramid. In terms of stylistic features the tombs of Thebes can be split into two large groups: the tombs of the Eighteenth Dynasty, and the tombs dating from the Ramesside period, to which can be added the later tombs, from the Saite period (seventh to fifth century BC) and the earlier tombs, far fewer, which date from the Middle Kingdom (2100–1750 BC).

*229 (right) This charming portrait of a Theban woman clearly shows the dress and hairstyle typical of the period of the Eighteenth and Nineteenth Dynasties. Her hair is pulled back and tied with a band of cloth around her temples. A braid covers her enormous round earring and falls down over her shoulder. Above her hair is a glimpse of the great cone of perfumed ointment that women usually wore on their heads, while her forehead is adorned with a lotus flower. Realism and poetry are merged in an intimate portrait of an extraordinarily modern face that seems to have been painted in defiance of the passing of the millennia.
(TT no. 69, Tomb of Menna, necropolis of Sheik Abd el-Qurna)*

A Medinet Habu
B Colossi of Memnon
C Ramesseum
D Necropolis of el-Khokha
E Temple of Sethos I
F Necropolis of Dra Abu el-Naga
G Assasif
H Deir el-Bahri

I Valley of the Kings
J Necropolis of Sheikh Abd el-Qurna
K Deir el-Medina: workers' village and necropolis
L Necropolis of Qurnet Murai
M Valley of the Queens

228 Three female musicians soothing the hearts of the mourners at the funeral banquet of Nakht. They are playing the harp, the lute and a wind instrument, and are one of the best known works in Theban painting. (TT no. 52, Sheikh Abd el-Qurna). Nakht was a

scribe and astronomer of Amun in the reigns of Tuthmosis IV and Amenophis II, possibly between 1396 and 1349 BC, a period when Egyptian art reached a high level of achievement. Music was an important feature of banquets, cheering the diners as it accompanied the elegant dancers.

*230–231 The vaulted ceiling of the burial chamber of the tomb of Sennedjem is painted with passages from the Book of the Dead and eight other scenes: this picture shows the deceased and his wife, Iyneferti, worshipping five star deities.
(TT no. 1, Tomb of Sennedjem, necropolis of Deir el-Medina)*

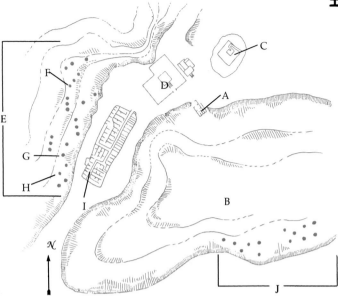

A Temple of Amun
B Qurnet Murai
C Great ditch
D Ptolemaic temple
E Necropolis
F Tomb of Pashedu
G Tomb of Sennedjem
H Tomb of Inherkhau
I Labourers' village
J Necropolis

Workers and artists who laboured on the construction of the Theban tombs lived in a village called *set maat*, an expression that can be translated as the 'Place of Truth' or the 'Place of Order', and which is now called Deir el-Medina. The village, the only permanent residential structure in the entire necropolis, was founded at the beginning of the Eighteenth Dynasty during the reign of Tuthmosis I, and it is one of the very few urban structures to have survived from ancient Egypt. Surrounded by a wall made of unbaked bricks, the village was composed of some 70 residences, and was connected to the Valley of the Kings and the Valley of the Queens by two paths that can still be used. The houses of the labourers all had more or less the same structure. The details of the everyday lives of the workers and their families can be reconstructed from the wealth of evidence that has been unearthed by archaeologists, and through epigraphic sources. The workers were highly organized and as members of the guild owned houses and had servants. To the west of the residential area, dug into the side of the mountain, were the tombs of the labourers, the decoration of which rivalled the finest tombs of dignitaries buried in the nearby necropolis.

232 (left) Sennedjem and his wife depicted before the sycamore goddess. Sennedjem's tomb was found, intact, in 1886, and most of the lavish funerary furnishings were taken to the Cairo Museum. (TT no. 1, necropolis of Deir el-Medina)

232 (above, left) The labourers' village of Deir el-Medina was called, in ancient times, set maat, meaning the 'Place of Truth'. This was the residence of the community of workers assigned to the construction and decoration of the royal tombs and the 'Tombs

of the Nobles'. The village, which was founded during the reign of Tuthmosis I, included some 70 dwellings within its walls, and about 50 more located outside. It has been calculated that around 400 people lived in Deir el-Medina during the era of the Ramessides.

232–233 (above) Sennedjem and his wife Iyneferti lived during the Nineteenth Dynasty, probably in the reign of Ramesses II. The painting on the eastern wall of their burial chamber shows them doing farm work in the Fields of Iaru, the place in the Afterworld where the deceased lived a second life, parallel to the earthly one, performing the same activities as the peasant. If the work became tiring, the deceased could always make use of the magic spells found in Chapter 6 of the Book of the Dead, and have the shabtis do the work for them instead. The shabtis were small statuettes that were placed in the tomb for this purpose.
(TT no. 1, necropolis of Deir el-Medina)

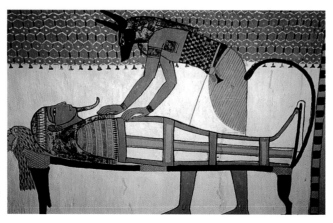

233 (left) The god Anubis, the Divine Embalmer, is shown here in the process of embalming the body of the deceased, and preparing the mummy.
(TT no. 1, necropolis of Deir el-Medina)

234 (top) Pashedu is shown here kneeling beneath a large animated udjat-eye offering candles. The udjat-eye, meaning, 'Made Healthy Again', was a powerful protective amulet that evoked the legend which told how Horus was wounded in one eye during the battle with the evil Seth, a wound which was subsequently healed by the god Thoth. (TT no. 3, Deir el-Medina)

234–235 (right) The eastern wall of the burial chamber of the tomb of Pashedu, 'the Servant in the Place of Truth in Western Thebes', at Deir el-Medina. The tympanum is dominated by a great central image of the god Ptah-Sokaris, shown as a hawk perched on a boat, surmounted by an udjat-eye. Below, left of the entrance, the deceased slakes his thirst from a small stream beneath a palm tree. To the right of the entrance are three registers in which the parents and various relatives of the deceased are shown. (TT no. 3, Deir el-Medina)

234 (below) Two depictions of the god Anubis in the form of a jackal dominate the narrow vaulted corridor that leads to the burial chamber of the tomb of Pashedu. At the far end (the west wall) are depicted the god Horus in the form of a falcon, Osiris, the lord of the Underworld, and a large udjat-eye.

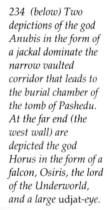

235 (left) Preceded by Anubis in the shape of a jackal, lying on top of a shrine, Pashedu, with his relatives, his wife Negemtebehdet and his two sons Menna and Kaha (shown at the feet of their parents), is shown worshipping before the god Horus (not visible here). Vertical panels contain passages from the Book of the Dead. (TT no. 3, Deir el-Medina)

236 (below) Work in the fields (including turning the soil, planting, cutting and harvesting wheat and flax and keeping accounts) is depicted in remarkable detail in the tomb of Menna, who lived during the Eighteenth Dynasty, probably around the time of Tuthmosis IV. Here, using special wooden implements, the peasants toss the threshed grain into the air to remove the chaff. Two colours dominate this agricultural scene: yellow, the colour of ripened wheat; and ochre, with which human bodies were painted. (TT, no. 69, Sheikh Abd el-Qurna).

236–237 (right) The cultivation of grain was probably the most important of the many agricultural activities in ancient Egypt. This scene illustrates one of the main stages in the harvest. Peasants standing on the ricks formed by the newly cut sheaves of wheat, scatter them across the threshing floor, using a three-pronged wooden pitchfork. A third peasant, holding a rod, drives two teams of oxen treading the sheaves of wheat to separate the kernels from the inedible chaff. (TT no. 69, Tomb of Menna, necropolis of Sheikh Abd el-Qurna)

237 (left) The entire wall with scenes of work in the fields: in the first two, Menna, 'Scribe of the Fields of the Lord of the Two Lands of Upper and Lower Egypt', can be seen overseeing punishment and also supervising the harvesting and threshing of the wheat. (TT no. 69, necropolis of Sheikh Abd el-Qurna)

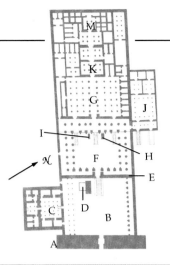

TEMPLES OF MILLIONS OF YEARS
THE RAMESSEUM

A First pylon
B First courtyard
C Royal Palace
D Colossus of Ramesses II
E Second pylon
F Second courtyard
G Hypostyle Hall

H Colossus of Ramesses II
I Colossus of Ramesses II, the head of which was removed and transported to England by Belzoni
J Temple of Tuya and Nefertari
K Hall of the Barques
L Hall of the Litanies

238 Aerial view of the second courtyard and hypostyle hall of the Ramesseum, the memorial temple of Ramesses II in western Thebes, described by the Greek historian Diodorus Siculus as the 'Tomb of Ozymandias'.

239 (right) The monolithic granite colossus of Ramesses, 'the Re of Rulers', stood 20 m (66 ft) tall. In the background is the first pylon, the gate of which has been temporarily sealed in order to increase the overall stability of the whole structure.

On the western bank of the Nile at Thebes the pharaohs of the Eighteenth, Nineteenth and Twentieth Dynasties had huge temples built. These are often referred to as funerary or mortuary temples – not wholly accurate terms as they were used by the living pharaoh. Called by the ancient Egyptians 'Temples of Millions of Years', they were associated with the cult of the divine king and linked to the principal deity of Thebes, the god Amun.

The pharaohs celebrated the *sed*-festival in these temples. A ceremony with ancient origins that took place in the thirtieth year of the king's reign, its purpose was to regenerate the strength of the ruler and – through him – the entire nation. In the 'Temples of Millions of Years', the deity and the pharaoh – considered the earthly son of the god – were closely linked in a form of worship that served to intensify the royal power. Built on the western edge of the Nile's alluvial plain, the temples all had an east–west orientation, corresponding to the axis of the sun and stars. Today, many of them – often built of unbaked bricks – are nothing but shapeless ruins, a sad fate which has befallen the temples of Amenophis III, Merneptah, Tuthmosis III, Tuthmosis IV and Ramesses IV.

The temple of Ramesses II, dubbed the Ramesseum by Champollion, is one of the most perfect and elegant examples of this form of architecture, though earthquakes, the passage of time and the plundering of structural material for use in later buildings have profoundly altered its original appearance. The complex of the Ramesseum, which to the ancient Egyptians was 'the Temple of Millions of Years of King Usermaatre-Setepenre-that is linked to Thebes in the estate of Amun, west of Thebes',

comprised a number of different buildings: the temple for royal worship; the royal palace, used by the king during ceremonies; a temple for the worship of the mother and the wife of Ramesses, Tuya and Nefertari respectively; and the large storehouses made of unbaked bricks. In these storehouses the products from the various temple estates were kept for use both in daily ritual sacrifices and to feed and clothe the priests of the temple.

On the western side of the first courtyard a giant monolithic statue in red granite from Aswan lies flat on the ground, portraying Ramesses 'Re of the Rulers'. This scene inspired Shelley to compose his poem, 'Ozymandias'. 'The Tomb of Ozymandias' is one of the names of the Ramesseum, from the Greek transliteration of the name of Ramesses II, Usermaatre. The Greek geographer Strabo called it the Memnonium, a word used for numerous buildings in antiquity,

taken from the Greek hero Memnon, the child of Aurora. In the second courtyard a splendid head of Ramesses II was found, called the 'Younger Memnon'. This was removed by Belzoni in 1816 and transported to the British Museum, where it can still be admired in the Egyptian Sculpture Gallery.

Abandoned at the end of the Twentieth Dynasty, the Ramesseum served a number of purposes in later years: a burial place for Theban priests during the Third Intermediate Period; a quarry for building material during the Twenty-Ninth Dynasty and a church for the Coptic communities who took up residence on the West Bank of Thebes in the fourth century AD. Currently, the Ramesseum is the subject of a huge campaign of study and restoration by the Franco-Egyptian team of the Centre National de la Recherche Scientifique of Paris and of the Centre d'Études et Documentations sur l'Ancienne Égypte of Cairo.

THE TEMPLE OF RAMESSES III AT MEDINET HABU

A Entrance
B Migdol
C Enclosure wall made of unfired brick
D Temple of the Eighteenth Dynasty
E Chapel of the Divine Adoratrices and Temple of Amenirdis
F Sacred Lake
G Royal Palace
H First pylon
I First courtyard
J Window of Appearances
K Second pylon
L Second courtyard
M Temple of Ramesses III
N First hypostyle hall
O Second hypostyle hall
P Sanctuary

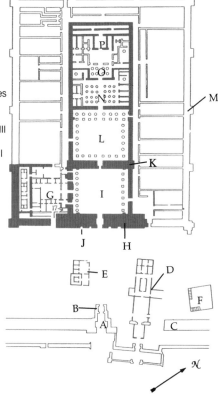

240 View of the second courtyard of the mortuary temple of Ramesses III at Medinet Habu, with the Osiris colossi that adorn the portico and the ramp that leads to the first hypostyle hall. This enormous temple for the pharaoh cult, called the 'Temple of Ramesses who Joins Eternity', was surely inspired by the Ramesseum; its structure includes two large pylons, followed by two courtyards and a series of three hypostyle halls, with a number of chapels.

240 (below) The first pylon of Medinet Habu, 63 m (206 ft) in length, is decorated with commemorative depictions of the victories of Ramesses III in the eighth year of his reign. The pharaoh is shown slaughtering his enemies (Asiatics and Sea Peoples) in front of Amun-Re (southern tower) and in front of Amun-Re-Harakhty (northern tower).

241 (opposite) The southern portico of the first courtyard of Medinet Habu is supported by a series of great columns. This portico marked the limit of the façade of the royal palace adjacent to the temple. A large aperture at its centre – the 'Window of Appearances' – allowed the pharaoh to watch the ceremonies that took place in the temple.

The vast complex of Medinet Habu contains numerous different buildings: the temple for the worship of Ramesses III; the royal palace; a second temple dedicated to Amun; an area of storehouses and lodgings of the priests. The temple of Ramesses III is without doubt the best preserved of all the Theban temples. It was built just half a mile to the south of the Ramesseum and was chiefly dedicated to the worship of the pharaoh, who was venerated as one of the forms of Amun-Re. Here the barque of Amun was transported during the 'Festival of the Valley', so that the god could visit the necropolis to confer his own vital energy to the dead. Unlike all the other mortuary temples, the monumental entrance takes the form of a military fortress of the type built by Asiatics, the so-called *migdol*. It is connected to the enclosure wall of the temple, over which it provided a ritual protective shield. In the southern section of the enclosure are the foundations of the royal palace, used by the pharaoh during ceremonies, and directly linked to the first courtyard of the temple through the 'Window of Appearances', where the pharaoh made his public appearances.

On the temple's outer northern wall, extensive reliefs depicted the battles fought by Ramesses III against the Sea Peoples (invaders from the north, probably from the Aegean–Anatolian region), while behind the southern pier of the first pylon, a splendid bull-hunting scene is illustrated, considered to be a masterpiece of the art of the Twentieth Dynasty.

242–243 One of the best-known reliefs from the temple of Medinet Habu is this splendid scene of bull-hunting, set in the marshes. It is carved on the western wall of the southern tower of the first pylon. Ramesses III, riding in his chariot and armed with a spear, is escorted by a line of young princes as he kills his prey.

To the northeast of the temple of Ramesses III, another temple was built during the Eighteenth Dynasty, dedicated to Amun by Hatshepsut and Tuthmosis III. During the first millennium BC, Medinet Habu was believed to be the place of burial of the Ogdoad, a group of eight deities made up of four couples, male and female. During a special feast, known as the 'Feast of the Tenth Day', the god Amun of Luxor, where the eight deities of the Ogdoad were born, would travel to Medinet Habu to celebrate the funerary rites for his ancestors, restoring life to them and thereby renewing creation itself.

During the Twentieth Dynasty, Medinet Habu became the administrative centre of the west bank of Thebes and a haven for the populace during the war between the high priest of Amun of Karnak and the Viceroy of Kush. Subsequently, during the Twenty-Fifth and the Twenty-Sixth Dynasties, special funerary-chapels were built in the southeast part of the sacred enclosure, for the divine adoratrices of Amun, priestesses of great prestige who formed part of the royal family. The complex of Medinet Habu was further expanded during the Graeco-Roman period, and its long history extended yet further, on through the ninth century AD, when the Coptic city of Djeme grew up there.

Since 1924, a team from the Oriental Institute of the University of Chicago has been working at the site, and has published the results of their studies, both archaeological and epigraphical.

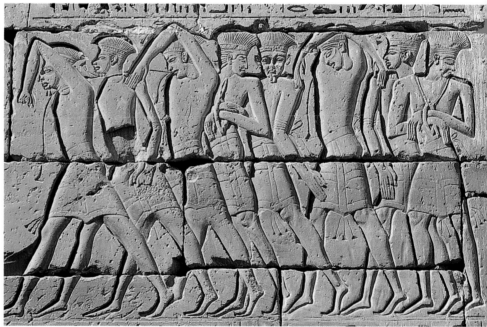

243 A relief in the first courtyard of the temple of Medinet Habu, depicting a line of Philistine prisoners, defeated by Ramesses III in a major battle which is portrayed on the outer northern wall of the temple. Philistines, together with other groups, formed the 'Sea Peoples', a loose confederation of people from the north, who increasingly threatened Egyptian territory. They had been defeated once by Merneptah, son and successor of Ramesses II, and they were defeated twice more by Ramesses III during the eighth and ninth years of his reign.

THE TEMPLE OF AMENOPHIS III

A Temple of Amenhotep, son of Hapu
B Temple of Amenophis III
C Temple of Ptah-Sokar-Osiris
D Brick enclosure wall
E Colossi of Memnon
F Processional boulevard (dromos)
G First pylon
H Second pylon
I Third pylon

244 The mortuary temple of Sethos I is the northernmost temple of Western Thebes. Since Ramesses I died after reigning for less than two years (1295–1294 BC), without having built a temple of his own, Sethos I added to his own temple a chapel for the worship of his deified father. The entire complex, completed by Ramesses II, originally included two pylons made of mud bricks, which were later destroyed. Today, nothing remains of the temple but the innermost part, consisting of the portico, the hypostyle hall with the side chapels, the sanctuary and an inner courtyard.

Almost nothing survives of what must once have been the largest temple in Western Thebes. Located far to the east of the Nile alluvial plain, the temple of Amenophis III, built of mud brick was probably eroded by annual floods, and was subsequently used as a source for building materials. The only indications of its long vanished glory are the two enormous statues of the deified pharaoh that stood on either side of the entrance, known as the Colossi of Memnon.

A similar fate also befell the immense royal palace of the pharaoh which stood at Malqata, about a mile south of Medinet Habu, which was linked to the Nile by an enormous artificial lake, the Birket Habu.

244–245 (right) These two enormous monolithic statues stood before the first pylon of the mortuary temple of Amenophis III; originally this was the largest of all the Theban temples built under the supervision of the great architect Amenhotep, the son of Hapu, subsequently deified. Sadly, this grandiose structure was entirely built of mud bricks, and was set in a badly chosen location – too close to the Nile – and was completely destroyed. These two colossi of Amenophis III are impressive evidence of what the temple must have been like. Made of quartzite, each stands approximately 17 m (55 ft) tall on a base standing in turn more than 2 m (over 6 ft) high. Greek travellers named them the Colossi of Memnon (the mythical son of Aurora). One of the statues, which had been badly damaged in an earthquake, probably during the first century BC, each morning, as the air began to heat up, emitted a sound that was interpreted as the groan of the hero, Memnon, who had been killed by Achilles. This phenomenon ceased abruptly when the statue was restored, at the orders of Septimius Severus.

THE TEMPLE OF SETHOS I

A First pylon
B Second pylon
C Portico

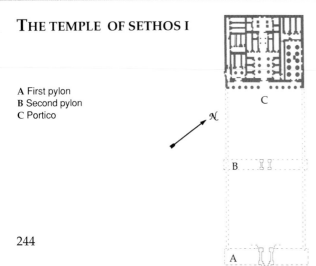

The northernmost of the 'Temples of Millions of Years' is that of Sethos I, the father of Ramesses II, built in the vicinity of the village of Qurna. Surrounded by a high enclosure wall, with an architectural motif that recalls those typical of the sacred enclosures of the Old Kingdom, the temple featured pylons made of mud brick, and only the innermost area, which alone has survived, was made of stone. Here the central chapel was intended to house the sacred barque of

Amun when it made its first stop in this temple during the annual ceremonial procession, while the side chapel housed the barque of the deified pharaoh. As Ramesses I, the father of Sethos I, died after a very brief reign without having built his own temple, Sethos I dedicated a chapel to the worship of his deified father. In the temple enclosure, much like at Medinet Habu and in the Ramesseum, there were storehouses and granaries. On the death of Sethos, the temple had not been completed, and construction was finished only during the reign of Ramesses II. Much later, a Coptic monastery and a church was built within it; and the inhabitants of the adjacent village of Qurna built their houses inside the enclosure, taking building material from the temple itself. For the past 20 years, specialists from the German Archaeological Institute of Cairo have been working to restore the entire complex.

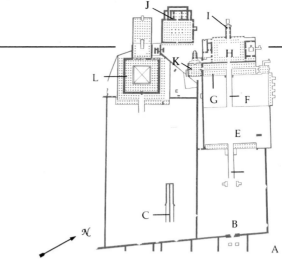

DEIR EL-BAHRI, THE 'MONASTERY OF THE NORTH'

A Processional causeway
B First courtyard
C Bab el-Hosan
D Ramp
E Second courtyard
F Ramp
G Portico of Punt
H Temple of Hatshepsut
I Sanctuary
J Temple of Tuthmosis III
K Chapel of Hathor
L Funerary temple of Mentuhotep

On the far side of the mountain that separates the Valley of the Kings from the hills of the necropolis of Qurna, directly opposite the temple of Karnak, opens the valley of Deir el-Bahri (an Arabic name which means 'the Monastery of the North', referring to a Coptic monastery built here). The valley, considered by the Egyptians to be sacred to the goddess Hathor, extends into the Theban mountain range for about a mile on a southeast–northwest axis and ends in a vast natural amphitheatre.

Pharaoh Nebhepetre Mentuhotep of the Eleventh Dynasty, who was responsible for the reunification of Egypt, had his mortuary temple built here, the only true mortuary temple on the west bank at Thebes. From an architectural point of view, this structure included some original features. For the first time the different parts of the construction were set at different levels, forming terraces lined by colonnades, possibly inspired by the building technique of the 'portico tombs'. As in all royal funerary complexes of the Old and Middle Kingdom, the mortuary temple is connected with the tomb proper by an underground passage leading to the burial chamber.

Very little survives of this temple and it is only possible to get an idea of its size and form by looking at it from above. Such is not the case, however, with the temple built alongside it by Queen Hatshepsut some five centuries later, in the seventh year of her reign. Indeed, this is the most grandiose of the 'Temples of Millions of Years' in the entire complex on the west bank of Thebes, and ancient Egyptians called it *djeser-djeseru*, or 'the sublime of the sublimes'.

246–247 At the head of the valley sacred to the goddess Hathor stands the complex of temples of Deir el-Bahri (the name means 'the Monastery of the North', from the important Coptic monastery that once stood there, long since destroyed). The complex is dominated by the temple of Queen Hatshepsut, designed by the renowned architect Senenmut. It was built on three successive terraces set into the slopes of the imposing cliff wall that separated this site from the Valley of the Kings. The chapel of Amun on the third terrace was the destination of the great procession that took place during the 'Beautiful Feast of the Valley', when the Amun of Karnak paid a visit to western Thebes. Alongside the temple of Hatshepsut stand the remains of a temple of Tuthmosis III, discovered in 1962, and the remains of the tomb-temple of Mentuhotep II, of the Eleventh Dynasty, the first pharaoh to build in this location. For a number of years now, a massive restoration campaign has been underway, with the participation of the Polish Archaeological Mission and the Egyptian Antiquities Organization.

The architectural scheme was conceived by the celebrated architect Senenmut, 'Chief Steward of Amun', utilizing ideas previously expressed in the construction of the temple of Mentuhotep. It consisted of a terraced structure on different levels, preceded by a great processional ramp leading from a valley temple that has since been destroyed. The result was an architectural solution that achieved a remarkable degree of harmony between the building and the savage beauty of the surrounding landscape.

Three great temple courtyards were connected by a system of ramps and separated by porticoes which covered the famous painted reliefs. Of particular note are scenes of divine birth and coronation, and of the transport on a ship of one of the two pairs of enormous obelisks and the

recounting of the famed expedition by land to the country of Punt, one of the most important events of the reign of Hatshepsut. A ceremonial visit was paid once a year to the chapel dedicated to Amun located on the third terrace, on the occasion of the 'Beautiful Feast of the Valley'. At that time, flowers were brought to the chapel and once they had been impregnated with the divine spirit they were placed before the tombs of the dead in the necropolis, in order to revitalize the souls of the dead.

The temple of Hatshepsut also suffered from the ravages of man and time, although to a lesser extent than Mentuhotep's. Almost immediately after the death of the queen, her successor Tuthmosis III defaced most of the images of Hatshepsut. Further destruction took place during the reign of Amenophis IV–Akhenaten, who spared only the images of the sun disk, under his rule venerated as the sole god.

In 1962 archaeologists discovered a third temple, the existence of which was completely unsuspected, built by Tuthmosis III and situated between the temple of Hatshepsut and that of Mentuhotep. Currently, a team of Polish archaeologists is working on the restoration of the whole complex, attempting to restore its ancient splendour.

248 Two phases of the expedition to Punt. The land of Punt, a place that has not yet been identified with any certainty, but was probably located in the Horn of Africa, supplied the rulers of Egypt with prized African products, such as animal skins, elephant tusks, fine woods and, especially, the much sought-after incense that was used in religious ceremonies in the temples. Hatshepsut organized a great expedition to Punt, illustrated in meticulous detail in the reliefs that appear in the western portico of the second terrace of the temple of Deir el-Bahri.

249 A splendid head of Queen Hatshepsut, made of painted limestone, found in the temple of Deir el-Bahri during the work of the Metropolitan Museum of Art of New York in 1926 and 1927. Hatshepsut, the daughter of Tuthmosis I, married her half-brother Tuthmosis II, who died early. She then assumed the regency on behalf of her nephew Tuthmosis III but, beginning in the second year of his reign, she proclaimed herself pharaoh of Upper and Lower Egypt and ruled for around 20 years, from circa 1479 to 1457 BC. (Cairo Museum)

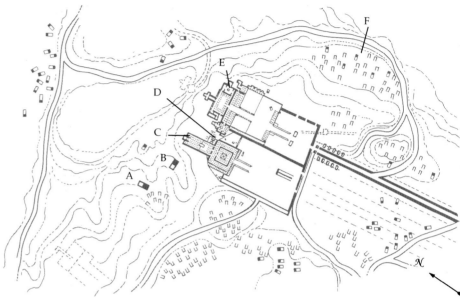

A Tomb of Meketra
B 'Royal cache' of Deir el-Bahri
C Temple of Mentuhotep
D Temple of Tuthmosis III
E Temple of Hatshepsut
F Necropolis

250 (left) In a rocky amphitheatre situated just to the southwest of Deir el-Bahri, Gaston Maspero found the renowned cache of royal mummies in 1881. The bodies of the most illustrious pharaohs were transported here in great secrecy by priests in the Twenty-First Dynasty because of the continual depradations of the tombs in the royal necropolis.

251 (right) Among the mummies in the cache of Deir el-Bahri was that of Ramesses II, placed in a simple wooden sarcophagus. The mummy, which was removed to the Cairo Museum with all the others, was attacked by parasites and microbes and, in 1968, was taken to Paris for a complex programme of restoration. (Cairo Museum)

252–253 On the side of the Theban mountain, between Deir el-Bahri and the western slope of the hill of Sheik Abd el-Qurna, in a place known as the Valley of Seankh-kare, a tomb was uncovered in 1919, during a campaign of excavations carried out by the Metropolitan Museum of Art of New York. The tomb belonged to a high official of the Eleventh Dynasty, about 2000 BC, whose name was Meketre. In the tomb, whose walls were not decorated, were 25 wooden models, of remarkable workmanship, which depicted all the details of everyday life as it was experienced 4000 years ago in Egypt. (TT no. 280)

252 (left) In the carpenter's shop, the various phases in working wood are shown. The central scene is dominated by the sawing of a log in order to make boards. The work is done with a large saw operated by two labourers. The boards are then roughed out and finished using other tools (axes, drills, chisels and so on), kept in a white case which can be seen at the far end of the shop. (Cairo Museum)

252 (below) In the courtyard of one of his properties, the deceased, sitting in a portico supported by four columns and accompanied by his son and by a number of scribes, inspects the herds of cattle that are driven along by peasants. (Cairo Museum)

253 (right) In the weaving room, a group of young women is busy spinning, gathered around two horizontal looms. (Cairo Museum)

254–255 Fishing on the Nile. The fishermen, aboard two papyrus boats propelled by oarsmen, are hard at work hoisting in the net filled with fish, held between the two boats. Other boats follow, transporting the deceased and his entourage. (Cairo Museum)

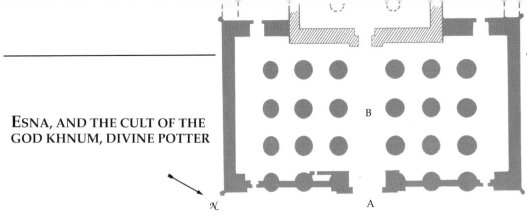

ESNA, AND THE CULT OF THE GOD KHNUM, DIVINE POTTER

A Entrance
B Hypostyle hall

At Esna, called *Iunit* by the ancients and now a small farming town about 50 km (30 miles) south of Luxor on the left bank of the Nile, a type of fish peculiar to the Nile, known as *Lates*, was considered sacred. This belief was the source of the Greek name for the city, *Latopolis*. Here, the principal god worshipped was Khnum – the divine ram-headed potter. Khnum was associated with both Neith and with Heqa, a personification of magic. The Ptolemaic temple of Esna, of the first century AD, was dedicated to these deities. Of the original building nothing survives but the hypostyle hall, built during the reign of Emperor Claudius. The hall is in an excellent state of preservation, even though it was converted into a Coptic church, and in more recent periods was used as a warehouse for storing cotton. Since the level of the inhabited area of the city has progressively risen the remains of the temple are now located at the bottom of a trench, 9 m (30 ft) deep, completely surrounded by the houses of the modern city.

The ceiling of this hall, with astronomical scenes and depictions of the zodiacal signs, is supported by two groups of nine columns, next to which are six large columns aligned with the two entrance portals. The capitals are particularly elaborate and elegant. The texts engraved on the walls of the temple and the columns contain not only hymns and litanies to Khnum, Heqa and Neith, they also provide valuable information on the feasts and important celebrations which attracted people from surrounding areas.

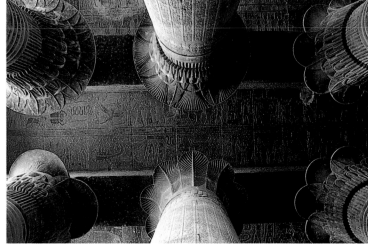

256–257 (left) The temple of Esna, built during Ptolemaic times and dedicated to the god Khnum, the divine potter who shapes human beings on his wheel, to the goddess Neith and to the goddess Heqa, the personification of magic. It is now situated in a trench in the midst of the surrounding modern city, the level of which has gradually risen over the centuries with the accretion of man-made structures of all sorts. All that remains of the temple is the great hypostyle hall built in the first century AD during the reign of Emperor Claudius. The ceiling is supported by a total of 24 columns, of great elegance and adorned with exceedingly elaborate capitals.

257 (above) The ceiling of the hypostyle hall in the temple of Esna is decorated with astronomical scenes and a calendar of the major religious festivals.

EDFU, THE REALM OF THE FALCON GOD

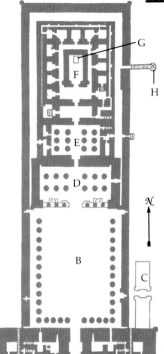

A First pylon
B Courtyard
C Temple of Ramesses III
D Pronaos (first hypostyle hall)
E Second hypostyle hall
F Sanctuary
G Granite naos
H Nilometer

N

Situated on the left bank of the Nile, close to the flowing waters of the river, Edfu was the capital of the second nome of Upper Egypt. The ancient Greeks – who identified Horus with Apollo – knew it as Apollinopolis Magna, and its importance is attested as far back as the earliest dynasties as the centre of the worship of the falcon god Horus.

258 (far left) The goddesses Wadjet and Nekhbet, wearing respectively the red crown of Lower Egypt and the white crown of Upper Egypt. They are placing the double crown on the pharaoh's head. The lengthy and complex hieroglyphic text engraved on the walls of the temple, make this in effect a library in stone, in which the religious rituals and theological doctrines of ancient Egypt have been carefully transcribed.

258 (left) The celebrated falcon with the double crown of Upper and Lower Egypt, symbol of the god Horus, stands alongside the great entrance to the pronaos of the temple of Edfu.

259 (right) The temple of Edfu, dedicated to the god Horus, is the largest temple in Egypt after that of Karnak; it is also the best preserved. The building, as it stands today, constructed on top of the remains of another, older temple, was begun in 237 BC during the reign of Ptolemy III Euergetes I, and was completed in 57 BC, during the reign of Ptolemy XII Neos Dionysos.

In 237 BC, during the reign of Ptolemy III Euergetes I, construction began on the great temple of Horus, built on the ruins of the temple that previously had existed there. Work continued under Ptolemy IV Philopator, and the outer hypostyle hall was not completed until the reign of Ptolemy VIII Euergetes II, in 124 BC, and the decorations were only completed during the reign of Ptolemy XII Neos Dionysos in 57 BC, 180 years after the start of construction. The temple, which formed part of a truly vast sacred precinct that extended under what is now the inhabited town, is unusual in that it is orientated towards the south and not along the east–west axis that most temples follow. The reason for this unusual orientation may be the specific geographic configuration of the site.

The temple includes a great pylon, a courtyard surrounded by a portico, leading into the first hypostyle hall, or

pronaos, in front of the entrance to which is a statue of Horus in the form of a falcon. A second hypostyle hall provides access to the offering room, which is followed by the vestibule, and finally the sanctuary is reached, the innermost part of the temple, in which stands a magnificent *naos* dating from the reign of Nectanebo II, which would have held a tabernacle containing the image of the god.

Around this central axis, a multitude of rooms opened, each with a specific function, described in the numerous texts that entirely cover the walls of the rooms. The temple of Edfu is still one of the largest and best preserved temples in all of Egypt; the entire complex was excavated by Auguste Mariette.

260 (right) A relief
engraved on a block of
sandstone from the
temple of Kom Ombo,
representing the two
deities to which the
building was dedicated:
crocodile-headed Sobek
and falcon-headed

Haroeris. Haroeris, a
Greek name which
derives from the
Egyptian name Heru-
our which means
'Horus the Elder', is a
form of Horus revered
at Kom Ombo as the
'Father of all the Gods'.

Kom Ombo,
THE TEMPLE OF THE HAWK AND THE CROCODILE

Kom Ombo (in Greek *Ombos*) was called *Nubt*, 'the City of Gold', due to the city's role in the trading of the precious metal. Kom Ombo is located around 65 km (40 miles) south of Edfu, not far from the mouth of Wadi Hammamat, the main artery between the Nile and the Eastern Desert, with its fabled gold mines. The temple of Kom Ombo was founded in the Eighteenth Dynasty, during the rule of Tuthmosis III, but construction of the building seen today was begun in the reign of Ptolemy VI Philometor, and continued under Ptolemy VIII Euergetes II. It was completed in the reigns of the Roman emperors Tiberius, Domitian and Caracalla, who ordered the construction of the two external chapels dedicated respectively to Hathor and Sobek. A distinctive feature that sets Kom Ombo apart from other Egyptian temples is that it is a double temple, split lengthwise and dedicated to two separate deities: Sobek, the crocodile-headed god; and falcon-headed Haroeris, or 'Horus the Elder'. Each of the two parallel axes

has its own entrance, but there is frequent access between them along their length. According to local theology, Haroeris formed part of a triad with Tasenetnofret ('the Good Sister'), his wife, and his son Panebtawy ('the Lord of the Two Lands'), much like Sobek who was in turn incorporated in a second triad, with Hathor and Khonsu. The division was not very strict, however, and at times the two mothers or the two sons were confused or assimilated with one another in extremely intricate theological constructs. Moreover, in all likelihood, the two principal deities, Sobek and Haroeris, were connected with two of the most ancient gods of the Heliopolitan theology – Geb and Shu.

On the exterior of the temple's mud-brick enclosure wall are the remains of a well dating from Ptolemaic times, a *mammisi* and a small chapel of Hathor, where hundreds of crocodile mummies are now stored. This animal was sacred to Sobek and they came from a sacred necropolis nearby.

260-261 The temple of Kom Ombo has a plan in many ways similar to that of the temple of Edfu, but its one distinctive feature is that it has a dual structure. Two entrances lead to two shrines with parallel axes, but which

communicate with each other along their length. The temple, on the right bank of the Nile, at the river's edge, is dedicated to two separate deities: Sobek, the crocodile-headed god, and Haroeris, also known as 'Horus the Elder'.

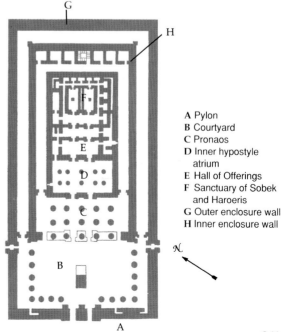

A Pylon
B Courtyard
C Pronaos
D Inner hypostyle atrium
E Hall of Offerings
F Sanctuary of Sobek and Haroeris
G Outer enclosure wall
H Inner enclosure wall

262 (right) The
famous Nilometer of
Aswan, on the
southeastern shore of
Elephantine island.
This structure allowed
the priests to
determine the exact
date on which the
annual inundation
began and its extent.

Both the land and the
people of Egypt
depended on the
flooding for their
survival. The waters
of the Nile ran
through an opening
and along a narrow
staircase, on the walls
of which graduated
scales were engraved.

ASWAN AND PHILAE, JEWELS OF NUBIA

ASWAN

A High Dam
B New Kalabsha
C Island of el-Hesa
D Old dam
E Island of Sehel
F Elephantine Island

G Rock tombs of the Old Kingdom
H Unfinished obelisk
I Granite quarries
J Island of Agilkia (current Philae)
K Island of Biga

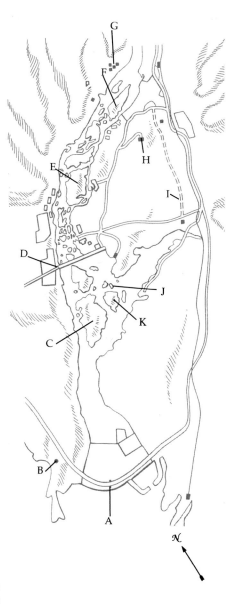

Aswan, the ancient Syene, from the Egyptian word *suenet*, meaning 'trade', is located on the right bank of the Nile immediately downstream from the First Cataract, beyond which stretches Nubia. In ancient times Aswan was an important trading city and the capital of the first nome of Upper Egypt. It was a commercial centre with its main market on the island of Elephantine, forming the point of contact between Egypt and the regions of equatorial Africa. The island of Elephantine takes its name from the fact that it was the centre of the ivory trade. At Aswan in 230 BC the Greek mathematician Eratosthenes calculated the circumference of the earth with a surprising degree of accuracy, taking account of the specific location of the city – precisely on the Tropic of Cancer.

Few traces of ancient Syene survive today; among them are the scattered ruins of a temple built by Ptolemy III Euergetes I, dedicated to 'Isis at the head of the armies', a theological innovation developed by that ruler, particularly well suited to the frontier location of the city. On the island of Elephantine there are a number of archaeological remains that testify to the importance of the site: the temple of Khnum from the reign of Nectanebo II (Thirtieth Dynasty); the remains of the temple of the goddess Satis, built by Tuthmosis III; and the Nilometer, a graduated staircase to measure the height of the floods of the Nile, located at the southeastern tip of the island, used in predicting the time and degree of the floods. The phenomenon of the Nile's floods was attributed to the god Hapy, a beneficent deity linked to the concept of abundance, and it was believed that the floods originated in the cataract

262–263 (above) On the island of Sehel, in the First Cataract, there is a stela called the 'Stela of Famine', carved on a granite boulder in Ptolemaic times. The text tells of a great famine that lasted seven years, and which befell the land during the reign of the pharaoh Djoser because of the limited extent of the flooding of the Nile. The famine ended, supposedly, due to the prayers of the king, which caused the intervention of the god Khnum, 'Lord of the Cataract', who returned the situation to normal.

264 (right) In the innermost section of the temple of Isis on Philae is the sanctuary, immersed in partial darkness, and lit only by two small openings high up in one of the side walls. On the granite pedestal, dating from the reign of Ptolemy III and his bride Berenice, the sacred barque of Isis was set. At Philae, Isis was associated with Sothis, the name of the star Sirius, the appearance of which signalled the beginning of the rise of the Nile. The cult of Isis had a close relationship to the flooding of the river.

itself. Indeed, it was thought that this was the location of the cavern from which water poured into the river, causing the seasonal overflow. The rock-cut tombs of the princes of Elephantine, carved in the rocky wall bordering the west bank of the river, date from a period between the Old and the Middle Kingdom, and prove the importance of Elephantine from this era forward. Elephantine and Syene reached their greatest splendour many centuries later, during Graeco-Roman times, when the temples of Philae were built on another of the islands in this turbulent stretch of the Nile. Structures on Philae include a temple dedicated to Isis, another to the worship of Hathor, and a kiosk – an open building for the temporary housing of sacred images during pauses in processions or jubilatory celebrations – of Trajan. These buildings were dismantled and rebuilt on the higher island of Agilkia.

264 (above) The eastern side of the temple of Isis, with, in the centre, the two pylons standing in front of the hypostyle hall, and, on the left, the kiosk of Trajan. This is a building of remarkably elegant proportions,

consisting of a portico with 14 columns with bell-shaped capitals. In ancient times it would have been covered with a wooden roof and was probably used during religious ceremonies, when the boat of Isis arrived at or departed from the island.

265 (opposite) The second pylon of the temple of Isis marked the entrance to the hypostyle hall, where the most sacred precinct of the building began. It was decorated with scenes of the ritual slaughter of enemies by Pharaoh Ptolemy XII Neos Dionysos.

The Aswan High Dam lies some 6 km (4 miles) upstream of Aswan, and is one of the most impressive pieces of hydraulic engineering ever accomplished. It is 3600 m (11,800 ft) long and its construction required a staggering quantity of material, equivalent to seventeen times the volume of the Great Pyramid of Cheops. Lake Nasser, created by the dam, extends for some 480 km (300 miles) behind it.

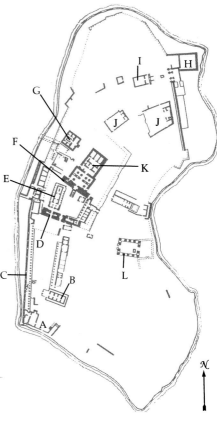

PHILAE

A Portal of Nectanebo I
B Temple of
  Arsenuphis
C Western colonnade
D First pylon
E Mammisi
F Second pylon

G Temple of
  Harendotes
H Gate of Diocletian
I Temple of Augustus
J Coptic church
K Temple of Isis
L Cloister of Trajan

*266–267 The first
pylon of the temple of
Isis, built during the
reign of Ptolemy XII
Neos Dionysos (first
century AD) includes
the great portal dating
from the reign of
Nectanebo I (Thirtieth
Dynasty) and marks
the entrance to the
sacred precinct of the
temple. In front are
two lions whose*

*features have been
defaced. To the right of
the portal are the three
chief gods who were
worshipped here: Isis,
Horus and Hathor.
The image of Isis, to
the left of the portal,
was almost entirely
chiselled away when
the atrium of the
temple was used as a
Coptic Christian
church.*

268–269 The island of Philae in the First Cataract is dominated by the imposing mass of the Ptolemaic temple of Isis, alongside which stand other religious structures, such as the temple of Arsenuphis, the temple of Hathor, the temple of Harendotis, and the kiosk of Trajan, which can be seen on the eastern side. To the left of the temple of Isis is a long portico, formed of 32 columns. Following the construction of the Aswan High Dam all these monuments were threatened with total submersion under the rising waters of the Nile. An international campaign was organized to save the Nubian temples, led by UNESCO. Between 1972 and 1980 the structures were dismantled, moved to the nearby island of Agilkia, and reassembled on higher ground.

Nubia: THE RESCUE OF THE TEMPLES

With the construction of the Aswan High Dam the temples that once stood on the banks of the Nubian Nile between the First and Second Cataracts faced the threat of submersion beneath the waters of the enormous expanse of Lake Nasser. In order to save these architectural treasures, UNESCO promoted an international campaign that culminated in the rescue of almost all the monuments within the area of the salvage programme.

The smaller temples were donated by Egypt to the countries (Italy, Spain, the Netherlands, USA, Germany) that had so generously contributed to the rescue operation. They were reassembled respectively in Turin (the temple of Ellesiya), Madrid (the temple of Dabod), Leiden (the temple of Tafa), New York (the temple of Dendur) and Berlin (Kalabsha gate).

The larger Nubian temples were entirely dismantled and reassembled in three different locations. The first site was called New Kalabsha, and is the only one that can be easily reached. It lies near the westernmost tip of the High Dam, and here the temples of Kalabsha and Beit el-Wali were rebuilt. The temple of Kalabsha was built by Emperor Augustus and dedicated to the Nubian god Mandulis; it originally lay 40 km (25 miles) further south, and was transported to its present location

between 1961 and 1963. The cliff temple of Beit el-Wali dates from the period of Ramesses II, and was dedicated to Amun-Re.

The second site, in open desert some 135 km (85 miles) away from the High Dam, includes the temples of el-Dakka, el-Sebua, and el-Maharraqa. The temple of el-Dakka dates from the Romano-Ptolemaic era, while the great temple of el-Sebua, built by Ramesses II, was dedicated to Amun-Re and Re-Harakhty, and to the deified Ramesses II. The Roman temple of el-Maharraqa was dedicated to Isis and Serapis. At the third site, some 40 km (25 miles) to the south of the second, the temples of Amada and el-Derr have been relocated, along with the rock-cut tomb of Penniut, from the site of Aniba. The temple of Amada, begun by Tuthmosis III and completed by Tuthmosis IV, Sethos I and Ramesses II, was dedicated to Amun-Re and Re-Harakhty. The cliff temple of el-Derr, built by Ramesses II, was dedicated to the same two gods, the deified pharaoh, and to Ptah. Despite the massive efforts, not all the Nubian temples were saved: the small temple of Horus at el-Sebua, one of the two temples of Tafa, Gerf Hussein, the fort of Quban of the Twelfth Dynasty, the fort of the Middle Kingdom, and the temple of the Eighteenth Dynasty of Aniba, Qasr Ibrim, are lost forever.

270–271 The temple of el-Maharraqa has now been reassembled at the same site as the rescued temples of el-Dakka and el-Sebua. This structure, dating from the Amarna period, originally stood at the site of the city of Hierasycaminos, the 'City of the Sacred Sycamore', on the southern border of the empire, about 40 km (25 miles) north of its current location.

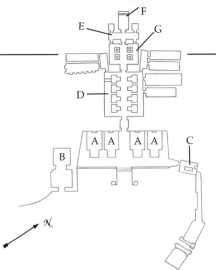

ABU SIMBEL:
THE TEMPLE HIDDEN IN THE SAND

A Colossi of Ramesses II
B Southern chapel
C Northern chapel
D Great hypostyle hall
   (pronaos)
E Vestibule
F Sanctuary
G Second hypostyle hall

272–273 *Aerial view of the complex of rock-cut temples of Abu Simbel, now set into the two man-made hills that protect the temples. To the north is the Small Temple of Hathor and Nefertari, while to the south, in all its majesty, stands* the Great Temple of Ramesses II, dedicated to Amun, Re-Harakhty, Ptah and the pharaoh himself. The entire complex was facing complete submersion by the waters of Lake Nasser, along with all the other Nubian temples. *Abu Simbel was the primary objective of the rescue mission organized by UNESCO, and in just four years, between 1964 and 1968, the entire complex was dismantled and moved to a site some 200 m (650 ft) away from its* original location. To achieve this incredible feat, the temple had to be cut into more than a thousand separate blocks, the largest of which weighed approximately 33 tons. Work was finally completed, down to the last detail, in 1972.

Abu Simbel is located on the west bank of the Nile at a distance of some 850 km (530 miles) from Cairo, not far from the Second Cataract and on the border with Sudanese Nubia. Here, in March 1813, the celebrated explorer and orientalist Johann Ludwig Burckhardt, who had already discovered the city of Petra in Jordan, found a huge temple whose enormous façade was partly buried in the sand. It had been built by Ramesses II, the most important pharaoh of the Nineteenth Dynasty (1279–1212 BC). A second temple, dedicated to Hathor and to Queen Nefertari, the wife of Ramesses II, stood not far away.

In October 1815, the English traveller and antiquarian William John Bankes, accompanied by Giovanni Finati of Ferrara (Italy), whom he had hired as a servant, visited Abu Simbel, and the pair made their way into the smaller temple. Of the larger temple, however, all that could be seen was the bust of one of the four colossal statues that adorned the façade, which depicted the seated pharaoh. In March 1816, the French consul, Bernardino Drovetti, accompanied by his agents Frédéric Cailliaud and Jean-Jacques Rifaud, also visited Abu Simbel, but did not succeed in hiring enough workers to be able to clear away the sand, a project which Bankes had considered too. Only Giovanni Battista Belzoni, accompanied by the English naval officers Irby and Mangles, succeeded, after a month's hard work, in removing the enormous mass of sand which blocked the temple's entrance. He entered the temple on 1 August 1817. If Belzoni was perhaps disappointed at not finding the treasures he had hoped for (the temple was practically empty), he was certainly excited at the beauty of

274–275 The Small Temple of Abu Simbel was built on a high promontory to the north of the Great Temple, and was dedicated to Hathor, considered in Nubia to be the bride of Horus, the hawk-god, protector of royalty and to Nefertari. The statues on the façade, 10 m (33 ft) tall, were housed in a series of niches. They depict Ramesses II and Hathor-Nefertari. The two statues of the queen, associated with Hathor, are flanked by four statues of Ramesses II and, in sharp contrast with all the conventions of royal statuary, are the same size as the statues of the pharaoh, in tribute to the prestige and importance of this royal wife. Thus, through the assimilation of the queen with Hathor, bride of Horus, of whom the pharaoh was the earthly representative, the clear legitimacy and continuity of the royal line is graphically expressed.

the painted reliefs depicting the military campaigns of Ramesses II in Syria, Lybia and Nubia, and the imposing size of the great pillars of the hypostyle hall, depicting the pharaoh. In commemoration of the event, Belzoni and his fellow workers carved their names and the date into the northern wall of the cella, where they can still be seen today.

The temple façade, carved into the rock, stands some 30 m (100 ft) tall and 35 m (115 ft) across, while the four colossal seated statues are around 21 m (70 ft) in height. Next to the legs of the pharaoh some standing statues depict Queen Nefertari and the royal princes and princesses. Above the entrance to the temple, in a central position is a sculpture representing the image of the falcon-headed god Re, while the upper cornice of the façade is adorned with a row of 23 statues of baboons.

On the interior, after the vestibule, is the great hypostyle hall supported by eight Osiris pillars. This leads to a smaller hypostyle hall and finally into a second vestibule that gives on to the cella; here, in a niche, stand four statues depicting the gods Ptah of Memphis, Amun-Re of Thebes, Re-Harakhty of Heliopolis and the

275 Beyond the entrance portal of the Small Temple of Abu Simbel, is a square pronaos, the ceiling of which is held up by six Hathor columns. These bear carvings of formulas of adoration dedicated to six deities: Hathor, Anukis, Isis, Satis, Mut and Weret-heqau. The walls of the pronaos are decorated with scenes

deified pharaoh himself: twice a year the rays of the sun pass through the long succession of halls and illuminate the statues in the cella. Rescue work at Abu Simbel, between 1964 and 1968, removed and reconstructed both temples, which were transferred to a distance of some 200 m (650 ft) from the original site and raised by some 65 m (215 ft) to safety.

of offerings made by Ramesses II and by Queen Nefertari. The pronaos is followed by a vestibule that leads in turn to a sanctuary, where there is a representation of Hathor in the shape of a cow emerging from the mountain.

276 (left) An intriguing detail of one of the Osiris colossi in the pronaos of the Great Temple of Abu Simbel. The four colossi on the south side depict the pharaoh wearing the white crown of Upper Egypt, his arms crossed, and holding the heqa-sceptre and the nekhakha-flail, while the colossi on the north side wear the double crown of Upper and Lower Egypt, almost as if to underline the dominant role of Upper Egypt over the rest of the land. Belzoni, who was the first European to penetrate the interior on 1 August 1817, described these colossi in the following terms: 'Up against each pillar stands a statue. These statues are carved with wonderful skill, and are little damaged by the ravages of time; they are not unlike the statues of Medinet Habu, and the tip of their crowns touch the ceiling, which is thirty feet tall.'

277 (right) The pronaos of the temple of Ramesses II, cut from living rock, is 18 m (60 ft) in length, and is decorated with eight colossi that stand 10 m (33 ft) tall and portray Ramesses II as Osiris. The temple was discovered by the Swiss orientalist Johann Ludwig Burckhardt in 1813, but Belzoni was the first European to clear away the sand and enter the temple, in 1817.

278–279 The impressive façade of the great temple of Abu Simbel is adorned with four immense colossi, representing Ramesses II. The first colossus to the south, to the left of the portal, collapsed long ago. At the side of each statue, and standing between their legs, are a number of smaller statues, representing the wife and the mother of the pharaoh, as well as the royal princes and princesses. Above the portal is a niche containing a statue of the god Re-Harakhty, with a hieroglyphic sign on his right which transcribes the word user, while to the left of the god is an image of the goddess Maat, which represent the praenomen of Ramesses II – Usermaatre.

GLOSSARY

AMULETS
Talismans that protected people during their lives and were placed with the dead to ensure that they would maintain their vital functions and be able to preserve certain qualities after death (health, beauty, knowledge, etc.).

AMUN

Regarded during the New Kingdom as the 'king of the gods', sometimes depicted as a human being (at times ithyphallic), with two tall plumes rising above his headdress, at other times as a ram, the animal sacred to Amun. Along with the goddess Mut and the god Khonsu, he formed part of the 'Theban triad'. He was also associated with the god Re, and venerated as Amun-Re. The chief centre of the Amun cult was Thebes.

ANKH

A hieroglyph symbolizing life; it was considered a very powerful amulet.

ANUBIS

Jackal-headed deity who presided over the embalming process and accompanied the dead in the Afterlife.

ANUKIS

Female deity, worshipped on the island of Sehel, near Aswan. She was considered one of the two wives of Khnum, along with Satis.

APIS
Sacred bull worshipped in Memphis, symbol of virility and fertility. The 'deceased Apis', (Osiris + Apis = Serapis) was believed to be buried at Saqqara in the underground structure of the Serapeum.

APOPHIS

Malevolent serpent of the Eastern Horizon that rises again each morning in order to combat the rising sun, but is always conquered.

ATEF (CROWN)

One of the typical head ornaments of the god Osiris, made up of a mitre surmounted by a sun disk, with an ostrich plume arranged on either side.

ATEN

The sun disk, elevated to the status of the sole deity (monotheism) during the reign of the heretic pharaoh Amenophis IV–Akhenaten.

ATUM

A deity representing the sun as Atum-Re; in particular this deity was considered as the form of the setting sun.

BA

An element of the human soul, portrayed as a human-headed bird; the other parts were the *akh* and the *ka* ('life force').

BASTET

Goddess of joy and music, depicted with the head of a cat (or in some cases the head of a lioness). Also a protective deity.

BES

Benevolent demon with a lion's skin disguise, protector of pregnant women and babies; his menacing appearance frightened off evil spirits.

BOOK OF GATES
A guide for the deceased on passing through the gates of the Underworld and past their guardians.

BOOK OF THE DEAD
Series of around 190 'chapters' containing magical and ritual spells, illustrated with drawings, intended to help the deceased survive in the Underworld. Popular from the New Kingdom on, the established chapters were written on papyri and placed near the deceased; during the Late Period, spells and drawings could also be traced on to the linen strips wrapped around mummies.

BUSIRIS
From the Egyptian, 'City of Osiris', a city in Lower Egypt, where the Osiris cult had its origins.

CANOPIC JARS

Vessels used to contain the liver, lungs, stomach and intestines removed from the body of the deceased during the mummification process. The viscera were put under the protection of the four sons of Horus (Imsety, Hapy, Duamutef and Qebhsenuef) and the canopic jars were sealed with lids which, from the era of the Ramessides, took the form of the heads of the four deities: human, baboon, jackal and hawk heads respectively and they were also linked to the four cardinal points of the compass.

CARTOUCHE

Originally a loop of cord with a knot at the base, which contained the written name of the pharaoh. The use of the cartouche, which symbolized the universal power of the sun god, and thus of the pharaoh, was reserved for the two most important of the five names held by the pharaoh, the nomen (the birth name, preceded by the title - -'Son of Re') and the praenomen (the most used, preceded by the title- -'King of Upper and Lower Egypt').

CENOTAPH
An empty tomb that did not contain the body of the deceased. A famous cenotaph was that built by Sethos I at Abydos so that he could rest symbolically near the tomb of Osiris.

COFFIN TEXTS
Series of magical and ritual spells intended to ensure that the deceased would survive in the Afterworld, painted on the sides of coffins during the First Intermediate Period and the Middle Kingdom.

COLUMNS

A number of different types exist in Egyptian architecture, classified by the shape of the capital: channelled or fluted column (or Protodoric, surmounted by a simple parallelepiped), the 'palm' column (with the capital in the shape of leaves of the date palm), 'lotus' column (topped by closed lotus buds), 'papyrus' column (with bound bundles of papyrus) and 'Hathor-headed' column (with a capital in the form of the head of the goddess Hathor).

COSMOGONY

Creation myths. According to the theology of the priests of Heliopolis, at the creation of the world there was a primordial ocean called Nun, from which issued the Sun God Atum, the creator of all things. The Sun engendered two deities (Shu, or dry air, and Tefnut, damp air), who in turn engendered Geb (the earth) and Nut (the sky); and their children were Osiris, Isis, Seth and Nephthys (see Ennead).

CROWN (ATEF, WHITE, BLUE, DOUBLE, RED)
See, respectively, Atef, Hedjet, Khepresh, Pschent, Deshret.

CUBIT
A unit of measurement of length in ancient Egypt: it was 52.3 cm (21 in) in length, and was broken down into seven palms, or 28 fingers.

DESHRET

The red crown which symbolized the power and rule over Lower Egypt.

DIVINE BEARD
False beard fastened to the chin of a pharaoh, deity or deified person. It may be simple or braided, and when worn by deities ends in a curl.

DJED-PILLAR

A pillar that symbolized stability and endurance, and represented the backbone of Osiris; a protective amulet.

ENNEAD
The nine deities of the cosmogony of Heliopolis: Atum, Shu, Tefnut, Geb, Nut, Osiris, Isis, Seth and Nephthys (see Cosmogony).

FAIENCE
An artificial glazed material obtained by heating a mixture of silica, alkali, lime and copper oxides. Generally dark blue in colour, it has an appearance not unlike glass.

FETISH
Animal hide on a stick, one of the symbols of Osiris and Anubis.

FIELDS OF IARU
Fields of the Underworld where the deceased could labour.

GEB
Personification of the earth, and brother-husband of Nut.

GENIUS
Geniuses often took the form of mummies, and could be benevolent or malevolent.

HAPY
See Sons of Horus and Canopic jars.

HAPY–NILE
Personification of the great river of Egypt, portrayed as an androgynous human being, with breasts and a prominent belly, symbols of prosperity and fertility.

HARAKHTY
See Re-Harakhty.

HARMACHIS
Sun god ('Horus on the Horizon'), guardian of the gates of the Underworld, depicted in the shape of a sphinx.

HAROERIS
A form of Horus: 'Horus the Elder'; identified with a falcon-god. The centre of the cult of Haroeris was Edfu.

HARPOCRATES
'Horus the Child', the youthful form of the god Horus; protects against bites from poisonous animals.

HATHOR
Goddess with the head (or just the ears) of a cow, she was a protectress of women and music and also the dead as she was assimilated with the goddess of the West.

HEDJET
White crown, symbol of dominion over Upper Egypt.

HEKET
Feminine deity depicted in the form of a frog; a goddess of fertility and of birth.

HELIOPOLIS
City in Lower Egypt, whose ancient Egyptian name was Iunu, the On of the Bible; it was the centre of the sun cult.

HEMHEM
Diadem composed of three atef-crowns joined together.

HEQA (SCEPTRE)
Sceptre in the form of a crook, crozier or staff, a symbol of royalty and linked to the god Osiris.

HES
An oval-shaped vase used to hold holy water.

HORUS
The hawk or hawk-headed deity. God of the sky and protector of the pharaoh, who was identified with this god. As the son of Osiris and Isis, Horus is often portrayed as a thumb-sucking child (Harpocrates).

IARU
See Fields of Iaru

IBIS
Bird sacred to the god Thoth; during the Late Period it was believed that the ibis was Thoth incarnate.

IMENTIT
Goddess of the West who welcomed the dead.

IMHOTEP
The architect who designed the funerary complex of the pharaoh Djoser (Third Dynasty); he was deified in the Late Period as a healer, and then equated by the Greeks with the god of medicine, Asclepius (Aesculapius).

IMSETY
See Sons of Horus

ISIS
Goddess – wife and sister of the god Osiris, mother of the god Horus.

KA
The part of the human soul representing the life force. It is also defined as the 'double'. It was created at the same time as its owner, but was immortal and provided the strength necessary for life in the Underworld.

KHEPRESH
Ceremonial crown, blue in colour and decorated with disks, worn by the pharaoh.

KHEPRI
The rising sun, depicted in the form of a scarab beetle.

KHNUM
Ram-headed potter deity, the god who created life and all living things, which he formed on his wheel. He was the protector of Elephantine and the area around the First Cataract.

KHONSU
Moon god in the form of a child; at Thebes Khonsu was considered to be the child of Amun and Mut. He is often depicted with the head of a hawk, adorned with a crescent moon surmounted by a lunar disk.

KNOT OF ISIS
See Tit.

KUSH
The name ancient Egyptians used to designate modern-day Sudan (Upper Nubia).

LOTUS
A symbol of creation, the flower was much used in rituals and festivals. Lotus columns were much used in Egyptian architecture.

MAAT
Goddess who personified the order of the universe, and also was connected with the concepts of truth and justice. She is depicted with an ostrich plume on her head, which is a transcription of her name.

MAMMISI
Birth-house. Small temples built to celebrate the birth of the deity whose cult centre it was.

MASTABA
Arabic word meaning 'bench'. A tomb, rectangular in plan, often with sloping sides and a flat roof, made of bricks or stone. Inside were one or more rooms for worship and a shaft leading to the burial chamber, often underground.

MEMPHIS
City in Lower Egypt, the capital of the Old Kingdom, founded, according to tradition, by Menes.

MENAT
A form of amulet used to counterbalance heavy necklaces.

MERETSEGER
Female deity, depicted in the form of a cobra. The centre of the cult was the village of Deir el-Medina, in the necropolis of Thebes.

MIN
A human or mummiform god, depicted as ithyphallic, with his right arm raised, carrying a flail, and wearing a cap adorned with two plumes. Min was considered the protector of fertility and of travel in the desert. The centres of his cult were at Coptos (modern Qift) and Akhmim.

MNEVIS
Sacred bull linked to the sun cult, worshipped at Heliopolis.

MONTU
War deity with a human body and the head of a hawk, often adorned with a sun disk and topped by two plumes; his cult was centred in the Theban area.

MUMMY
Desiccated dead body, eviscerated and wrapped in narrow strips of cloth. The word comes from the Arabic *mumiyah*, meaning bitumen, though this was used in the mummification process only during Roman times.

MUT
Goddess originally portrayed as a vulture and later depicted in human form. The wife of Amun, her cult was based at Thebes.

NAOS
Stone or wooden tabernacle where a statue of the deity was housed inside the sanctuary.

NEB
Hieroglyph that can be translated as 'all'; also used for precious metal.

NEFERTUM
Male deity, personification of the Primordial Lotus upon which the sun was created at the beginning of the world.

NEITH
A goddess, originally worshipped at Sais in the Delta, linked both to war and to weaving; she served a protective role and as such exercised an important part in the funerary cult, along with Isis, Nephthys and Selkis. From the New Kingdom, she was considered to be a creator deity, mother of the sun. She is depicted with the red crown of Lower Egypt; in some cases she wears a shield on her head with two crossed arrows.

NEKHAKHA
Flail, made of interlaced leather, symbol of authority, associated with the god Osiris.

NEKHBET
Goddess portrayed as a vulture, worhipped at Nekheb (modern El-Kab); protectress of Upper Egypt.

NEMES
A sort of striped headcloth worn by rulers of ancient Egypt: it enveloped the head and fell on either side of the face.

NEPHTHYS
Sister of the goddess Isis and wife of Seth.

NILOMETER
Built near the most important temples, this instrument measured the level of the Nile's floods, upon which the religious and economic life of Egypt depended.

NOME
A word of Greek origin, which was used to indicate the various administrative provinces (which varied in number from 38 to 42, depending on the era) of ancient Egypt. This system of administrative division of the country probably dates from the Early Dynastic period, and it was preserved until Roman times.

NUBIA
Territory that extended from the First to the Fourth Cataract. It was divided into Lower Nubia, situated between the First and the Second Cataracts (the ancient Egyptians called it Wawat), and Upper Nubia, known as Kush.

NUN
Deity representing the Primordial Ocean, the original chaos from which creation began (see Cosmogony).

NUT
Personification of the celestial vault, wife of the earth-god Geb, and daughter of Shu and Tefnut. She was portrayed as a woman with an arched body studded with stars. Often she was depicted as a protective figure in royal tombs or on the covers of coffins.

OBELISK
Word of Greek origin – 'little roasting spit' – indicating a monolith with four faces, tapered toward the apex, topped by a pyramidion (see Pyramidion). Obelisks were often arranged in pairs before the pylons of temples and may be interpreted as symbols of the sun.

OCCIDENT, OR WEST
This represents the kingdom of the dead as it is where the sun sets and is also where the souls of the deceased go.

OFFERING-TABLE
Stone or terracotta table, painted or carved in relief with depictions of various types of offerings for the deceased; these tables were placed in the tomb so that they could magically supply the deceased with food and drink for their sustenance for eternity.

OPENING OF THE MOUTH
An important ceremony by means of which life was imparted to statues and to mummies symbolically, by the touch of a small adze. A scene often depicted in tombs.

OPET
Great religious feast that took place in Luxor during the second and the third month of the period of flooding (*heket*) during which the image of the god Amun left the temple of Karnak and was transported on a religious visit to the temple at Luxor, which was called *Ipet-isut*.

OSIRIS
One of the greatest Egyptian gods, ruler of the Underworld. The centre of his worship was at Abydos. He was murdered by his brother Seth and brought back to life by his wife and sister Isis. Their son was Horus.

OSTRACON
A shard of a terracotta vase or fragment of stone, used as a writing surface.

PAPYRUS
Aquatic plant (*cyperus papyrus*); the fibres of its stalk were used to make writing paper.

PHARAOH
The word is derived from the Egyptian term *Per-a*, meaning great house, and was used to indicate the royal palace. In the first millennium BC it became the word used to describe the king.

PRONAOS
Vestibule of a temple or a tomb.

PSCHENT
Double crown symbolizing dominion over Upper and Lower Egypt, formed of the white crown (Hedjet) set within the red crown (Deshret) (see Hedjet and Deshret).

PTAH
Creator god of Memphis, husband of the lioness goddess Sakhmet, depicted as a mummiform man with the *was* sceptre. Subsequently Ptah was overlaid on the other funerary god of Memphis, Sokaris, and was worshipped in the syncretistic form of Ptah-Sokaris.

PYLON
Monumental entrance to temples, formed of two massive towers with trapezoidal shapes, flanking the portal.

PYRAMID
Funerary monument containing the tomb of the pharaoh. Its practical role was protective but symbolically it represented a stairway to heaven or the angled shaft of the sun's rays. The earliest examples were step pyramids (Third Dynasty), from which true pyramids (Fourth Dynasty) developed. On the south side of the monument were one or more satellite pyramids (some of which were of queens) while on the east side, the funerary temple

usually stood, connected by a processional ramp to the temple in the valley, used for the ceremonies during the pharaoh's burial.

PYRAMIDION
Small stone pyramid, a sun symbol, which was set upon the apex of an obelisk, or else which was used as the tip of a pyramid. It was often coated with sheets of gold or electrum – an amber-coloured alloy of gold and silver.

PYRAMID TEXTS
Series of spells for funerary rituals specific to the pharaoh, first carved on the walls of the burial chamber of pyramids at the end of the Fifth and during the Sixth Dynasties.

QEBHSENUEF
See Sons of Horus.

RE
An extremely ancient deity representing the sun, which was identified with many other deities (Atum, Khepri, Horus, Harakhty); the centre of the Re cult was Heliopolis. Re was depicted as having the head of a falcon, surmounted by the sun disk or with the head of a ram during his nocturnal navigation. Beginning in the Fourth Dynasty, the pharaoh took the appellation of 'son of Re'.

RE-HARAKHTY
Sun god – Horus of the Horizons. Depicted as a hawk and sun disk, and combines the qualities of Re and Horus.

REGISTER
Horizontal subdivision of the wall decorations in tombs and temples, and on objects such as stelae.

RENENUTET
Female deity, depicted with the body of a woman and the head of a cobra, protectress of agriculture and of fertility. During the Middle Kingdom, her cult was documented in the Faiyum, at Medinet Madi.

SATIS
Female deity, worshipped on the island of Elephantine at Aswan; with Anukis, considered to be one of the two wives of Khnum.

SCARAB
Beetle associated with solar rebirth (phonetically, its sign signifies 'to be born' or 'to become'); it represents the rising sun (see Khepri).

SCEPTRE
See Heqa, Sekhem, Wadj, Was.

SED
Festival marking the pharaoh's 'jubilee' and celebrated at the end of thirty years of rule, thereafter celebrated every three years.

SEKHEM
Sceptre symbolizing authority.

SEKHMET
Feminine divinity, depicted with the head of a lioness, at times surmounted by the sun disk; protectress of the pharaoh's royal power, assimilated to Hathor, Bastet and Isis.

SELKIS
Goddess serving a protective function in the funerary cult, as Isis, Nephthys, Neith. On her head is a scorpion that transcribes her name.

SERAPIS
Deity from the Ptolemaic era who combined the Egyptian features of Osiris–Apis and the Greek features of Zeus–Pluto. The Serapea, buildings dedicated to Serapis, at Saqqara and at Alexandria, were famous.

SERDAB
Closed statue-chamber in a mastaba where the statues of the deceased were preserved.

SEREKH
Stylized depiction of the façade of the royal palace, within which the first of the five names of the pharaoh were written.

SETH
God of chaotic forces, brother and murderer of Osiris and rival of Horus. He is represented as an animal of unidentified type.

SHABTI OR SHAWABTI
A figurine placed in an ancient Egyptian tomb to serve as a a a slave for the soul or as a substitute for the soul in performing forced labour. The name is taken from the verb *shwbty* meaning 'to respond', since each day it was meant to respond to the call to labour.

SHU
Masculine deity, personification of dry air, twin-brother of Tefnut in the Heliopolis cosmogony.

SISTRUM
An ancient Egyptian percussion instrument consisting either of a box in the form of a *naos*, or else of a looped metal frame set in a handle and fitted with loose crossbars that rattled when shaken; sacred to the goddesses Hathor and Bastet.

SOBEK
Crocodile god, depicted with an animal or with a human body, and animal head with the *atef* crown. His cult centres were Kom Ombo and the Faiyum.

SONS OF HORUS
These are four deities in the form of mummies, respectively with a human head (Imsety), the head of a baboon (Hapy), a jackal (Duamutef)

and a hawk (Qebhsenuef). They serve to protect the viscera of the deceased, which are contained in the four canopic jars deposited in the tomb (see canopic jars).

SPHINX
Usually takes the form of a lion with a human head, the incarnation of royal power and protector of the doors of temples. The most famous sphinx is the Great Sphinx of Giza, which may be a portrait of king Chephren (Fourth Dynasty), and which was later identified with the god Harmachis ('Horus of the Horizon').

STELA
Slab of stone or wood, of various shapes, bearing decorations and inscriptions with funerary applications or for political propaganda on the part of the pharaoh ('royal stelae' or boundary stelae).

SYCAMORE
Tree sacred to the goddess Hathor and to the goddess Nut. Its very hard wood was used in the manufacture of furniture, of sarcophagi and other funerary accessories.

TEFNUT
Female deity, personification of humidity, twin-sister of Shu.

TIT
Protective amulet, also known as the 'knot of Isis'. Normally made of semiprecious red stone such as jasper. It is mentioned in chapter 156 of the Book of the Dead, which describes the ceremony accompanying the correct placement of this amulet on the neck of the deceased, so as to protect the body. Although the significance of the shape of this amulet is not yet entirely clear, it is believed that it represents the knotted girdle of the goddess Isis.

THOTH
The god of learning and wisdom, depicted as an ibis, or with a human body and the head of an ibis, alternatively he was depicted as a baboon. As the inventor of writing and science, Thoth was the protector of scribes; the centre of his cult was at Hermopolis.

UDJAT
The eye of the celestial hawk god Horus; it means 'that which is in a good state'. The motif of the *udjat* was used as a protective amulet, often incised on the plaque that was placed over the embalmer's incision on a mummy.

URAEUS
Royal cobra that symbolized light and royalty, it was found, in a rearing position, on the forehead of most deities and pharaohs. It was sacred to the goddess Wadjet and to the sun god; it was believed to be the eye of the latter.

VIZIER
Title that indicated the head of executive power in ancient Egypt; the vizier acted for the pharaoh in every aspect of the administration of the country.

WADJ
Sceptre which took the form of a papyrus stalk, characteristic of feminine deities.

WADJET
Goddess depicted as the *uraeus*, worshipped in Buto (modern Tell el-Farain) in the Delta, protectress of the royal authority over Lower Egypt.

WAS
Sceptre characteristic of male deities.

WEIGHING OF THE HEART
After death, the soul of the deceased, represented by the heart, was weighed in a balance: if it was as light as the feather (symbol of truth and justice) placed on the other side of the balance it was admitted to eternal life; if not it was devoured by the monster Ammit.

ANCIENT EGYPT AND ITS PROVINCES

The hieroglyphs that appear at the top of each page indicate the nome to which the sites and towns belong that are discussed in that particular section of the book. Ancient Egypt, in administrative terms, was broken down into a number of different districts – known as *sepat* – which the ancient Greeks referred to as nomes. Each nome was marked by an emblem (related to animals, tutelary deities, fetishes or symbols of a magical nature) which were probably originally, prior to the unification of Egypt, the identifying standards of the people who inhabited the territory in question. The division into nomes was connected with considerations of agriculture, economics, and taxation, and must originally have been based on the irrigation of a specific territory, as the

hieroglyph ▦ indicated. This hieroglyph was found in the names of all the nomes and it represented a system of canals. Each nome had its own capital and was governed by a nomarch, described in ancient times as 'he who digs the canals'. During the Old Kingdom, there were 38 nomes, but in time the number rose to 42 (22 in Lower Egypt and 20 in Upper Egypt); this number also bore a certain relationship with Egyptian theological beliefs, inasmuch as there were 42 judges in the tribunal of Osiris when the soul of the dead came before them to be assessed. The oases, the Faiyum and Nubia upstream of the First Cataract were not counted among the 42 nomes, and were considered separate territories.

LOWER EGYPT

First nome: *ineb heg*, 'White Walls', Giza, Saqqara, Memphis

UPPER EGYPT

First nome: *taseti* 'Land of Nubia', Elephantine, Kom Ombo, Philae

Second nome: *utches-tor* 'Throne of Horus,' Edfu

Third nome: *nekhen* 'Rural' (?) Esna

Fourth nome: *waset* 'Sceptre', Thebes, Luxor, Medinet Habu, Valley of the Kings, Valley of the Queens

Sixth nome: *iker*, 'Crocodile', Dendera

Eighth nome: *ta ur*, 'The Great Land', Abydos

Nineteenth nome: *imety pehu* 'Lower royal infant', Tanis

Fifteenth nome: *unu* 'Hare', Amarna

Twenty-First nome: *naret pehetet* 'Lower Nâr Tree', Dahshur, Meidum

Mer-ner, 'The Great Lake'; the Faiyum

Nubia, Abu Simbel

Sema Tawy a symbol indicating the 'union of the two lands', that is Upper and Lower Egypt.

BIBLIOGRAPHY

GEOGRAPHY AND TOPOGRAPHY

Baines, J., Malek, J., *Atlas of Ancient Egypt*, Oxford and New York 1980

Porter, B. and Moss, R.L.B., *Topographical Bibliography of Ancient Egyptian Hieroglyphic Texts, Reliefs and Paintings* I–VII, Oxford 1927

EXCAVATIONS, VOYAGES AND DISCOVERIES

Belzoni, G.B., *Narrative of the Operations and Recent Discoveries within the Pyramids…*, London 1820

Burckhardt, J.L., *Travels in Nubia*, London 1819

Carter, H., *The Tomb of Tut.ankh.Amen*, London 1922–1933

Clayton, P.A., *The Rediscovery of Ancient Egypt. Artists and Travellers in the the 19th Century*, London 1982

Schiaparelli, E., *Relazione dei lavori della Missione archeologica italiana in Egitto: I, la tomba intatta dell'architetto Kha*, Turin 1922; *II, L'esplorazione della Valle delle Regine*, Turin 1927

Siliotti, A. (ed.), *Belluno e l'Egitto*, Verona 1986

Siliotti, A. (ed.), *Padova e l'Egitto*, Florence 1987

Siliotti, A. (ed.), *Viaggiatori Veneti alla scoperta dell'Egitto*, Venice 1985

Vercoutter, J., *The Search for Ancient Egypt*, London and New York 1992

HISTORY AND CIVILIZATION

Aldred, C. *Egypt to the End of the Old Kingdom*, London 1965

Clayton, P.A., *Chronicle of the Pharaohs. The Reign-by-Reign Record of the Rulers and Dynasties of Egypt*, London and New York 1994

Dawson, W.R. and Uphill, E.P., *Who Was Who in Egyptology*, London 1972

Gardiner, A.H., *Egypt of the Pharaohs*, Oxford 1974

Grimal, N., *A History of Ancient Egypt*, Oxford and New York 1992

Hobson, C., *Exploring the World of the Pharaohs. A Complete Guide*, London and New York 1987

Kemp, B.J., *Ancient Egypt. Anatomy of a Civilization*, London and New York 1989

Posener, G., Sauneron, S., Yoyotte, J., *Dictionary of Egyptian Civilisation*, London 1962

Quirke, S. and Spencer, A.J. (eds), *The British Museum Book of Ancient Egypt*, London and New York 1992

Spencer, A.J., *Early Egypt. The Rise of Civilisation in the Nile Valley*, London 1993

RELIGION AND MAGIC

Aldred, C., *Akhenaten, King of Egypt*, London and New York 1988

Andrews, C.A.R., *Egyptian Mummies*, London 1984

Andrews, C.A.R., *Amulets of Ancient Egypt*, London 1994

Cerny, J., *Ancient Egyptian Religion*, London 1952

D'Auria, S., Lacovara, P., Roehrig, C.H., *Mummies and Magic. The Funerary Arts of Ancient Egypt*, Boston 1988

Davis, A.R., *The Ancient Egyptians, Religious Beliefs and Practices*, London 1982

Dawson, W.R. and Gray, P.H.K., *Catalogue of Egyptian Antiquities in the British Museum I: Mummies and Human Remains*, London 1968

El Mahdy, C., *Mummies, Myth and Magic in Ancient Egypt*, London and New York 1989

Faulkner, R.O., *The Ancient Egyptian Book of the Dead*, rev. ed., London 1985

Goyon, J.C., *Rituels funéraires de l'ancienne Égypte*, Paris 1972

Hamilton-Paterson, J. and Andrews, C., *Mummies: Death and Life in Ancient Egypt*, London 1978

Hart, G., *Egyptian Myths*, London 1990

Lurker, M., *The Gods and Symbols of Ancient Egypt: An Illustrated Dictionary*, London and New York 1982

Quirke, S. *Ancient Egyptian Religion*, London 1992

Roccati, A. and Siliotti, A., *La magia in Egitto ai tempi dei faraoni* (papers of an international conference), Milan 1987

Spencer, A.J., *Death in Ancient Egypt*, London 1982

Wilkinson, R.H., *Symbol and Magic in Egyptian Art*, London and New York 1994

ART AND ARCHITECTURE

Aldred, C. *Egyptian Art*, London and New York 1980

Curto, S. and Roccati, A. (eds), *Tesori dei faraoni*, exhibition catalogue, Milan 1984

Edwards, I.E.S., *The Pyramids of Egypt*, rev. ed., Harmondsworth 1991

James, T.G.H., *Egyptian Painting*, London 1984

James, T.G.H. and Davies, W.V., *Egyptian Sculpture*, London 1983

Lucas, A. and Harris, J.R., *Ancient Egyptian Materials and Industries*, London 1962

Robins, G. *Egyptian Painting and Reliefs*, Aylesbury 1986

Robins, G. *Proportion and Style in Ancient Egyptian Art*, Austin and London 1994

Schäfer, H., *Principles of Egyptian Art*, Oxford 1974

Wilkinson, R.H., *Reading Egyptian Art. A Hieroglyphic Guide to Ancient Egyptian Painting and Sculpture*, London and New York 1992

LITERATURE

Gardiner, A.H., *Egyptian Grammar*, Oxford 1957

Lichtheim, M., *Ancient Egyptian Literature*, Berkeley 1973–1980

Parkinson, R.B., *Voices from Ancient Egypt*, London 1991

ARCHAEOLOGICAL SITES:
TANIS

Montet, P., *La Nécropole royale de Tanis, I, Les constructions et le tombeau d'Osorkon II à Tanis*, Paris 1947

Montet, P., *La Nécropole royale de Tanis, II, Les constructions et le tombeau d'Psousennès à Tanis*, Paris 1951

Montet, P., *Les énigmes de Tanis. Douze années de fouilles dans une capitale oubliée du delta égyptien*, Paris 1952

Montet, P., *La Nécropole royale de Tanis, III, Les constructions et le tombeau d'e Chéchanq III à Tanis*, Paris 1960

Stierlin, H., and Ziegler, C., *Tanis, Trésors des Pharaons*, Paris 1987

GIZA

Curto, S., *Gli scavi italiani a El Ghiza*, Rome 1962

Dunham, D. and Simpson, W.K., *The Mastaba of Queen Mersyankh III*, Boston 1974

Junker, H., *Gîza*, I–XII, Vienna and Leipzig 1929–1955

Reisner, G.A., *Mycerinus. The Temple of the Third Pyramid at Giza*, Cambridge 1931

Reisner, G.A., *A History of the Giza Necropolis*, I–II, Cambridge 1942–1955

Simpson, W.K., *The Mastabas of Kawab, Khafkhufu I and II*, Boston 1978

Zivie, C.M., *Giza au deuxième millénaire*, Cairo 1976

ABU GHURAB

Edel, E.and Wenig, S., *Die Jahreszeitenreliefs aus dem Sonnenheiligtum des Königs Ne-user-Re*, Berlin 1974

ABUSIR

Borchardt, L., *Das Grabdenkmal des Königs S'a-hu-rel*, I–II, Leipzig 1910–1913

Ricke, H. et al., *Das Sonnenheiligtum Des Königs Userkaf*, I–II, Cairo 1965

SAQQARA

Bresciani, E., *La tomba di Ciennehebu, capo della flotta del Re*, Pisa 1977

Duell, P. et al., *The Mastaba of Mereruka*, I–II, Chicago 1938

Goneim, M.Z., *Horus Sekhem-khet. The Unfinished Step Pyramid at Saqqara*, I, Cairo 1957

Lauer, J.P., *Saqqara. Royal Cemetery of Memphis*, London 1979

Martin, G. T., *The Hidden Tombs of Memphis*, London and New York 1991

DAHSHUR

de Morgan, J., *Fouilles à Dahchour*, I–II, Vienna 1895–1903

Fakhry, A., *The Monuments of Sneferu at Dahshur*, I–II, Cairo 1959-1961

MEIDUM

Petrie, W.M.F., *Medum*, London 1892

THE FAIYUM

Bresciani, E., *Rapporto preliminare delle campagne di scavo 1966 e 1967*, Milan and Varese 1968

Vogliano, A., *Rapporto degli scavi … Medinet Madi*, I–II, Milano 1936–1937

EL-LAHUN

Petrie, W.M.F., *Kahun, Gurob and Hawara*, London 1890

Petrie, W.M.F., *Illahun, Kahun and Gurob 1889–1890*, London 1891

BENI HASAN

Newberry, P.E., Griffith, F.L. et al., *Beni Hasan*, I–IV, London 1893–1900

EL-ASHMUNEIN

Roeder, G., *Hermopolis 1929–1939*, Hildesheim 1959

TUNA EL-GEBEL

Gabra, S. and Drioton, E., *Peintures à fresques et scènes peintes à Hermopolis Ouest (Touna el-Gebel)*, Cairo 1954

EL-AMARNA

Aldred, C. *Akhenaten. King of Egypt*, London and New York 1991

Davies, N. de G., *The Rock Tombs of El Amarna*, I–VI, London 1903–1908

Martin, G.T., *The Royal Tombs at el-Amarna*, I, London 1974

Peet, T.E., Woolley, C.L., Pendlebury, J.D.S., *The City of Akhenaten*, I–III, London 1923–1951

ABYDOS

Calverley, A.M. et al., *The Temple of King Sethos I at Abydos*, I, London and Chicago 1933

Mariette, A., *Abydos*, I–II, Paris 1869

Petrie, W.M.F., *The Royal Tomb of the First Dynasty...*, London 1900

DENDERA

Chassinat, E. and Daumas, F., *Le temple de Dendara*, I, Cairo 1934

Daumas, F., *Dendara et le Temple d'Hathor*, Cairo 1969 .

Mariette, A., *Denderah*, I–IV, Paris 1870–1873

LUXOR AND KARNAK

Barguet, P., *Le Temple d'Amon-Rê à Karnak. Essai d'exégèse*, Cairo 1962

Brunner, H., *Die südlichen Räume des Tempels von Luxor*, Magonza 1977

Golvin, J.C. and Goyon, J.C., *Les bâtisseur de Karnak*, Paris 1988

WEST THEBES

Carter, H., *The Tomb of Tut.ankh.Amen*, London 1923–1933

Hornung, E., *Valley of the Kings*, New York and London 1990

Leblanc, C., *Ta Set Neferou*, Cairo, 1989

Naville, E., *The Temples of Deir el Bahari*, I–VI, London 1894–1908

Reeves, N. *The Complete Tutankhamun*, London and New York 1990

Reeves, N. *Valley of the Kings*, London 1990

Schiaparelli, E., *L'esplorazione della Valle delle Regine*, Turin 1927

Siliotti, A. and Leblanc, C., *La tomba di Nefertari e la Valle delle Regine*, Florence 1993

ESNA

Downes, D., *The Excavations at Esna 1905-1906*, Warminster 1974

Sauneron, S., *Esna*, I, Cairo 1959

EDFU

de Rochemonteix, M. and Chassinat, E., *Le Temple d'Edfou*, I–XIV, Paris 1892

KOM OMBO

De Morgan, J. et al., *Kom Ombos*, I–II, Vienna 1909

ASWAN AND ELEPHANTINE

Bresciani, E. and Pernigotti, S., *Assuan. Il tempio tolemaico di Isi. I blocchi decorati e iscritti*, Pisa 1977

Edel, E., *Die Felsengräber der Qubbet el-Hawa bei Assuan*, I, Wiesbaden 1968

PHILAE

Junker, H. and Winter, E., *Philä*, I, Vienna 1958

Giammarusti, A., Roccati, A., *File. Storia e vita di un santuario egizio*, Novara 1980

BEIT EL-WALI

Ricke, H. et al., *The Beit el-Wali Temple of Ramesses II*, Chicago 1967

KALABSHA

Siegler, K.G., *Kalabsha. Architektur und Baugeschichte des Tempels*, Berlin 1970

ABU SIMBEL

Desroches-Noblecourt, Ch., Kuentz C., *Le Petit Temple d'Abou Simbel*, I–II, Cairo 1968

Save-Soderbergh, T. (ed.), *Temples and Tombs of Ancient Nubia*, London and New York 1987

ILLUSTRATION CREDITS

INDEX